PARALLEL LINES

PARALLEL LINES

or

journeys on the railway of dreams

or

every girl's big book of trains

Ian Marchant

BLOOMSBURY

First published in Great Britain in 2003
This paperback edition published 2004

Copyright © 2003 by Ian Marchant

Illustrations © Jonny Hannah
Photographs © Paul Williams

The moral right of the author has been asserted

Bloomsbury Publishing Plc, 38 Soho Square, London W1D 3HB

A CIP catalogue record for this book
is available from the British Library

ISBN 0 7475 6584 8

10 9 8 7 6 5 4 3 2 1

All papers used by Bloomsbury Publishing are natural,
recyclable products made from wood grown in
well-managed forests. The manufacturing processes
conform to the environmental regulations of the
country of origin.

Typeset by Hewer Text Ltd, Edinburgh
Printed in Great Britain by Clays Ltd, St Ives plc

www.bloomsbury.com/ianmarchant

For Christine Kidney

CONTENTS

The Train Now Standing. . .

'Hello.'

A girl was talking to me, a pretty black girl. She was twenty, maybe a year or two younger.

'Hello,' she said again. I was trying to look at St Pancras Station, from the opposite side of the Euston Road by Camden Town Hall, and I was embarrassed to be caught by girls on my first day as a train enthusiast, and I wished she'd go away. But where I come from it would be rude not to say hello back.

'Hello,' I replied.

She smiled. She wasn't wearing many clothes, I couldn't help but notice.

'What are you doing?'

'I'm just looking.'

'You look all you want, love.'

'I will. Thank you.'

Her friend, younger still, a blonde in a pink mini-skirt, seeing that I had been engaged in conversation, came hurrying up.

'Hello,' she said.

'Hello,' I replied again.

'We've got a place we can go,' said the blonde girl. 'Hundred and fifty quid for both of us.'

'That seems reasonable,' I said.

The girls smiled, the black girl took my arm, and I realized what they were offering.

'Ah, no. Sorry. I thought you meant that you had a place which *cost* you both a hundred and fifty pounds . . . Sorry . . . I'm not interested in . . . I mean, obviously I am, but . . . when I said it seemed reasonable . . . I didn't mean that you seemed reasonable. Though

I'm sure you are. Very reasonable. But I like stations, you see. I'm here to look at the station.' I nodded towards St Pancras.

The black girl let go of my arm.

'Wanker,' said the blonde.

I had not handled this well, and I scuttled down the subway to the safety of the Underground.

A fascination with railways, I have discovered, is one of those things almost guaranteed to put a woman off, like socks with sandals. They see themselves (not without some justification) spending weekends in engine sheds, or looking after the flask and sandwiches on the end of the platform at Crewe, or spending a fortnight's holiday visiting the Great Little Trains of Wales. Women and trainspotting don't mix, you might imagine. Mostly, you would be right.

But not entirely. Sometimes you do meet lasses at platform's end. I did. It was only when I started dating a lady trainspotter, a trainspotterette, that I became interested myself. At weekends, when I came to London to visit her, we would set off for Steam on the Metropolitan open days, or travel on the newly opened Jubilee Line, getting off at all the new stations to admire the architecture. What red-blooded guy hasn't dreamed of a girlfriend with a passionate interest in Underground trains? Just imagine – a girl with the same interest in hard facts and figures as yourself. So what if her facts and figures aren't as interesting as yours? At least she won't get at you for pointing out that Birmingham has more miles of canal than Venice, or tell you you're boring just because you know the titles of all Elvis Costello's B-sides. How can she, when she wants to talk about abandoned Underground stations, or about how the District Line used to go to Windsor?

I'd always known, secretly, that I had a train buff in me somewhere; it just needed awakening, nurturing, and when the relationship died, a soft spot for trainspotting was one of the things that I took away with me.

And then – rail disaster piled on top of rail disaster, an astounding indifference from our political masters, corruption and gross mismanagement at the highest level of the rail industry, strikes and delays and breakdowns. After Hatfield, rail travel became intolerable for several months. We all heard the stories; nineteen hours from Nottingham to Sunderland, fourteen from London to Exeter.

It was while sitting on a post-Hatfield train from Manchester to London, a journey which would normally take a couple of hours, but which on this occasion took eight, that I realized all the trainspotters were still there, there on the end of the platform at Stafford and Crewe, still eating egg sandwiches from greaseproof paper packages, still writing who knows what in their little black books. They didn't care about a bit of horror, didn't see it somehow. The passengers on the trains were full of righteous hatred, but the spotters' hearts were still bursting with love. I began to think about the two railways; about how there is this railway that we use and hate, and about how there is this railway that we remember, or imagine we remember, and love.

The railway has been a national obsession since 1825.

The British have lived with the railway for 175 years. For a long while, it was a love affair. For the first 100 years of its existence, the steam-hauled railway was the height of modernity. Steam traction was at the cutting edge of technological development in the 1820s and 1830s. The Railway Mania of the 1840s was the dot.com bubble of the Victorian Age. In its time the railway has symbolized complacent mercantile prosperity, imperial power, architectural splendour and industrial innovation. It was seen to promote freedom of movement, the growth of the middle class, the mushrooming of the suburbs and the birth of mass leisure.

Filippo Marinetti, in the Futurist Manifesto of 1909, claimed that the railway was the living, breathing apotheosis of futurity and hence of aesthetic possibility. Marinetti would rather watch an engine enter a great metropolitan terminus, steam and sparks flaring from its smoke stack, than see any amount of Old Master paintings, and for him the gargantuan breath of boilers, the gasping pistons and the screech of brakes were the authentic symphonic music of the time.

The railway was it.

Until it became the killing engine of the Western Front, the most effective weapon of war yet devised by man, as millions of soldiers entrained for the Somme. The love affair turned sour.

We've never forgiven it; but nor have we ever forgotten what it was. Now there are two railways: the real railway, and the railway of our dreams.

The first is just shit.

Your wallet £75 lighter, you are sitting outside the bog on an Inter-City 125 (125 refers to the speed at which the engine travels – one mile every twenty-five minutes) with Rod and Doug from Motherwell, they cheerily talking about what they'd like to do to the English and sipping Tennants from tins with pictures on them of girls called 'Shona' or 'Fiona', their paps oot fe th'lads; you trying not to laugh, or whimper, trying to focus on your book, but having to get up every time someone wants a piss.

The seat of your trousers clammy and cold, you lurch through carriages stuffed with those bastards who actually got a seat for their money, stopping only to press your groin into old ladies' ears to allow the train manager to squeeze past. You make your way to the buffet for a plastic cup of hot water, an enfeebled teabag clinging inside like a wee brown limpet with a silver foil foot, two plastic containers of 'Tastes Like Real Milk', a bag of peanuts and a whortleberry jam doughnut. Now £6 the poorer, you rejoin Rod and Doug.

Doug has been sick.

There are leaves on the line, the wrong kind of snow, and the Emergency Services have been called to scene after scene of horrific injury and death: King's Cross, Clapham, Paddington, Hatfield, Selby, Potters Bar.

In the good old days, Two Jags would come on the news wearing a hard hat and express his sympathy for the bereaved in his special-sympathy-for-the-bereaved voice. He would promise a Public Inquiry.

Then we got Stephen Byers. He would come on and say it wasn't his fault, he wasn't there, and anyway, it was the Civil Service, they just briefed him wrong, so it's nothing to do with him at all. He refused to take responsibility, and felt that a public inquiry would be a mistake, at a time like this when we should be thinking about the preservation of his career.

Now we've got Alastair Darling, so everything is going to be fine.

And on the station the staff would be just as happy to kill you as you would be to kill them.

I've sat on stations for what must by now be a measurable percentage of my life. I've cried on stations, fought on stations, cursed and sworn and yawned and slept on stations. I've waited on stations for girls who didn't come almost as often as I've waited for cancelled trains. When I was a child, I would travel across the country by train to be met by my father for his access weekends, at Didcot, Southampton, Paddington. Now I wait anxiously for my daughter at Victoria, Preston, Exeter.

I can never decide which is the worse kind of station: the terminus, thousands of anxious travellers staring up at the information board for news which never comes about trains which never leave, or the suburban station, sitting in an open-sided shelter in a howling gale with a weeping girl, staring up the deserted track for a glimpse of a lighted headboard, destination a home which seems further away every minute.

All human life passes through the station. What's not to be fascinated by?

But we feel contemptuous of trainspotters, pitying at best.

In America, train buffs are cool. You can still hear Woody Guthrie singing in the rails. Neil Young has his own locomotive and Whoopi Goldberg travels everywhere in her own private rail-car. The guy who told me this, an American, works in one of London's top railway bookshops. He's written a book himself, about a line in Texas which mostly carried apricots.

'Can you tell me why railway buffs are considered nerds here, and cool over there?' he asked, somewhat defensively.

'No idea,' I said.

His voice sank to a whisper, presumably to avoid offending his customers.

'I tell you what,' he said, 'if you saw the weirdos we get in here, you'd begin to understand.'

The other railway, the railway of our dreams, is beautiful, romantic, brimful of nostalgic promise. This is the railway that trainspotters like.

Those same stations, the packed terminus, the lonely suburban platform, still have something about them of Marinetti's Futurist amphitheatres. Modern trains snake under the great Victorian arches, passengers disgorge, lovers meet. Trevor Howard takes coal dust from Celia Johnson's eye. There are spies on the Night Train.

The abandoned railway hotels still ring with the memory of grandees; of the directors of the line, sucking cigars; of the Queen and Albert, racing up to Balmoral; of leather-bound luggage and the traffic of Empire. The modern train leaps across great bridges, dives into tunnels, thunders through towns, just like it does in *Every Boy's Big Book of Trains*. The countryside glides by; through pastoral England, mysterious Wales and magnificent Scotland, the best view is still to be found from the window of a train.

In the Railway Arms there are photographs of railwaymen, watch in hand, whistle in mouth, waving away a steam engine that always runs on time.

You can still ride steam trains, on beautifully preserved lines. You can still buy tea in a china cup and a scone and jam in the buffet from smiling matrons in smocked aprons. The fireman still wears a shiny peaked cap, his cheerful face streaked with coal dust and sweat; the porter still has his watch on a chain; and apple-cheeked children still chat with the driver, who leans from his cab with a grin.

But the line only goes three miles; the porter is really your dentist, the fireman your Independent Financial Adviser, and the driver is Ron from the pub. Their mums are serving the teas.

And isn't there something odd about the apple-cheeked children? What will they turn into?

Trainspotters.

Model-railway enthusiasts.

Capital A anoraks.

The railway for which we might feel mild nostalgia is for them the very stuff of life. It wants looking into.

St Pancras again, the day after the working girls chased me off, and the day after the release of the Cullen Report on the Ladbroke Grove rail disaster.

I kept getting drawn back to this station in particular. Everyone knows the Gothic front on the Euston Road, or the view of the great clock tower as you come down Pentonville Hill. When I first moved to London, most days I took the North London Line from Canonbury to Gospel Oak, and was thrilled by the view of St Pancras from the northern heights. It looks like one of mad King Ludwig's fairytale castles from up there, or a bloated *hôtel de ville*. It is one of the great buildings of London; or rather, *two* of the great buildings, for that is what it is, two remarkable buildings stuck together: the train shed and the hotel.

Along the Euston Road are some of the great London stations: Euston, King's Cross and St Pancras. Marylebone is hidden away along there, too. Euston was the first to be opened, the London terminus of the London and Birmingham Railway, which was the largest engineering endeavour since the construction of the pyramids. Such a vast undertaking needed a suitably grand station, and Euston was built with a Doric façade, 1830s neo-classicism designed to reflect the grandeur of the project. This temple in praise of progress was swept away in the 1960s and replaced with the current functional modern station, which resembles nothing so much as an airport terminal.

King's Cross, the next to arrive, also impressed by the scale of its engineering. I still think it impressive now. Built in the 1840s, it looks to me as though it were built in the 1930s – it is a very modern building, function and form indivisible.

St Pancras was the last of the three to be built, by the Midland Railway Company. In the 1850s the Midland was the greatest and grandest of train companies. Its headquarters were in Derby, and its directors, prototypes of the complacent fat-cattery that we see almost as *de rigueur* in the people who run our railway system today, decided that their London terminus should be the grandest and most up-to-date of all.

It had been hard for them to get an entry into London. Their trains had been sharing the metals of the Great Northern, running into King's Cross. For a company with such grand notions of self-importance, this would not do at all, so they resolved that they must have their own terminus, despite the attendant difficulties, not least of which was the St Pancras burial ground, from which hundreds of bodies would have to be moved to allow the line through. As the work started, onlookers were scandalized to see fragments of bone and locks of hair lying about in the old graveyard. The architects, to prevent further outrage, sent an assistant to supervise the removal of the dead. His name was Thomas Hardy, and he wrote several poems about the event:

> O Passenger, pray list and catch
> Our sighs and piteous groans
> Half stifled in this jumbled patch
> Of wrenched memorial stones.

> We late-lamented, resting here,
> Are mixed to human jam,
> And each to each exclaims in fear,
> 'I know not which I am!'

('The Levelled Churchyard')

The first part of St Pancras to be built, by W. H. Barlow, was the vast train shed. Finished in 1868, its great arcing cast-iron roof, 100 feet high and 240 feet wide, was for almost 100 years the largest structure of its kind in the world. Supported on almost 700 columns, the space of a beer barrel apart, the uninterrupted sweep of the roof sheltered seven platforms. Under the platforms, the beer from Burton was unloaded and stored – so important were the Burton brewers as customers to the Midland Railway that the train shed was purpose-built for the handling of beer. The train shed is still impressive now; look at the cast-iron ribs, each with its blue and white painted *Butterley Company of Derbyshire 1868* maker's mark, or, as you walk up the platform towards the hotel, at the remarkable station clock which looks like a huge inverted saucer, the hours marked with lozenges, the edges decorated with the kind of faux Indian patterning so beloved of designers after the Great Exhibition of 1851.

The second building, the huge Gothic hotel, is the one that first comes to mind when we think of St Pancras. When it was finished in 1872, it was as up-to-date and contemporary as the Lloyds building or the Guggenheim in Bilbao are today. The architect, Gilbert Scott, was a follower of John Ruskin, the most important architectural theorist of his time. It was Ruskin who advocated the Gothic as the most appropriate building style for northern climates and northern lights. If you catch the westbound North London Line train at sundown, and watch out after Caledonian Road station, you may see what he meant, get a feel for his aesthetic.

Difficult to imagine the directors of the Midland worrying too much about aesthetics. What they wanted was a terminus to symbolize their power and wealth, and in the train shed and its attendant hotel they felt that they had got it. The Midland Grand Hotel was the most modern and luxurious on earth. It was the biggest building ever to have been constructed featuring hydraulic lifts, or 'lifting rooms'. It had over 500 bedrooms, each sumptuously decorated, each warmed by its own coal fire and lit by gas. There is a sea of chimneys up there on the roof.

And it was almost immediately obsolete. When it was built, running water was not available in that part of London, so the people who could afford to stay there preferred to continue their journey into town and stay at a place with taps. Gas lighting was just about to be replaced by electricity; central-heating boilers were beginning to be installed. The hundreds of chambermaids required to supply hot water and keep the fires alight were redundant right from the onset. Even the plutocratic Midland couldn't afford to run this white elephant, the Centrepoint of its time, and it quickly became the problem that, to some extent, it still remains.

John Betjeman, remembered as everyone's favourite Poet Laureate, was also one of the most influential architectural writers of the twentieth century, and we owe him a debt as the foremost advocate of Victorian architecture. He helped to shape our idea of St Pancras as beautiful, worth preserving, a problem worth solving. The problem is, what to do with such an impractical building? It is a building of the imaginary railway that the English so adore; its tragedy is that it is of no use to the real railway that it is forced to accommodate, the railway that we hate.

On the day of my second visit, the old hotel (hotel no longer of course; it stands largely empty) was fenced around with netting, and access was denied. The station is in the process of being renovated so that it will be ready to act as the new terminus for Eurostar. Inside the train shed the green and white Midland Mainline trains looked like malevolent toads; dirty toads at that. There was a food shop, a buffet, the Shires Bar, a Smith's and a couple of food outlets, each accommodated in a shabby hut erected under the high roof. There was no great arrivals and departures board; instead, at the end of each of the platforms, tawdry monitors flickered with what passed for information about the trains. In yet another temporary hut, a grim-faced woman in a green hat sat telling passengers the time of the next train to Wellingborough.

The ticket hall is splendid, lined with linen-fold panelling, and the huge tiles on the ceiling are wonderful, but when you get to the front of the queue, you still face a bureaucratic nightmare and the prospect of taking out a second mortgage before you can buy a ticket, just as in less impressive ticket offices.

I couldn't help feeling that the destinations were anti-climactic. The trains ran to Sheffield, Barnsley, Matlock, Derby, Leicester and Kettering. In such imperial surroundings only great engines pulling elegant cars to Istanbul, Paris, Teheran or Moscow would be fitting. I like Kettering, I love Sheffield, but St Pancras is too overpowering for them. It makes them seem silly. Calling the trains the *Robin Hood* (for Nottingham) or the *Master Cutler* (for Sheffield) does not help. I hope that when the fast link to the Channel Tunnel arrives in St Pancras, the station will get the trains it deserves, and that the Trans-Siberian will start from there.

Brighton station, another of the glories of Victorian railway architecture, has just been restored and renovated, and it is a triumph. The glass in the roof has been replaced, the columns repainted in Brighton blue, and the whole station shows what can be done with these termini. They needn't be unloved liabilities.

Drinking a couple of pints and reading the Cullen Report in the Shires Bar, I was thrilled at the idea that Network Rail executives might face prosecution for their part in the systematic rundown of our railway. They should all be locked up; hanged, better yet. Cars should be illegal for politicians and Network Rail management: no single piece of legislation would improve the railway more efficiently, or more readily.

Beer during the day, no longer from Burton, does not suit me. I was becoming aggressive, and I walked up the platform to look back into the train shed. There was a spotter at the end of the platform. He was about forty, quite sharply dressed, with shades. He was muttering numbers into a tape recorder, and there was an open notebook on his lap, full of still more numbers.

'Hello,' I said brightly. He looked up with no great enthusiasm. Perhaps in view of my earlier experience, I should have been wary of saying hello to strangers at St Pancras.

'Hello,' I continued. 'I'm thinking about becoming a trainspotter. Er . . . have you seen any today? Trains . . . and that? Well . . . trains, obviously . . . but interesting ones?'

He shrugged, and pointed to his notebook. I leaned over his shoulder, looked at the numbers, and nodded sagely.

'I've been reading the Cullen Report. Awful, isn't it?' I said.

'What is?'

'The Cullen Report.'

'I dunno.' He turned back to his notebook, and I slunk away from St Pancras with my tail between my legs for the second time in two days.

But the dormant fascination with trains that slumbers within the breasts of all big boys had come to life. I knew that I wanted to ride some trains, and hang out with some spotters, and visit some stations, and try to track down the romantic railway, the railway of dreams. It would be the equivalent of the aborigine's walkabout, I imagined, except not walking, but on trains. And not sleeping in an improvised bivouac under the stars, but in two-star hotels with tea-making facilities and a trouser press in the room.

I would not be travelling alone. I would take, as friend and philosopher, a book published in 1862 called *The Railway Traveller's Handy Book*.

No one has ever been able to find out who wrote this wonderful book, ostensibly written as a 'How To' guide for railway travellers but actually an unsung classic of High Victorian comedy. It is divided into short sections, one each on the perils that face the traveller, such as 'Fixing the Time of Departure', 'Travelling Costume' and 'Procuring Ticket'.

All these issues worry us still, as might the author's view of going through tunnels:

Male passengers have sometimes been assaulted and robbed, and females insulted in passing through tunnels. And this has been most frequently the case when there have been only two occupants in the carriage. In going through a tunnel, therefore, it is always as well to have the hands and arms ready disposed for defence, so that in the event of an attack, the assailant may be instantly held back or restrained.

I have some sympathy with the author's feelings about talking to strangers in trains, as well:

Why should half a dozen persons, each with minds to think, and tongues to express those thoughts, sit looking at each other mumchance as though they were afraid of employing the faculty of speech? Why should an Englishman ever be like a ghost, in not speaking until he is spoken to?

The Railway Traveller's Handy Book is a link between the two railways. It speaks to us of the Victorian railway of lost content, of porters and *Bradshaw's* and locomotives steaming into the station; but it is also hard-nosed and cynical, always expecting the worst, always alive to the reality of the state of the trains. I shall refer to it at need.

A note on what Victorian railway writers would call 'this present volume'.

Although the railway would not exist without steam engines, I think people are put off railway books by the way they go on about 'GNR Gresley 2–6–0 1000 Class' locomotives, or whatever. I'm going on a lot of journeys by rail, and I'm not going to care what sort of locomotive is pulling the train. Most especially, I'm not going to record their numbers. I hope that the enthusiasts will forgive me, and that in return they will gain the understanding of a hostile public and will henceforth be left in peace to watch the trains go by!

Oh, and the bloopers thing! Railway books use lots of bloopers!! Lots and lots of them!!! I hope that railway enthusiasts will forgive me their absence too!!!!

Other conventions of railway literature I'm happy to conform to. The first chapter, or introduction, of any self-respecting railway book is always called something along the lines of 'Departures' or 'The Train Now Standing . . .' The last chapter is always, always, always called 'All Change' and is invariably about Beeching. Fans of the genre will find these aspects of my book, at least, reassuringly familiar.

Newhaven, Gateway to Europe

All my journeys begin from Newhaven, I guess.

The ugly old town sits on a hill at the mouth of the River Sussex Ouse, in the only real gap of any size in the range of chalk cliff which runs otherwise unbroken between Brighton and Eastbourne. It is a new town, as the name suggests, a largely Victorian town. The River Sussex Ouse could never settle on the exact spot in the shallow bay where it should meet the sea. Its mouth used to be in Seaford, an associated Cinque Port, three miles to the east along the beach, but 400-odd years ago the river burst through the shingle bank which holds the sea back from the low-lying, waterlogged farmland behind it, and made a fresh confluence, known as the New Haven. Over a period of 100 years, the river was canalized, a harbour entrance built, and Meeching, the cluster of fishermen's cottages lucky enough to find itself with a fine new harbour, changed its name to Newhaven in honour of its new-found status.

The railway arrived in 1847 to connect London with the recently opened regular steam-packet boat to Dieppe, and it was this which sparked the growth of the modern town. Newhaven lies almost due south from London, and Dieppe is the nearest seaport to Paris. The sea journey between the two small towns is longer than that from either Dover or Folkestone to Calais, but, as the crow flies, the shortest London to Paris route is via Newhaven–Dieppe. By the 1880s, regular passenger and cargo boats ran between Newhaven, St-Malo, Caen, St-Nazaire and the Clyde, as well as Dieppe. In terms of the amount of money it earned, Newhaven was the sixth most important port in Victorian Britain. It was the Gateway to Europe; from Victoria to Newhaven Harbour, from Dieppe to the Gare du Nord. The last king of France, Louis Philippe, spent his first night in exile in Newhaven, in 1848.

Newhaven itself was criss-crossed by railways on both sides of the river; to the harbour and along the shingle bank to Seaford, across the old swingbridge and down towards the new breakwater, and up to the chalk quarries with horse-hauled trains. The cliff which overlooks the harbour entrance had been an embattlement since the Napoleonic Wars, and continued to be heavily fortified until after 1945. The low, flat beach of Seaford Bay was a tempting target for invaders, and Newhaven Fort stood ready to repel them. Newhaven was also, therefore, an important military town. The world's first armoured train underwent its trials in Newhaven on the East Beach rail track, in 1894.

Armoured trains seemed like a great idea. This first train carried a forty-pound gun and two armoured carriages for troops. Armoured trains were used in action for the first time in the Boer War. The designers had overlooked the fact that a few loosened nuts at a points crossing, never mind leaves on the line or the wrong kind of snow, are enough to stop a train; in the case of the soldiers on the trains, enough to stop them dead in their tracks. Winston Churchill was taken prisoner of war during the South Africa campaign while trying to defend a hapless disabled armoured train. They were as much use as elephants in the Alps. Nobody bothered building armoured trains after that. No, the glory of the train as a weapon was that you could carry millions of men and countless thousands of tons of *matériel* up to the front, easily and quickly. They were meat wagons.

> *Down the close, darkening lanes they sang their way*
> *To the siding shed,*
> *And lined the train with faces grimly gay.*
>
> *Their breasts were stuck all white with wreath and spray*
> *As men's are, dead.*
>
> *Dull porters watched them and a casual tramp*
> *Stood staring hard,*
> *Sorry to miss them from the upland camp.*
> *Then, unmoved, signals nodded, and a lamp*
> *Winked to the guard*

So secretly, like wrongs hushed up, they went.
They were not ours:
We never heard to which front these were sent.

Nor there if they yet mock what women meant
Who gave them flowers.

Shall they return to beatings of great bells
In wild train-loads?
A few, a few, too few for drums and yells,
May creep back, silent, to still village wells
Up half-known roads.

(Wilfred Owen, 'The Send-off')

Aged seventeen, my stepfather watched from Newhaven Bridge as hundreds of dead Canadian soldiers were unloaded from barges returning from the Dieppe Raid and lifted on to trains at the Harbour station.

I moved to Newhaven when I was ten (cue sound-track: 'Last of the Steam-powered Trains', by the Kinks, from *The Village Green Preservation Society*, 1968) and moved away when I was eighteen, but it will always be my home town, if only because my parents still live there.

Our primary school was called Meeching County in honour of the lost fishing village, but it has vanished too, knocked down to build a swimming pool. The kids' dads worked on the railways or docks if they were well-to-do, and on the industrial estates if they were less well-off. By the time we went up to the big school, Tideway Comprehensive, high on the hill and overlooking the ruined Fort on the clifftop, me and my mates were allowed to go into Brighton on our own, by train, a twenty-five-minute journey, even though a guy in my class had a kid brother who was fried, playing on the live rail. We used to go into town to sit on cushions and listen to 'Tubular Bells' through headphones in Virgin Records, or to buy stack-heeled shoes from Saxone. Now we sit on Virgin Trains, thankful at least that we never have to hear 'Tubular Bells' again. Our children are wearing our stack-heeled shoes, which they found in Grandma's loft space.

I started following Brighton and Hove Albion, and would meet the same gang of wannabe boot boys every Saturday down Newhaven station to go to the Goldstone, or away, to QPR, Fulham, Portsmouth. We ran up and down the train, chanting; at Brighton we crushed on to the train to Hove, just one stop, and I could still do the walk from Hove station to the Goldstone blindfold, though the ground is long gone. Sometimes we would chase small groups of opposing fans, and sometimes we would be chased by large groups of opposing fans. We kicked in a phone-box window on the platform at Hove after a home defeat by Crystal Palace. I had my first can of Guinness sitting in the luggage rack on the way back from a shit goalless draw with Torquay. Ooh, we were hard.

As we got older still, we took the train in to go and stare at girls in Sherry's, or to see a band in the Students' Union at Sussex University. The train was boss; the alternative bus was slow and dull as it bumped along the coast road through the horror that is Peacehaven. We liked pissing about on Brighton station; we liked the way the announcer sounded like the Queen Mother as he called the stops: 'London Road . . . Falmer . . . Lewes . . . Southease and Rodmell . . . Newhaven Town . . . Newhaven Harbour . . . Bishopstone and Sea-fawd'. We liked the train because it got us where we wanted to be, not because it had a particular kind of carriage, or headcode, or number. Or because it was the great invention of the Victorian age, the one that had changed the world beyond all recognition. We hardly noticed its strangeness and charm. The romance was lost on us.

The longest journey I took alone was on my father's access weekends, when I had to get from Newhaven to Didcot, changing in London. I took this trip every month, but it was exciting only because my dad was waiting to meet me the other end, and I couldn't wait. The journeys dragged by, I remember. I read a lot.

Then, when I was eighteen, I went to college, at Lampeter in Dyfed. It was, and still is, Britain's smallest university, high up the Teifi valley, hidden in the foothills of the Cambrian Mountains.

I went there because it was a long way from Newhaven and you didn't need French O-level to get in.

I got there by train and bus. And I loved the journey, nine times taken there, nine times back, still the most romantic I have ever taken; from childhood into adulthood, from restriction to liberty – and back again.

I left our house with my bags and walked down Newhaven High Street, past Fine Fare where I had worked after school, past the Co-op where my mum still worked, and where she got me a Saturday job cleaning out the bacon fridge and tobying up the cut-out discount vouchers after I got sacked from Fine Fare for pissing about, past Noise, the record shop where I spent what I earned in the supermarket, over the river bridge by the North Quay where my stepfather worked as a fork-lift truck driver unloading timber and stone from coasters and Channel boats, and down to Newhaven station.

There were always a couple of staff on the remembered station: a booking clerk and a porter. There was always a coal fire burning in the grate of the dark wood-panelled waiting room-cum-ticket office. I always bought a pink pasteboard return ticket to Carmarthen, valid for three months. In those days, you didn't have to book weeks before you travelled. You bought the pasteboard ticket and hopped on the train. It was a ticketing system which at that time was already 140 years old.

There is a steel case in the Warehouse at the National Railway Museum in York with drawers full of these old pasteboard tickets. There are thousands of them, from and to a host of different stations, and in all the various classes and types: first-class smoking, second-class ladies only, third-class parliamentary, special tickets for servicemen, for theatrical companies, for fish porters. They are called Edmundson tickets, after their inventor, Thomas Edmundson, a Lancaster Quaker.

The early railways had never really been prepared for the volume of passenger travel that their construction had created. Imagining that they would carry about as many passengers as the stage-coaches, they used the same ticketing systems as the coaches themselves. The tickets, or way-bills, were handwritten and torn out of a book by the guard (hence, 'booking a ticket'). The railways of the late 1820s and early 1830s didn't have stations as we know them, and tickets could be bought from a local inn or hotel. Edmundson was appointed station-master at Brampton station on the Newcastle and Carlisle Railway in 1836, and realized the inefficiency and opportunity for corrupt practice the old system represented. The railway was creating new traffic, not merely replacing the old, and the stage-coach tickets were inadequate for the task. The Duke of Wellington expressed his concern about the new-fangled railway when he said: 'it will only encourage the lower orders to move about.' And he was right.

Edmundson's answer to this new demand was to make tickets, each pre-printed with a destination, and each with an individual serial number, together with a simple press for date stamping. The booking-office clerk, instead of writing out the ticket and then copying it into his ledger, chose the appropriate ticket from a rack, already marked from his station to the most popular destinations, stamped it with the date, and wrote the serial number in a ledger. Edmundson became the world's first ticketing expert, and in 1839 he was head-hunted by the Manchester and Leeds Railway to solve their problems; by the 1840s, at the instigation of the Railway Clearing House (the first regulatory body), most railways had adopted his system, and Edmundson was able to set up on his own. Each of the companies that used his tickets paid him a royalty of ten bob a year per mile of line.

British Rail issued their last Edmundson ticket in February 1990, but independent and revived lines use them still. The Train Operating Companies (or TOCs) now use a thing called APTIS (All Purpose Ticket Issuing System). Those bulky terminals in the ticket office are connected to a central computer in Nottingham, which downloads the day's sales information from each of the APTIS machines. They look fantastically complex, which probably accounts for the amount of time the booking clerk spends pressing keys and faffing about and feeding little bits of cardboard into the body of the machine. I'm sure it's much better than Edmundson, but I swear it takes five times longer now than it did in the Seventies.

The British, you see, can even generate nostalgia about small pieces of pink pasteboard.

The ticket is proof of a contract between you and the TOC. It is an unequal contract. On the back of every ticket you buy it says 'Issued subject to the National Rail Conditions of Carriage' in tiny letters. You are not issued with a copy of the National Rail Conditions (though, if you ask for one, the ticket seller is obliged to give you a copy), so you don't know what the Conditions are, do you? But the companies do. Have no fear; they do all right out of the deal. But ask for a copy of the National Rail Conditions. It's dull, I admit, but it is worth reading the small print, so you know what you're getting into. The print is very small, and a legal background will be of benefit in understanding it. For example:

> *Where relevant these Conditions apply to the carriage of passengers and their property in road vehicles which a Train Company owns or which are operated by any other party on its behalf unless notice is given to show that different conditions apply. For these purposes, the term 'train' includes any road vehicle owned or operated by a Train Company or on its behalf.*

Legalese exists to make people powerless. It's not meant to be clear. It is not just semi-literacy, endemic in our half-educated culture, which makes it difficult for people to read this guff. Like all legal documents, it is designed to be read and fully understood only by a lawyer. That's how lawyers make money, translating. That paragraph could say something like, 'These rules still apply on Replacement Bus Services', but that would probably be too easy.

Buying your ticket has always been fraught. *The Railway Traveller's Handy Book* has a great deal to say on the subject. The modern British queue was born in the railway booking offices of the 1840s and 1850s, and the anonymous author is keen to introduce his audience to the newly evolving niceties of queuing etiquette. He suggests, for example, that instead of chatting to the clerk when you get to the front of the queue, 'you should apply for your ticket somewhat after this manner, "Bath – first class – return", or whatever it may be.'

Still fairly sound advice, I guess.

He also recommends having the correct change ready when you get to the window. His portrait of a traveller who ignores his tips is horribly familiar, especially given the extra opportunities for queueing afforded by supermarkets and cashpoints, and is worth quoting in full. It hardly needs updating at all, except perhaps to change 'gingling' to 'jingling', and to replace 'An elderly lady' with a non-gender-specific hate figure of your choice.

An elderly lady presents herself at the ticket counter, and expresses a wish to go to some place at a small distance, say Putney. She first of all inquires what is the fare; first, second and third class; upon being told that, she hesitates a few seconds, and then thinks she will travel first class. Being asked whether she requires a single or return-ticket, she appears to be astounded at the proposition, ejaculates 'Eh! Oh! Ah!' at wide intervals, and finally decides upon a single ticket, giving at the same time her reasons for doing so. Having been informed the fare is ninepence, she dives for her purse into some apparently unfathomable chasm connected with her dress, and after considerable rummaging, accompanied by a gingling of keys and the production in succession of a pocket-handkerchief, smelling bottle, a pair of mittens, spectacle case, a fan, and an Abernethy biscuit, she at length succeeds in drawing forth an article which resembles an attenuated eel. Thrusting her long bony fingers into this receptacle, she draws out what she conceives to be a shilling, but on nearer inspection she discovers it to be a sovereign. She makes another dive and discovers a half-crown, as she supposes, but this proves to be only a penny piece: finally, she manages to fish out sixpence, and connecting this with the penny piece, and vaguely wondering whether she can find twopence more to make up the required amount, but without arriving at any satisfactory conclusion, she is at length constrained to give over further search and to lay down the sovereign. Upon receiving her change, she examines each piece leisurely to ascertain if it be genuine; satisfied on this point, she counts her change over, repeating the process some four or five times, and on each occasion arriving at a different result. At length she makes out the matter to her own satisfaction, then after having carefully stowed away her change in such a manner that the first pickpocket may abstract it, she looks about her to make sure she has left nothing behind, and after remarking how wonderfully the clerk resembles her nephew who has gone to the Indies, she somewhat reluctantly makes way for the next person.

A perennial subject for humorous writers, I admit, but surely this is the first such piece.

Pasteboard in pocket, I waited on the platform at Newhaven. A bell would ring, and the gates across the road would close. And the train would come and take me away for another ten weeks of freedom.

It's not pretty as you pull out of Newhaven station. On one side of the line is the North Quay, with dunes of graded aggregate sucked from the sea bed piled under gravel hoppers, and a sprawling car scrapyard, half wrecked Mondeos layered on rusting Cortinas, a giant club sandwich built from abandoned cars. On the other side of the line are factories: imperious Parker Pen, the concrete slab of Concord Lighting, the brick-gabled furniture warehouses, car-body places, lorry parks. But soon the line passes into the flat, empty valley of the Ouse, where our geography teacher loved to take us on field trips.

'There!' he would say out in the wet fields. 'Look at that! An ox-bow lake,' or 'That's a text-book example of a knoll.' As ever on school trips, we cared for nothing but Jackie Sinclair, very much the first girl in our class to develop secondary sexual characteristics; we found out years later that the geography teacher had shared this enthusiasm, and with a great deal more success than us.

I continue to press Lewes District Council to promote the Ouse valley as 'Bloomsbury Country'. After all, here's Charleston, where Clive and Vanessa Bell lived with Duncan Grant; here's Berwick church, with its murals by Vanessa and Duncan, there's the Monk's House where Virginia and Leonard Woolf lived; ooh, and look, there's the exact place where Virginia threw herself in the thick salt waters of the River Sussex Ouse. You could have tea rooms, and coach parks, and a daily reconstruction; get some poor cow dressed all in white and fresh out of RADA to chuck herself in at three in the afternoon, every afternoon. You could go to the lighthouse at Newhaven, and watch the waves. Not only would it go a bundle with the better classes of Japanese and American tourists, thus bringing lots of money to the area, but the Bloomsburies would be spinning in their godless graves at the idea of the hoi polloi trooping through their houses and gawping at their things. Win-win, I call it.

I changed at Lewes, seven miles up the line. Lewes is a funny old town, inhabited in equal numbers by posh county types and hippies not quite far out enough to cut it in Totnes. A few middle-class kids from Newhaven whose parents didn't want them to enter the scrum of Tideway were sent to school here, and to the Newhaven mind, this is enough to condemn the place for ever. We don't trust it. But I love the old station. Going to and from London, you always have to change at Lewes, which means I spent a lot of time there, one way or another.

On Lewes station, October 1975, I saw my first punk, Jordan, who was not the Brighton fan with the pumped-up *embonpoint* currently beloved of the *Daily Star*, but little Pam Brookes from Seaford, whom I had met briefly on a school outing a few years before, and who was now the shop assistant in Malcolm McLaren's King's Road shop, Sex. Resplendent in a leather tutu and torn fishnet tights, her hair piled into an impossible white floss beehive, with great streaks of mascara over her dead-white skin, she sat in the waiting room by the platform for Newhaven and Seaford while the other passengers queued up to stare at her. One even took a photograph.

Oscar Wilde, after his conviction, wrote to Lord Alfred Douglas about his transfer from London to Reading Gaol by railway and about having to wait, in 'convict dress and handcuffed', for half an hour on the central platform at Clapham Junction:

> *Of all possible objects, I was the most grotesque. When people saw me, they laughed. Each train as it came up swelled the audience. Nothing could exceed their amusement. That was of course before they knew who I was. As soon as they had been informed, they laughed still more. For half an hour I stood there in the grey November rain surrounded by a jeering mob.*

This was Jordan's daily commute to work, Seaford to the King's Road, via Lewes, and I was part of the mob. But I wasn't jeering – she rocked my world. I didn't have the courage, of course, to remind her of the acquaintance, and I still hate myself for my timidity.

The train to Victoria from Eastbourne or Hastings came curving into the platform, where I would be anxiously pacing about. Some people wait calmly for a train, but I am not one of them. I smoke, I walk up and down, I peer up the line, muttering. Fellow travellers watch me, and laugh at me, and resolve to get in a different carriage. Some people, knowing that in the 170-odd years of railway travel in Britain a train has never once left a station early, turn up two minutes before departure time, take their place on the platform with a show of studied equanimity, and stand quietly waiting for the train to arrive. I always turn up at least twenty minutes before departure, and begin my famous impersonation of a mad bloke. It is punctuality that is the politeness of princes, not turning up early. It's a bad habit that I have never been able to master; I think, what if, *just this once*, the train leaves fifteen minutes early? Who's laughing then?

The run from Lewes to the Thames is mostly mundane. The train passes through the Sussex commuter towns of Haywards Heath, Burgess Hill, Three Bridges, through Gatwick Airport, and into a seemingly endless succession of South London suburbs. The best part of the trip is just north of Haywards Heath, where the line crosses the Ouse Valley Viaduct, at one time the largest brick-built building on earth. It has classical pretensions, and is capped by stone urns. This crossing of the wide green valley was always my last farewell to home. On all often-taken journeys, there is a familiar marker which tells you that you are leaving home, and the Ouse Valley Viaduct was mine.

But it was when we crossed the Thames by Battersea Power Station that my romantic juices started to flow. I loved the sight of London from the railway bridge. And I loved arriving in Victoria station, collecting my bags, walking down the platform, anonymous and free in a crowd. Victoria was the terminus not just of the old London, Brighton and South Coast Railway, but also of the London, Chatham and Dover. The two companies were bitter commercial rivals. This is why Victoria is in two halves; it is really two stations, stuck together, each rebuilt in varying styles at different times. Until 1923, you had to go out of one station and into the next; there was no interconnecting arch, as there is now. But the two halves are still quite distinct. Most people now think of the side where the trains run to Brighton, but on the Chatham, the so-called Continental side, until the 1970s you could catch the *Golden Arrow* to Paris, via Dover. Custom control was done at the station, so that on arrival at Dover, passengers could get straight from the train on to the ferry, and then on to the *Flèche d'Or* in Calais with the minimum of delay. The Continental departure board read Paris, Berlin, Basle, Vienna, Split; and Venice, Athens and Istanbul, for this was the starting point of the Orient Express.

Victoria was thus the most romantic of stations, in a way it is no longer. A romantic journey, perhaps all romance, is something that happens in memory. It is difficult now, waiting on the Continental side of the station for a commuter train to Queen's Road, Peckham, to connect with the ghosts of the thousands of travellers who waited here for a train to Istanbul.

I felt, at eighteen, like a real traveller, diving into the Underground and catching the Circle Line to Paddington. This was the only Tube journey I had ever taken alone, when I went to visit my dad, so I knew all the short cuts down to the platform. I imagined that people saw me either as a hip London street kid, an accomplished user of the Tube, or as a spotty speccy twat, off to college for the first time in an ex-RAF greatcoat and filthy Wrangler flares. What I know now, of course, after many years of Tube travel, is that no one saw me at all. No one sees anything down there.

Paddington was the terminus of the Great Western Railway, the only London terminus with no exterior. The recently restored hotel was not part of the original plan. Rather, the station was built in a cutting, with a sweeping roof of iron and glass. Ramps from the street carried passengers down on to the platforms. It was designed and built, like the railway itself, by the one great Victorian engineer that everybody has heard of, Isambard Kingdom Brunel.

There was no precedent for the scale of the first railway boom of the early 1830s. The Liverpool and Manchester Railway, opened in 1830, had sparked a nationwide realization of the potential of the new steam-hauled train, and three immense and wildly ambitious railway building programmes grew directly from its success. These were the Grand Junction, which ran from Warrington (where it joined the Liverpool and Manchester line) down to Birmingham, engineered by Joseph Locke, and far and away the easiest line to build: the London and Birmingham, which joined the Grand Junction at Birmingham, and ran on to London at Euston station, engineered by Robert Stephenson and the most difficult to build of the three great lines, and the Great Western, from London to Bristol, which was to provide the stage for the most dynamic and innovative engineer of his day, Brunel. Locke, Stephenson and Brunel were the great triumvirate of railway engineers; when they began on these vast engineering projects, Stephenson was thirty-five, Locke thirty, and Brunel just twenty-seven. The railway couldn't be built by cynics. Our romantic feelings about it arise partly because it was built by romantics. The pioneers were all starry-eyed about what the railways might bring. Isambard Kingdom Brunel was the greatest romantic of them all.

His father, Marc Brunel, was one of the most famous engineers of the previous generation. He invented a machine called the tunnelling shield, which enabled tunnels to be built faster and more safely than by any previous method. He claimed that thanks to his invention it was now possible to build a tunnel under the Thames, and in 1824 a company was set up to build the world's first underwater tunnel, between Wapping and Rotherhithe. Construction started a year later. Marc Brunel laid the first brick of the cylinder which would be sunk into the shaft at Rotherhithe; the project's resident engineer, Marc's nineteen-year-old son Isambard, laid the second. They sank the shaft, installed the shield, and started to dig forward towards the river. Almost at once the water started to leak in, and for the first year progress was slow.

In 1826 Marc Brunel was taken seriously ill, so, at the age of twenty Isambard found himself effectively in control of this unique undertaking. The tunnel flooded, and steam pumps were installed in an attempt to keep it dry. Work was slower than ever, and the Tunnel Company, worried by lack of cash flow, started selling tickets to the curious who wanted to visit the works. Isambard knew that there would be a massive breach, and he could only hope that this would happen when there were no visitors in the tunnel. On the night of 18 May 1827 the river burst through the roof, and a wall of water swept through the tunnel. The navvies fled; Brunel stood at the foot of the shaft, urging his men to safety. A quick headcount showed that one man was missing, an old pump operator called Tillet. Brunel could hear faint cries for help; he tied a rope around himself and forced his way through the water. Finding Tillet, he tied him to the rope and pulled him to safety. No one had been killed in the breach. Brunel wasn't merely a romantic figure; he was straightforwardly swashbuckling.

So now the tunnel was full of water. Brunel went down to the bottom of the Thames in a diving bell and saw where the river had broken through. He decided to plug the hole by dropping thousands of sacks filled with clay and hazel twigs into the riverbed above the tunnel. The work took months. The breach had to be sealed, the water pumped out, and then the shield had to be cleared of hundreds of tons of mud. By November Brunel was ready to start digging again, and to celebrate he ordered a banquet to be served in the tunnel for the navvies, his family and friends. Entertainment was provided under the river by the band of the Coldstream Guards.

Digging began again, but in January 1828 the river burst through once more. This time Brunel was not so lucky. Hearing the water rushing through the tunnel, he tried to help Ball and Collins, two of his men who were trapped, but his foot was caught under some timbers, and he was unable to reach them. Brunel was washed out from the tunnel to the top of the shaft, badly injured; Ball, Collins and four others were drowned in the tunnel.

By 1828 Marc Brunel was sufficiently recovered to take charge of the tunnel again, and Isambard was sent to recuperate from his injuries at Clifton, near Bristol. So it was that the younger Brunel was in the right place when it was decided by local worthies to go ahead with the long-planned Clifton Bridge. Isambard's health was never good after the Thames Tunnel experience, but he still managed to visit Telford's Menai Bridge, between North Wales and Anglesey, to see the suspension principle for himself. With some help from his father, and after a deal of opposition from the engineering establishment, Brunel submitted the winning design for the bridge which spans the Avon Gorge today. He was therefore already well known in Bristol by 1832, when a committee of local businessmen proposed a railway from that town to London.

The committee originally had it in mind to choose the cheapest design, but Brunel, at twenty-seven already a master at handling committees, treated this approach with contempt. He said, 'It is quite obvious that the man who has the least reputation at stake, or who has most to gain by temporary success, and least to lose by the consequences of disappointment, must be the winner in such a race.' Brunel would build them the best railway, not the cheapest, and the committee were persuaded by his argument. It took three years to survey the route and gain Parliamentary approval for Brunel's chosen line. He was also fighting a personal battle with his committee on the previously uncontroversial subject of gauge; that is, the distance between the rails. The earliest railways were built to a gauge of four feet, eight and a half inches, for reasons that we will come back to. But Brunel thought that this was inadequate for the fast running of locomotives, and he wanted to build his railway with rails seven feet apart, the so-called broad gauge. He won this argument, too, and construction began in 1835.

Between London and Swindon, the railway is almost flat. Railways, like Daleks, have difficulty in getting up hills. Metal wheels running on metal rails mean that there is very little friction between wheel and track, so large loads can be hauled at high speed. It also means that there is little adhesion between wheel and track; fine on the flat, but highly problematic on hills. Leaves on the line mean the wheels don't stick; the wrong kind of snow isn't sticky enough.

The Great Western main line was so flat that it was known as Brunel's Billiard Table. The main obstacle in Brunel's path on the first part of his line was the Thames, which the railway crosses at Maidenhead. When you cross the river today, it is difficult to appreciate the beauty of Brunel's solution to the problem. The Maidenhead Railway Bridge needs to be seen from the river. The elegance of its three arches looks so appropriate in this setting that it is hard to conceive of the revolutionary nature of Brunel's design. No bridge had ever been built with arches that were so flat in profile. His critics said that it couldn't work; that the bridge would never be able to support the weight of a fully laden train. They were wrong; it is still there, still supporting far higher tonnages than it was designed to carry. Turner's famous painting, *Rain, Steam and Speed*, first exhibited at the Royal Academy in 1844, shows a broad-gauge locomotive chasing a hare across the Maidenhead Bridge.

The one place that Brunel couldn't avoid the hills was outside Bath, and his solution was once again bold and innovative. The steepest part of the line would have to have a gradient of one in sixty, and Brunel decided to hide it underground, in his masterly Box Tunnel. The portals of this tunnel, which is one mile and 1,452 yards long and took three years to build, reflect the Georgian grandeur of Bath itself. The last part of the line to be completed, it opened in 1841. The tunnel is also a testament to Brunel's cheek; one might almost say his arrogance. One in sixty was a steep gradient, and the fact that its line ran underground has led to operational problems which continue to this day. Most audacious of all, the tunnel is aligned so that on the morning of Brunel's birthday, 9 April, the rising sun shines through it end to end – or so says the myth. I have met railway enthusiasts who have sworn to me that they have witnessed this phenomenon; but in fact, Brunel did not take into account the effects of atmospheric defraction, and the sun only really shines right through the tunnel on the mornings of 6, 7 and 8 April. As a man who struggles to put up a flatpack Ikea Billy bookcase, I regard this as a remarkably close call. And the imagination and nerve necessary even to attempt such a thing boggle the mind.

Nor is this the only amazing thing about the Box Tunnel. Conspiracy theorists insist that there is a network of secret tunnels that lead from inside Box to the government installation at Rudloe Manor, which is reputed to be the centre for research into UFOs. Ufologists claim that the powers that be store alien spacecraft down there. There are railwaymen too who claim that there are secret tunnels hidden behind steel doors in Box, but that they hold, not UFOs, but steam locomotives, the so-called Strategic Reserve. The argument runs that in time of nuclear war it would be almost impossible to move about the country, and that diesel and electric trains would be immobilized. Steam trains, which need only coal, water and a box of matches to operate would be the best way to transport people and materials. The engines that have been preserved for this purpose wait, painted black and without identification numbers, in a vast underground siding, accessed through Box. Gangers have long reported 'phantom trains' in Box Tunnel, and in the last days of steam, they became reluctant to work underground. There is supposed to be a secret underground city down there, prepared for the government against an all-out thermonuclear attack.

The huge locomotives which worked the railway were designed and built by another young man, the Great Western's locomotive superintendent, Daniel Gooch. The company was worried that so much responsibility rested on the shoulders of two such young men, but Brunel had faith in Gooch, and Gooch's majestic engines were the fastest on the British railway system at that time. It is a pity that the experiment failed; seven-foot trains would run much faster than standard-gauge ones, of that there can be no doubt. But it was a battle that was lost before it really began; the Great Western, proud of its identity, clung to the broad gauge until 1892 before succumbing to the inevitable and changing its tracks to the standard. The broad-gauge experiment failed, not because Brunel was mistaken in thinking that a seven-foot gauge would enable much faster running, but because the narrower four foot, eight and a half inches was already so well established. Every time goods were transported from, for example, Liverpool to Plymouth, it was necessary to trans-ship them from one gauge of wagon to another halfway through the trip, incurring loss of time and extra expense.

Brunel's romantic vision extended across the Atlantic. His idea was that passengers would embark at Paddington for New York via Bristol, and he engineered a series of remarkable steamships, the *Great Britain*, the *Great Western* and the *Great Eastern*. You can still visit the *Great Britain* in Bristol Docks; Brunel built those too. Everywhere you travel by train in the west, you can see Brunel's hand; most famously, as you cross the Tamar Bridge at Saltash. The stations still bear the hallmark of the man who designed them. I conducted a straw poll, where I asked for people's favourite station, and Bristol Temple Meads came a clear second. (St Pancras, of course, was the winner; Edinburgh Waverley was third.) I'm not sure about it; the main line has been moved to the north, and runs through Bristol Parkway, and I find Temple Meads anti-climactic, much of the building given over to offices, the concourse a drab car park. Brunel's real legacy is the romance that continues to cling to God's Wonderful Railway. At eighteen, standing on what is still called 'The Lawn' at Paddington (the area where people stand staring at departure boards, waiting for platforms to be announced), I certainly felt that romantic power. Or perhaps it was just the prospect of sex, drugs and rock and roll at the end of the trip that made me feel so excited.

At Paddington, the almost-brand new InterCity 125 train would be waiting on the platform. They were an innovation then, those high-speed trains with their cheese wedge-shaped nose. On the first trip, I got into a non-smoking compartment; on all subsequent journeys, I found a seat in the smoker. If college taught me anything, it was how to smoke. Often, on the outward run, I would go for breakfast in the restaurant car, paid for with the cash my mum had given me to see me through the first days before my grant arrived. On the way back, I starved.

Didcot Power Station was the last familiar marker on the journey – that was where my stepmother worked – and Didcot Parkway was the station where my father would meet me for my weekend visits. After that, it was unknown territory. Not terribly inspiring territory, I always felt; Brunel's Billiard Table is flat because it runs through flat country, though there are green downs to the south, and the first foothills of the Cotswolds to the north. The highlight was Swindon, oddly. This was where Daniel Gooch built the locomotives that made Brunel's broad-gauge vision come to life. There is a museum in the attractive old engine sheds by the line. Swindon was one of the greater railway towns, as Newhaven was one of the lesser, but it is not such a spotter magnet as Derby or Crewe.

The line to South Wales bypasses Bristol now and leaves England by the Severn Tunnel. This has always been a wet tunnel; it is only constant pumping that keeps it merely very damp. The train runs through the heart of South Wales, from Newport to Cardiff, and almost passes into the great steel-works at Port Talbot before it terminates in Swansea. I changed at Swansea for a little diesel train to Carmarthen. My almost-home sign in West Wales was always Llanelli, because of the name, the double '(llch)'. You couldn't be anywhere but in Wales. It stands at the far western end of the South Wales conurbation, and beyond it the real deep country starts. So from there on the ride was beautiful and isolated and properly Welsh, I always thought. The line follows the beach at Cefn Padrig where Amelia Earhart landed after her solo flight across the Atlantic, and from Kidwelly into Carmarthen, the line hugs the estuary of the River Towy, looking over to Laugharne (Llareggub), where Dylan Thomas sat writing in his shed . . .

The little train stopped at Carmarthen, the line into Lampeter having fallen under Beeching's axe in the Sixties. There was an old-fashioned single-decker brown bus, 'Edwards of Pencader', waiting outside the station for the twenty-mile ride into Lampeter, which was my Shangri-La when I was eighteen. And what could be more romantic than a journey to your own private Shangri-La?

Snag is, no one works in Shangri-La, and neither did I. I am one of a tiny handful of people alive today who failed a degree. Not easy, I promise you.

So after I failed to graduate, I moved to Brighton with my student band. That didn't work out, so some of us moved to Manchester to play in a new band. That was horrible, so I moved back to Brighton and got a day job as a boardmarker in a bookie's. I started playing music with a five-piece Newhaven band, a kind of supergroup of the best players in or from the town, all head-hunted and forced to play nicely together by our cynical bass player. Real bands all come from the same cul-de-sac, he reasoned, and he was almost right. We were pretty good. Radio Caroline called us 'the best unsigned band in Britain' and had our demo on their playlist. We stayed unsigned. We rehearsed three nights a week, in Newhaven, where all the others still lived, so on these nights I caught the train from Brighton to Newhaven and walked from the station across the bridge and along the river wall to the place where we rehearsed. After rehearsal, I walked back beside the black river, crackling with cat ice under the fishing jetties in winter, across the bridge, past Newhaven Town station, which closed at midnight, and all the way to Newhaven Harbour station, where the last train, the 00.25 boat train, stopped.

I must have taken this journey by that last train 500 times; and on no more than five occasions did anyone else board it at Newhaven Harbour station. The other 495 times I took that trip, there was just me getting on, and waiting for me in the carriage the only other passenger, a skinhead who wore a smart Crombie in winter and a Harrington in summer. He had clearly got on at Bishopstone or Seaford, probably after seeing his girlfriend, or so I deduced. It was just us on that night train, but we never spoke, in five years. Mind you, who does strike up casual conversation with a full-dress skinhead? Especially someone who, in five years, was never once allowed to stay over with his girlfriend. I imagined that he was in a bad mood, judging from his scowling face.

He got out at Lewes. Sometimes, one or two people would get on to take his place, but more often than not I would be alone until the next station, Falmer, where students from Brighton and Sussex Universities would pile on to the train for the last few stops into Brighton. The only exception was Bonfire Night, when Lewes station looked like Tokyo Central; hundreds of wrapped-up-warm bonfire fans jammed together on the platform, waiting for the last train.

There was nobody on the boat train because the boats had stopped, at least in winter. Even when they did run, in high summer, everyone seemed to be car passengers, the existence of the connecting train forgotten by all but a handful of foot passengers; on average, one a year. The link between the ferry and the train had been broken, to their mutual loss, and to the ruin of the town. By the 1980s Newhaven was over; the supermarkets where I had worked were closed down; Noise, the old record shop, was a ratty car-spares place; my stepfather had been made redundant from the Quay and was lucky to find work on the line in a soap-dispenser factory on the industrial estate. Newhaven Fort had been turned into a low-rent visitor attraction which didn't attract many visitors. There was, and is, a thriving smack culture. Bruce, a pal from school, was a user. He supported his habit by working as a ganger on the permanent way – he was killed by a train.

When I felt the band had gone as far as it could, we split up 'due to musical differences', as they say. So I head-hunted my own Ouse Valley supergroup, casting my net as far afield as Peacehaven and Lewes, but trying to stay true to the same cul-de-sac principle. This time there were ten of us, an insane hippy orchestra. We still rehearsed in Newhaven, and I still had to catch the 00.25 boat train home. The new band had another singer apart from me, one of the hard, pretty girls who had been in my year at school. I loved her voice, breathy and flat, like Astrid Gilberto's, and I loved the way it sounded next to my own. We spent a lot of time laughing and talking together at rehearsal and at gigs, waiting for the horn section to learn a part, waiting for the guitarists to tune up, and for the piano-player to turn up. We sat together in the van on the way to gigs, playing backgammon. We stood next to each other on stage, staring into each other's eyes, singing to each other, singing the love songs that I was writing, writing for her . . .

We were both married. She lived with her husband in a terraced house by the Harbour; we walked to the station together after rehearsal, and she would wait with me on the platform for the last train before crossing the tracks to go home. We had our first kiss on that platform, said a hundred desperate goodbyes on that platform, waiting for the last train. She was the one I watched from the window, receding into the distance, as she stood watching my train pull away. She was the one who ran into my arms at Brighton station when she could get away to meet me. She was Celia Johnson to my Trevor Howard.

One night, we were joined on the platform at the Harbour station by a foot passenger from the ferry. As I've said, this was highly unusual. He was tall and thin, and wore a grey anorak. Like me, he was one of those who pace up and down. We ignored him; we didn't let a stranger burst our bubble of momentary happiness, waiting for the crossing gates to close, waiting for the train that would keep us apart for another day or two. When it came, I leaned from the window, as was my custom, to watch my girlfriend standing under the platform lights.

Then I clocked the skinhead, sat down, and opened my book. The tall, thin guy with the grey anorak walked past me and went into the loo. He had an old-fashioned knapsack with a Canadian maple-leaf badge sewn on to one of the pockets, I noticed.

Lewes came, and the skinhead got off. I read my book and thought about the girl I'd left at the station, and the girl who would be asleep in bed when I got home. As we came out of London Road, the last stop before Brighton, I looked up and saw a large pool of thick bright red liquid coming from under the lavatory door. I had no clue what it could be. I looked back down at my book. As the train pulled into Brighton, I stood up and put my book in my pocket. The pool had grown much larger, and was oozing towards me over the floor of the train. It was bright pillar-box red. I bent down and dipped my finger into the soupy pool, and touched the tip of my finger with the tip of my tongue. It was blood.

The train pulled to a stop beside the platform, and I ran to find help. I told the ticket collector at the platform's end what I had found, and he hurried back with me the length of the train. We collected the guard on the way; I showed them the blood, and the ticket collector took me off to the Transport Police. They sealed off the platform and took me to a little interview room. I told them everything I remembered of the tall, thin guy, which was very little. Another Transport policeman came in to say that they had found a dead body, a Canadian national from his passport, in the lavatory compartment of the boat train. I was sent home after a couple of hours.

The next morning, I told my wife that I was leaving her. I packed a bag and went to stay with a friend. For good measure, I told my song-writing partner, Gary, that I was leaving the band.

I phoned the police to ask if they knew what had happened. The Canadian guy was a junkie and had been jacking up. For whatever reason (usually it's because of good gear), he had passed out. In falling forward, he had hit the bridge of his nose on the rim of the bogpan. While he was unconscious, he bled to death through his broken nose.

I still find it strange that I had been witness to the last few moments of a life, and that I sat reading while he bled to death six feet away. We pass strangers by the thousand every day, at least some of them minutes from death. Strange, too, that I chose that moment to end my marriage and what I had always thought of as my career. Why then? I'm still not clear. We all have self-destruct buttons; this was my moment to see what would happen if I pressed mine, I guess. My girlfriend left her husband and went to stay with her mother while we sorted things out. For four weeks she would take the train into Brighton after work and we would sit and talk for hours in the buffet. We didn't have anywhere else to go; and Brighton station is cold, the coldest place I know. We talked mostly about how guilty we felt about the terrible thing we had done. We were miserable as sin.

One night I met her from the train, and she didn't run into my arms. She told me that she was going back to her husband, because she couldn't live with how much she had hurt him. When she hugged me before she caught the last train back to Newhaven Harbour, I knew that I would never see her again. She didn't lean from the window to see me standing on the platform. I went crawling back to my wife, and she laughed at me. I went crawling back to the band, and only two of the old ten-piece lineup were willing to work with me. We got a new band together, with players from Brighton, so I didn't have to catch the night train home, which was just as well, because there wasn't any home to go back to any more.

Eighteen years and more later, I was waiting on the Continental side of Victoria with a large group of railway enthusiasts to catch a train to Newhaven Harbour (Newhaven Marine, they call it now). The train was called 'The Brighton Breezy', and it was to be steam-hauled. This is what is known as a rail excursion, a special train hired by a company to give enthusiasts the thrill of a steam run on a main line. These trips are run by various private companies; this time it was Past Time Rail, the market leaders. At one time, until very recently in fact, all these charters were run by a company owned by Pete Waterman, the man who gave the world Kylie. He's a huge railway fan, and we owe him a great debt. That must say something, surely?

It was exciting to see a steam engine again in Victoria, with smoke puffing idly from the stack, and steam hissing softly from the valves. It is a somehow familiar and comforting sight, though I guess I have never actually seen a steam engine here before. All I've seen is trains on film: we take other people's nostalgia for our own, sometimes. The enthusiasts enthused, hundreds of them. They were a funny-looking bunch, on the pipe and slippers side of forty, by and large. Two teenage nu-goth girls who'd been reading *Ghost World* started calling after one of the enthusiasts, 'Hey, Mister! Mister! I know you!'

'Yeah,' says her friend, 'you're famous! You're in a band!'

'Yeah, that's right! You're Lemmy from Motorhead! Aren't you?'

'Lemmy, can we have your autograph?'

I couldn't help grinning. He did look a lot like the Reverend Kilminster, but whereas Lemmy wears a leather jacket covered in motorbike badges, this guy was wearing a stained old engine-driver's coat covered in train badges; and his mutton-chop whiskers, rather than paying homage to Gene Vincent, recalled the mid-period Fred Dibnah.

Some of the enthusiasts gathered around the engine, taking photos, crowding one another out like crazed paparazzi, or trying to catch the driver's eye for an invitation to hop up into the cab, like they hoped to when they were lads. The main body, many of them accompanied by wives and grandchildren, baggsied themselves the best seats in the old-fashioned carriages, and cheerfully started popping their flasks and unwrapping sandwiches from greaseproof paper. As the time of departure came closer, the photographers reluctantly folded away their tripods, and the groupies realized that, once again, they were going to have to ride in a carriage rather than on the footplate. They crammed into the few remaining seats. The steam-hauled train from Victoria to Brighton, via Lewes and Newhaven Marine, was packed to the gunwales.

I never took the train. I meant to. I bought a ticket. But when it came to it, I couldn't face it. I realized that I had no real stake in the day out to Newhaven, just as the men who liked the trains had no stake in their destination. Their romance was not my romance. So instead, I stood on the platform. I watched the driver send steam from the boiler to the valves, heard the first burst of effort, saw the pistons start the attempt at turning the great driving wheels, watched the wheels resist, and the pistons insist, until the Brighton Breezy pulled its load of cheerful excursionists out of the Continental side of Victoria, all bound for Newhaven Marine, fifty-five miles away, the passengers leaning out of the windows, waving at those of us who stood watching them go.

As I said, the boats hardly run at all now, but the sign at the half-deserted ferry terminal still reads 'Newhaven – Gateway to Europe'. The council want to build a rubbish incinerator on the North Quay. They hope to attract garbage from France into the port. Half the shops are boarded up as the factories struggle on, at best. Some of the people I played with in bands work in those factories, recently on short time. One of the guitarists is a truck mechanic, and he can't find work in a town that was once full of trucks, work which he badly needs to feed his smack habit. The police station is permanently understaffed, and is regarded as the worst posting in Sussex. My mum doesn't go up the town any more. She goes to the out-of-town Sainsbury's, or my stepfather drives her into Seaford.

'The town is dead,' they say.

The Port of Newhaven is essential to the life of the Port of Dieppe. It can't be allowed to die. So Dieppe Town Council bought it last year. Newhaven is the first French-owned town in England, and a good thing too. If there's hope for Newhaven, there's hope for us all.

The cloud of steam dissolved away from under Victoria station roof, and the train was gone. I bought a newspaper and caught the 38 bus from outside the station.

My mobile chattered. It was my girlfriend.

'Hello?'

'Hello, darling. Where are you?'

'I'm on the bus.'

'Why aren't you on the train?'

'I couldn't hack it.'

'Hack what?'

'Newhaven. I'm coming home.'

The Railway Age – The Family Destination

From the 1920s until well into the 1960s, children were expected to be interested in trains. If you didn't want to be a train driver, you were gay or something. Girls wanted to be train drivers too, but they couldn't be, because they were girls. Kids who didn't like trains were weird. Children's annuals all had pictures of steam locomotives, together with a vast amount of technical information. Girls' comics had them too; I have a copy of the *Swift* Annual from 1961, which has a two-page full-colour piece on 'Great Trains'. Pretty well anybody could identify the more famous engines, and if you talk to anyone over sixty, they will still be able to tell you the sort of steam engine that used to take them on holiday. Trainspotting was normal. As late as the 1970s, aunties always sent you birthday cards with pictures of steam trains on them, and 'Happy Birthday Dear Nephew' embossed in gold ink. My aunties did, anyway.

There were hundreds of illustrated railway books for children, which were still being published in the 1960s. Every boy worth his salt had at least one of these books. They had titles like *Every Boy's Bumper Book of Trains*. As an example of the genre, I give you *The Book of Railways* by Arthur Groom. The style of illustration is now mostly familiar to us from 'Black Bag' or 'Jack Black' from *Viz* comic. A father who works on the railway takes his two children, Billy and Betty, on a 'two weeks' railway holiday'. Billy and Betty are very keen on the railway – a little overkeen, perhaps, but the book was published sometime between 1948 and 1952, when spottermania was at its height, so maybe they can be excused. As the trip starts, Betty says of their visit to Waterloo station, 'Oh, Daddy, I can't think of anything nicer than this.'

Betty must be aged about eleven. Try taking a twenty-first-century eleven-year-old girl for a day out in the signal-box at Waterloo, or round the major London termini to watch trains depart, and see how you get on. Billy and Betty, however, were made up. Their dad doesn't just take them spotting, he takes them for train journeys too; for example, on a sleeper to Cornwall. Billy and Betty are very excited. They wake up early and watch the train cross Brunel's Saltash Bridge over the Tamar. They 'whoop with glee' as the train pulls into Penzance. You might think that they then spent a few days by the seaside; not a bit of it. All Groom tells us of Penzance is that, 'The stay in Cornwall was quite short but, as they had the long day journey back to Paddington to look forward to, the children did not mind that.'

Parents were obviously less scared of kids in those days. If I'd taken mine to Penzance on a sleeper, and then turned round and taken them straight back to Paddington, they would have brained me. One thing that Betty and Billy's father does try is a trip on the Romney, Hythe and Dymchurch Railway, a miniature railway which runs along the Kent coast. It sounded such fun that I decided to take my own thirteen-year-old on it at some point. This would be a useful test, I felt, of the degree to which children's interests have changed over fifty years.

One thing that hasn't changed much is that *Blue Peter* is still on the telly. These days, they have pieces about checking your testicles for cancer, and the perils of crack smoking, but when the show started in 1958, its first presenter, Christopher Trace, was chosen because of his interest in model trains. The original idea behind *Blue Peter* was that it would show girls how to make dolls' clothes, and boys how to extend their model railways. I can remember watching *Blue Peter* in the Seventies, and they still used to get the train layout down to play with, at least once a month. A genial modeller would come on and show Peter Purves how to make convincing hedges from cotton wool. It's long gone now, has the *Blue Peter* railway, as has the endemic interest in railways and all things railway that it grew out of. Ours is the generation that knows least about trains and the railways of any since 1830.

Hey, kids! Let's find out!

If there are any places left where the old feelings about trains remain, they must be York and Crewe. York is famous for many things; ask the average Joe about York, and he will tell you about Vikings and the Minster, with railways maybe making it into the top five. Crewe is famous for nothing else. I was off to both.

I arrived in York station to find a huge queue for taxis outside, so I went back into the buffet for a cup of Ritazza coffee. *Blue Peter* was playing on the TV set; and they were doing a piece about kilts. Peter Purves may have been able to carry a kilt, but today's presenters look like men in skirts. You've got to have a bit of beef on you to carry off a kilt. Today's presenters are willowy, epicene creatures; they should try lugging the old train-set out of storage. That would build them up.

The worst of the queue passed off, and I eventually got a taxi out to my hotel.

'What brings you to Yark, mate?' asked the driver.

'To visit the National Railway Museum.'

'Trainspotter, are yer?'

'No, I'm researching a book about trains.'

'You want to try writing about something interesting, mate.'

We were sitting in traffic on George Hudson Way. Hudson was 'the Railway King', an extraordinary figure who saved York from fading into obscurity, like Lincoln or Norwich, two other medieval cities which fared badly in the newly industrialized Britain. Hudson's wealth, tenacity and willingness to play politics at the highest level ensured that York came to be at the centre of the spreading railway network during the 1840s. The companies he controlled were rolled up into the mighty Midland Railway Company, in 1844. He returned high dividends to his shareholders, who loved him. He was also one of the great creative accountants; he would have been happy at Enron. After he was forced to resign from yet another of the companies he controlled, the Eastern Counties, a Commission of Enquiry found that the reason for all the high dividends was the fact that he had been paying them out of capital. The great plutocrat fled abroad to France. Hudson's exile brought to an end the years of 'Railway Mania', when people panicked if they did not own railway shares, and the railways entered the first real slump in their fortunes, which had been on the ascendant for the first fifty years of the century. But people in York are proud of Hudson, and rightly. He did all right by them. This not very clever taxi driver would not be picking up passengers from the station and sitting with them in traffic jams on George Hudson Way if the old rogue had not done his sums in York's favour.

'What would be interesting?' I asked the driver.

'What?'

'What would be interesting for me to write about?'

He fell silent for the rest of the journey. Perhaps he's still mulling that one over.

A night in a hotel meant that I could be at the National Railway Museum (NRM) in the morning for opening time. It's an offshoot of the Science Museum in Kensington. It was European Museum of the Year for 2001, and it is the best museum I've been to outside London. Shortly after opening time, it was already busy. Today was York Day, when residents of York could get into all the city's visitor attractions free; clearly, many of them had decided to take advantage of this to visit the NRM, even though it's free anyway.

I began my visit in traditional style; I went for a cup of tea in the museum café, which is in the middle of the old engine shed. I sat drinking tea and eating cake, surrounded by a fabulous collection of old railway carriages, nut-brown *wagons-lits*, a superb Midland Railway dining car whose destination was Glasgow St Enoch. I tried not to be overwhelmed by nostalgia for a past that wasn't mine. More than anything, I wanted to find some bits of old track. The carriages could wait while I wandered off to find the roots of the railway.

The NRM has a huge new circular building with an engine turn-table at its heart. This is where the curators display their collection of locomotives. I didn't want to see those, either. Along one side of the Turn-table Hall, largely overlooked by the people who were climbing up to have a look at the engines, was a selection of different lengths of railway track, which show the evolution of the railway over its first 200 years. I found this exhibit, lit a metaphorical pipe, and gazed down at the rusty old rails.

Railway literature (actually, I should say 'railway books', because there is precious little actual literature on the subject) is excessively interested in steam locomotives. This is understandable, because they are big and smoky and fast, all things that boys like. There must be a book by a woman in the thousands of titles I have seen, but I have never found it. The *Swift*-reading girls of the 1950s and 1960s did not go on to write *Branch Lines to East Grinstead*. This obsession with steam means that school memories of history will tell you that the Stockton and Darlington Railway was the world's first. It was not, not by a long chalk. It was the world's first public railway to use steam-hauled trains for part of its operation, which is a completely different thing. By the time the Stockton and Darlington opened in 1825, railways had been operating in Britain for over 200 years.

The builders of the pyramids, and perhaps even Stonehenge, must have used sleds with rollers which were supported on trackways of wood. There is some evidence that the Babylonians used, if not railways, then rutways; grooves cut into rock which allowed the smoother running of wagons or sleds. If you walk through deep snow, it is easier if you follow the footprints of someone who has gone before. If you are dragging huge blocks of stone through the desert, it will be easier to drag them in the compacted ruts of the poor saps who went first. There is some evidence in Malta of groove-cutting for sleds, which dates from about 2000 BC.

The first documentary record we have of regular use of wheeled vehicles running on track is Agricola's *De Re Metallica*, published in 1556. Agricola's aim was to publish an encyclopedic work which contained all of man's knowledge about metal and metal-working. The illustrations clearly show German miners pushing wagons full of ore back to the surface on wooden tracks. It is less clear how the wagons stayed on the tracks; it looks as though the wheels had guiding pins of some kind.

German miners had probably been using underground railways for hundreds of years before Agricola recorded them, and certainly British mines would have used the trackways too, often running for several hundred yards, from the face up to the pithead. Rivers were the best and most reliable method of transport in the medieval world, and tracks may also have run down from the pithead to the river. It is a good bet, but there is no real evidence of this until Huntington Beaumont, a wealthy mine owner, built a two-mile line from his pithead down what is now Wollaton Lane, in Nottinghamshire, in 1603. It was not the first in the world, we can be fairly sure; but it is the oldest railway site whose existence is beyond doubt. Beaumont was a man interested in 'new and extraordinary events and practices', and when he acquired an interest in some mines in Northumberland it was natural for him to take the idea of wagons running on 'rayles' with him.

These early railways were called tramways, or wagon ways. Horse-hauled over the flat, and helped by winding-gear up inclines, these tramways almost always ran from a pithead down to a trans-shipment point by a river. Throughout the seventeenth century tramways were built in the industrialized areas of Shropshire, and down from the mines in South Wales; but it was in the north-east, from Durham and down the Tyne to Newcastle, that they were most widely used. The only remaining physical evidence for a seventeenth-century tramway is at Ryton Moor in Co. Durham.

By the end of the seventeenth century, the tramways were so widespread in the north-east of England that they became known as 'Newcastle Roads'. The best-known memorial of these is the Causey Arch, built in 1727 to carry the Dunston railroad. Causey still stands today, the world's oldest extant railway bridge. Throughout the eighteenth century, the north-east developed its system of railways. The tracks were all made of timber. In the South Wales coalfields and the heavily industrialized parts of Shropshire, the track tended to be L-shaped, so that ordinary wagons could be guided along the track. In the north-east, however, the rails were straight, and known as edgeways; it was flanged wheels which kept the wagons on the track. By the middle of the eighteenth century, stationary steam engines were used to pull trains up the inclines. If the line had to go downhill, the horse would hop into the 'dandy cart' and get a ride behind a gravity-run train.

Wood sticks on wood; metal slides over metal. Metal is stronger than wood, and metal-tyred wagons running on metal creates less friction than wood, which meant that heavier loads could be hauled by the teams of horses without the rail buckling. I doubt that horses are particularly nostalgic about this period in early railway history, despite the occasional spree in the dandy cart. They preferred steam, when they got to ride in elegant horse-boxes. The first metal rails were built in the 1760s, at first as protection for the wooden tracks from iron tyres. Cast- and wrought-iron-only rails started to be laid widely during the 1790s, prompted by an explosion in tramway-building, itself prompted by the growth of English canals.

Canals are made of flat water, and flat water is difficult stuff to get hold of. It is expensive. You use locks to keep it flat when you go up hills. Sometimes, you have to take the water under hills in tunnels in order to preserve its flatness. Canals were not cheap to build. To get right up steep hillsides, to get the coal from the mine, you needed tramways, which were much less expensive to construct. Tramways spread away from the canals like frost on glass. The canals meant that more coal could be sold, more iron could be founded. Prices of raw materials dropped markedly as a result of the canal's opening; demand rocketed. More iron and coal had to be mined, and tramway technology responded accordingly.

Some of the tramways reached epic proportions. The greatest of them was the High Peak Tramway, built by Josiah Jessop to link the Cromford and Peak Forest Canals, carrying the line over 1,000 feet high. This was built as an L-shaped line, rather than an edgeway. By 1800, the canal system as it remains today was three-quarters finished, and there were hundreds of miles of tramway, linking mines and factories to the cut.

There was only one part of industrial England where there was no major canal-building, and that was the north-east. Good links with London by sea was one reason, of course, but perhaps the north-east needed canals less, given the widespread extent of their edgeways, climbing up from the Tyne and the Tees to the mines. One of these Newcastle Roads was called the Wylam Wagonway. George Stephen- son was born in a cottage two yards from the line in 1781. The first job he remembered as a child was stopping his younger brothers and sisters from getting under the horses' hooves as they pulled loads up the line.

'You all right, sir?'

I jumped. A volunteer member of the museum staff touched me on the arm.

'Yes, I'm fine.'

'Interested in the rails, are you?'

'Yes.'

'Ooh, you should come and look at the engines; great big engines we've got here, sir. Come on, sir, you don't want to spend your day looking at those rusty old things! Come and see the engines, sir.'

'I'm fine. I like beginnings.'

'Come on, sir, come and see the engines. They're just about to operate the turn-table! Theres a lovely engine on the turn-table. You must see the turn-table.'

An announcer announced, 'There will be a demonstration of the turn-table in the Engine Hall in five minutes. Please stand well back from the rail.'

'There y'are, sir. What did I tell yer, sir? Come and see the turn-table.'

I went to see the turn-table. A commentator sat on the old steam engine on the turn-table spouting turn-table facts through a radio mike. Her colleague operated the turn-table. The engine went round on the turn-table. The commentator waved at the children standing watching her go by. This was a change from the normal arrangements on roundabouts, where it is the children who go round, while the grown-ups stand and watch. The children at the NRM were less than enthusiastic in their response to the cheery commentator. Clearly, it was they who should be riding on the thing. Railway enthusiasts (as we must learn to call them, never trainspotters) can be a passive bunch. There are volunteers who work on the preserved lines, of course, and a handful of them will go on to drive trains, but mostly, your railway enthusiast is something of a bystander. You can't really have a go on a train, or a train turn-table. You have to stand well back from the rail. All you can do is watch, or play, like here at the NRM. I wandered around, watching things and looking for something to play on.

There are some beautiful engines in here, though, old and silent, massive and cold as icebergs. Here is the dolphin's curve of *Mallard*, the fastest of all steam engines (126 mph in 1938). Here is a vast blue English *Electric Deltic* diesel/electric, the prototype from 1951, with go-faster chevrons, post-austerity modernism in the raw. Here is the elegiac *Evening Star*, mournful in black, the last steam engine built by British Rail, in 1960. They are precious things. You can't really get in and start pissing about with the levers.

What there is to play on, is a Japanese Shinkansen 'Bullet Train'. You can go and sit in one of its carriages and see how cool it is. I climbed aboard. The seats were great; all airline style, with fold-down tables. Lots of leg-room. You'd be thrilled if it turned up at Milton Keynes Central and whisked you up to Manchester Picc to see Aunt Alice. A smashing and really modern and comfortable train, which came into service in 1964. The Japanese were starting to develop the Bullet Train at the same time that we were building *Evening Star*. Ours is an old railway, you see. I stretched out and watched a video about how good the Shinkansen is, and how good InterCity could have been.

My mobile tittered. It was my girlfriend.

'Hello?'

'Hello, darling. Where are you?'

'I'm on the Bullet Train.'

'What are you doing?'

'Watching a video about the Bullet Train. It's great. All the attendant railway staff wear white gloves.'

'Is that good?'

'I don't know. I suppose so. Hang on . . . we're going into a tunnel . . . hello . . . hello?'

But she had gone. Two Japanese tourists were taking photos of themselves inside the train, just like we'd take a photo of ourselves standing on London Bridge, Arizona. Remember how superior you felt when the Yanks bought London Bridge, thinking it was Tower Bridge? That's how these Japanese visitors must have felt, looking at our railway. A bit smug.

The announcer announced again. 'The Platform Four Theatre Company will shortly be staging a short play on the early history of the locomotive in the Turn-table Hall.'

That was a good play. It was two-hander, very well done and enjoyable. It was a play about the early days of steam, and the building of the Stockton and Darlington Railway. The actors were skilled; the script was light-hearted and funny as well as interesting and informative. They used period songs and contemporary dialogue. The British people watching it were embarrassed and discomfited, as British people always are when confronted by street performers of any description, which was fun. In short, the whole experience was great. If this really were *Blue Peter*, you would now be able to see this play, perhaps with the presenters playing a part. If this had been an illustrated children's book of the 1950s, there would be a picture-strip novelization, with lantern-jawed George Stephenson, clever but feckless Trevithick, and perhaps some sinister Luddites who try to stop the construction of the line, but who are eventually foiled by our hero, helped by his dog Sparks. As it is, I can only give you the rough outline of the plot. You must write your own play, or draw your own pictures. Still, come with me now as we go back . . . back . . . back to the story of railways as we left it, in around 1800, with the young George Stephenson growing up by the lineside . . .

(Cue harp music and wobbly lines over the screen) . . . in the first decade of the new century, two radical steps towards the modern railway were undertaken. First was the appearance of the public railway. All previous railways had been privately owned, and the wagons which used them were restricted as to what they could carry. Canals had the status of roads; they were free to all who would use them, in return for payment of mileage tolls to the canal companies. A road, in this sense, is not a strip of land; it is a right of way. Tramways were not.

In 1801 the Surrey Iron Railway was opened from the banks of the Thames at Wandsworth to Croydon in Surrey. The road was open to anyone who paid the toll. It was a fully public road which just happened to be a tramway. The wagons that used it did not have flanged wheels, but ran between the L-profiled rails used in Shropshire and South Wales. It was a very popular and successful venture. The iron rails ensured a smooth, low-friction ride. Large amounts of goods were carried, and there was talk of a through route to Portsmouth. It was the first time that the tramways had really taken on the canals.

Similar public railways sprang into existence from 1801 until right into the 1830s. One early example was the Oystermouth railway, running along the shoreline of Swansea Bay, which opened in 1807. This was probably the first of the public railways to carry passengers. It was certainly the scene of the first known account of railway travel, as described in the journal of Miss Elizabeth Isabella Spence, in 1808.

I never spent an afternoon with more delight than the former one (02/08/08), in exploring the peculiarly romantic scenery of Oystermouth. I was conveyed there in a carriage of singular construction, built for the conveniency of parties who go hence from Swansea to Oystermouth to spend the day.

This car contains twelve persons, and is constructed chiefly of iron, its four wheels run on an iron railway by the aid of one horse, and is an easy and light vehicle.

This is also the first record of 'railway' and 'romantic' in close proximity. It was not the railway that was romantic, you will note, but the scenery at Oystermouth. The railway was too new to be romantic; it was a concept of the railway which would come to have increasing potency.

It was not romanticism but sound Quaker commercial sense which caused a group of mine owners to build just such a public railway from Stockton to Darlington. Promoted in 1821, the line would be almost thirty miles long and would link the mines of south-west Durham with the River Tees at Stockton. The north-east, you will remember, was the home ground of the edged rail. And by a series of accidents, the new company had acquired George Stephenson, a forty-year-old millwright and one of the first steam-locomotive enthusiasts, as their surveyor and engineer. Stephenson was well known in the area. He had invented a safety lamp for miners, and was in dispute with Sir Humphrey Davy over priority. He was chief engineer to the 'Grand Allies', a powerful group of north-western pit owners who were involved in the promotion of the line. He had built and run several lines down from pitheads to staithes on the riverbank for the trans-shipment of coal. And he had been doing it, at least in part, with steam locomotives. This was the second great innovation of the early nineteenth century.

There are always wayward geniuses trembling on the brink of insanity and penury who are the midwifes of a new idea, and who don't get the recognition they deserve until after their death or destruction, when they achieve iconic status – John Aubrey, William Blake, Syd Barratt. The railway's own such martyr/guru figure was a Cornish mining engineer called Richard Trevithick. Like several people on the Continent (most notably Cugnot in France), he had been experimenting with steam vehicles which ran on the road during the late eighteenth century. Unlike the others, Trevithick saw that the vehicles would run better on a tramway, where they could pull loads, like an iron horse. To satisfy a bet, he built just such a steam locomotive, in 1804, and ran it over the Pen-y-Darren Tramway, near Merthyr Tydfil. The engine did very well, pulling loads of up to ten tons. The rails did less well; they buckled under the weight of the wheels, and the engine had its wheels taken off, and was used as a stationary winding engine. A similar locomotive was bought by a colliery owner to run over the Wylam Wagonway, beside which Stephenson had been born. Again, the wooden rails split. It was Trevithick who realized that only iron rails could carry an iron horse. He saw that there would be sufficient adhesion between the slipping of the metal wheels and the metal rail only if the engines were heavy, and the rails strong. To prove his point, Trevithick built a circular track in North London, almost exactly where the forecourt of Euston station is today, on which he ran his locomotive, *Catch Me Who Can*. Nobody seemed interested in it, however, other than as a novelty ride.

But groups of engineers in the north and north-east had been fascinated by the Trevithick engine which had come to their area and failed. In Leeds, Murray and Blenkinsop built a light steam locomotive which could run on existing rails. Because it was too light to stick to the rail, it used a geared cog to pull itself along. Also in Leeds, on another railway with claims to being the world's first, the Middleton, the famous *Puffing Billy* came into service in 1813.

Stephenson and his friends in Tyneside saw themselves as the best steam engineers in the world, and they were probably right. In 1813 they received the funding to build their first locomotive, the *Blucher*. So in fact Stephenson did not build the world's first steam locomotive. He always acknowledged that Trevithick was first, and years later, the penniless and broken Trevithick used to claim friendship with Stephenson, saying that he had sat many nights in George's cottage, dandling the infant Robert on his knee and talking steam engines. Stephenson's main innovation seems to have been that he was the first to use the idea of the Newcastle Road with locomotives; flanged wheels running on straight rail. He said, 'I will do something in the coming time which will astonish all England.'

And he did. He brought arguably the world's most advanced steam engine to the newest and finest of the public railways. His steam engines had been running successfully for several years on short colliery lines, with lines cast to his design. William James, the first man to survey the Liverpool–Manchester route, and the railway's first visionary, the man who saw that all the lines should be linked together to form a national network, said of Stephenson's engines in 1821, 'The locomotive engine of Mr Stephenson is superior beyond all comparison to all the other engines I have seen . . .'

With Stephenson as their engineer, the promoters of the Stockton and Darlington Railway felt that they could take a risk. This was therefore the world's first public railway authorized by Parliament to use steam-hauled trains alongside the tried and tested horse. The line continued to use horses throughout its length, and at steep places it still used inclined planes. But much of its ore traffic was steam-hauled (by Stephenson's *Locomotion*), with great success. All subsequent railway projects would have to take the Stockton and Darlington as their lead.

The Stockton and Darlington Railway may have been overshadowed by the first fully modern railway, the Liverpool and Manchester. But it taught all subsequent railways important lessons, not the least of which was that the company owning and operating the engines had to be the same one that owned and maintained the rails. Private owners might own wagons, but everything else had to be owned by the company, run together in railway-controlled trains, pulled by company engines over company metals. Otherwise the potential for catastrophic accident was too high. This was the most important lesson that was thrown away at privatization, after almost 170 years of proven worth . . .

The play ended, and the crowd drifted off mumbling. They were unsettled by theatre, and wanted to get back to watching information films about trains from the 1930s, which would now be running again in the Turn-table Hall.

In England, we punctuate each task completed, each shift of gear, each change of emphasis with another cup of tea. I went back to the café and sat with the hundreds of people who were having a little tiffin. Then I wandered around the old engine shed and looked again at the antique railway carriages on display. I wandered alongside the old royal trains, and no, you can't see Queen Victoria's lavatory. Frosted glass. Still no answer . . . do the Royal Family go? The NRM won't tell you.

I looked at the horse-boxes which had replaced the dandy carts. More horses became sporting items and less straightforwardly beasts of burden as the railway network spread. The popularity of hunting increased throughout the nineteenth century, because people who lived in towns could get out to the smart county hunts using these horse-boxes.

And I looked, in particular, at the various classes of carriage.

If ever uppity friends from elsewhere in the world would like to understand something of 'the exquisite cruelty' of the English Class System, why not take them on a day trip to the NRM? By 1865, there were seven distinct classes of rail travel: first class, second class, third class, fourth class, first-class express, second-class express, and work-men's trains. Then you had Pullman, which was another class altogether. Then there was Ladies Only, and Smoking. And if you were very rich, like the Dukes of Sutherland, you had your own private carriage. This carriage is in the NRM, a fabulous opulent saloon, like the drawing room of a great country house on wheels. It was built in 1899 and was used by the Dukes of Sutherland up until 1948, when silly old nationalization came in, and they had to give it up. One

Duchess of Sutherland had a steam locomotive named after her. Remember them, the Duke and Duchess of Sutherland. Somewhere between Inverness and Kyle of Lochalsh, I'll tell you what they did to pay for the best darned train-set in the world, twelve inches to the foot.

There is a carriage from the Midland Railway beside the museum café in the old engine shed. You can walk alongside it on a raised platform so that you can see through the windows. It has all three main classes, divided off from each other. I peered through the windows of the first-class compartment. It looked very comfortable. There was a civilized-looking lavatory. The seats were very comfortably upholstered, and they all had arms. Behind was a bulkhead wall (this was not a corridor train). Second class looked welcoming too. There were no arms between the seats, and the lavatory had to be shared with an identical second-class compartment behind it, but it looked like a pleasant way to travel. The seats were also comfortably upholstered.

Almost as well upholstered were the third-class compartments. Whereas second-class seats were formed so that one's buttocks did not have to touch those of a stranger's, third-class seats were flat. Other than that, third class seemed identical to second, with just the same lavatory facilities. You weren't really paying for that much extra comfort, certainly not on the trains of the Midland, which took a progressive view of third-class travel. You were paying to make sure that you didn't have to sit next to a person of a different social order. You were paying to sit next to People Like You. As the *Railway Traveller's Handy Book* points out, 'There is but little distinction between second and third class, the main difference being in the quality of the company.'

This was too silly even for England. Something had to go. Fourth class was short-lived; nobody wanted to travel in open wagons if they could sit inside. There were enough people who were willing to pay to go first. It was third class which was the most popular, and second class which died.

The railway created new traffic which it had not been expecting. In the 1870s 60 per cent of rail passengers travelled third class. Third class was a huge money spinner. The Midland, competing with the other companies who were running services to Scotland and the North, announced that it was dropping second class from 1874. Third-class facilities were dramatically improved. Many of the other companies watched the Midland's revenues soar for ten years, before ditching second class themselves. Second-class carriages hung on, however, until after nationalization in 1948, when some boat trains still had second-class compartments.

It was not until 1956 that someone thought of changing the name of third to the much nicer second. Better to be second-rate citizens than third-rate ones. We've come up in the world! And now it's even better yet; since 1987, we've been second no longer. Now we are standard citizens. Our masters are improving their PR skills, of that there can be no doubt.

I walked up from the NRM to York station. Arriva trains had been on strike the day before. The day after strikes can be completely chaotic, as rolling stock is all over the system, where it was left instead of being where it should be. I was lucky that my train to Manchester was only delayed by half an hour. I was going to stay with a chum in Stockport, so that I could see some more evidence of early railways, and then I was going to Crewe, home of spotters, to visit another museum for some more re-education. If I am successful, everyone will know about trains again, romance will return, and aunties can rescue from the attic their stash of 'Happy Birthday Dear Nephew' birthday cards with pictures of steam engines on them. I settled in a corner of the carriage to think.

I was trying to follow the journey from York to Manchester in my railway atlas. Railway enthusiasts trace their journey in railway atlases like music lovers follow a score, but it is not easy. I want you to know that I am an accomplished map reader, and that my knowledge of British topography is sound. I want you to know that the fault does not lie with me. The fault lies with the maps. Railway books are not bursting with maps and it can be difficult to follow a writer's line without them. When there are maps, they are uniformly bad. Often they come without a key, so that it becomes difficult to see which line is which, which a single track and which a double, for example. This is annoying enough. Most railway atlases do not show any representation of the countryside that they are passing through; this can be frustrating, and underlines some railway enthusiasts' lack of interest in anything except trains. Most annoying of all, one page of the atlas does not overlap on to the next. In road atlases, each new page has about an inch of the last map on its margins, so that you can trace your journey, but I have never yet seen a railway map that does this. I've seen maps that go out of their way to avoid it; maps which will daringly go a couple of millimetres over the margins, in order to avoid overlap on the next page. This makes it easy to lose your place when you turn a page, and in an area where there are lots of lines, this is a real problem. In fact, I think this map thing helps us to understand something of the mind of a true railway enthusiast. The way people choose to represent the world must help us to understand how they see it.

What train buffs like is accuracy, above everything else. By making the maps easier to follow, they would be ruining their pristine loveliness. This page does exactly what it says on the tin; the last page showed you everything you needed to know about this map, and if you can't follow it, why, then you can't be a real railway enthusiast. The bad maps tell us that you are supposed to know stuff already.

And the indexes in railway books would drive a saint to distraction. Where they exist at all, they seem designed to make it harder to find what you are looking for, rather than easier. Some railway books even have bizarre page-numbering systems, obviously devised by the author in an attempt to update old-fashioned 1, 2, 3, 4 . . . These books are not for outsiders. There are very few entry-level books about railways, and hardly any proper history worth the name. There are histories by the million, yes, histories of lines, histories of engines, of coaches, of signalling, but hardly any are by academic historians, and all but a handful exclude any attempt to set the railway in a social context. L. T. C. Rolt was probably the most lucid writer on railways, but he was not an academic historian, although his series of books on engineers (the Stephensons, Telford and Brunel) are still the standard works. Jack Simmons is a lonely beacon; any of his books are worth reading. It was he who edited *The Railway Traveller's Handy Book* for its 1971 reprint. His *The Victorian Railway* is the best single-volume railway book I've read, and also one of the best books about Victorian England. Most railway books are not like this. They bear titles such as *Thirty Years of Steam on Dartmoor*, or *Branch Lines to East Grinstead*. They are largely by enthusiasts for enthusiasts. The books reflect the interests of those who are already in the know, rather than those who might like to find out.

Railway enthusiasts remind me of heavy metal fans. If you watch a heavy-metal fan in a record shop, you will see him walk untroubled past records by The Velvet Underground, Scott Walker, Aretha Franklin or The Beach Boys. Eyes straight ahead, he does not relax until he is faced with a choice of records by such artists as Iron Maiden, Metalica or Pantera. They know what they like, do metalists, and they are not going to let nonsense like critical judgement get in the way. They think you are a twat because you like Marvin Gaye. They simply ignore everything that isn't metal, except Queen. They think Queen are great, and, like Ben Elton, turn a blind eye to the Sun City thing. After all, can't we forgive them one lousy trip to apartheid South Africa, in return for all the great records they gave us, like 'Fat-Bottomed Girls' or 'Innuendo'? Lots of metalists, in my experience, come from happy, stable families with no real musical tradition (often with a *soupçon* of evangelical Christianity thrown in). Many of them went to grammar schools and the like, so that it was difficult for them to decide what cool is. When, therefore, they decide to kick over the traces a bit, they somehow accidentally think that metal is cool, or interesting even. Hey, they eat bats! They must be good! That'll teach our parents not to try to make us happy!

Railway enthusiasts also seem to come from stable, happy backgrounds, even more so than the childhood homes of heavy-metal fans. So happy and stable are the families of people who grow up to be railway enthusiasts that they never feel the need to kick over the traces at all. As one enthusiast said to me, 'I often think that railway enthusiasts have gone straight from being twenty to being middle-aged men without an intervening period.'

They latch on to a hobby that doesn't worry their mums. I much prefer the company of trainspotters to that of heavy-metal fans, who think they are cool. The railway enthusiast knows that he's not, and doesn't care. Isn't interested. This I find admirable. But railway enthusiasts are very good at shutting out the non-railway world, sometimes.

My friend Johnny met me at Manchester Piccadilly. At least, he was there, and so was I. The station was in the middle of modernization works due to be in place by the start of the Commonwealth Games. The whole station was one vast construction site. All the places I knew in Piccadilly seemed to have disappeared. The Smith's where I was to meet Johnny wasn't there. Neither was the ticket hall. I decided to wait outside the station. Johnny decided to wander about looking for me inside. After a while, I got antsy and went back into the station. Johnny, meanwhile, had made his way up to the platform where the train from York had been due. I stood by the temporary hut that housed Smith's, thinking that this made most sense. Johnny went outside. I stayed inside. Half an hour had passed since we were due to meet. I was getting annoyed with him; he was getting annoyed with me. We discovered this when I went outside again, just as Johnny was coming in.

'Where the fuck have you been?' said Johnny.

'Where the fuck have *you* been?' I replied.

We went for a coffee, to untangle our respective movements. Then we walked towards Castlefields, to the Manchester Museum of Science and Technology. We walked down Ducie Street and Canal Street. Johnny, a lifelong Stockport lad, which is only five miles down the road from central Manchester, turned left, and right and left again.

'Where are we, John?'

'It's down here somewhere.'

We passed the library, the Corn Exchange, the Arndale.

'You're lost, aren't you, John?'

'No! It's just behind the G-Mex.'

'Where's the G-Mex?'

'I thought it was down here.'

Yes, you can't beat a local guide if you really want to see a place. We found a wall map for tourists, which put us right. Why can't men ask for directions?

What I wanted to see at the museum was the London Road station, supposedly the oldest surviving in the world. The line has gone, but the station is still there. We walked through the museum site; as I remember, we couldn't find the old station at first, and I swear I remember wandering through a multi-storey car park, but we found it in the end, a simple, classically proportioned building, with separate booking halls for first and second class. Mannequins dressed to look like travellers of the late 1830s were trying to buy tickets from mannequins dressed as ticket sellers. No change there.

This was the terminus of the Liverpool and Manchester Railway. When it was opened in 1830, it was the world's first public railway to use steam haulage for all its services. This was the first modern railway, and the Railway Age was born on the day it opened for traffic. London Road was the first station on the first modern railway. This is where those bits on *Blue Peter* about how to make sheep from pipe-cleaners to add realism to your layout took off. Two hundred years of development, environmental pressures, accidents of birth, and now zing, here we were, 1829, and we were racing off over Chat Moss at 28 mph!

'Johnny?'

'What?'

'Standing here in the world's oldest station . . .'

'What?'

'I don't know what. I feel . . .'

'What?'

'Weird. Like I'm going back . . . back . . . back . . .'

Welcome back to 1821. The Stockton and Darlington was under way at the same time that a group of promoters were considering building a line between Liverpool and Manchester. William James, that railway visionary who had been such a supporter of Stephenson's, did a survey of the line, and took the young Robert Stephenson with him. Visionaries must give way to practical men of genius; in 1824, James was sidelined, and George Stephenson brought in as engineer. But practical men of genius must give way to smoothy-chops who can persuade politicians and investors that the job's a good 'un. So Stephenson in turn was sidelined, and one of the great firms of civil engineers, the Rennies, together with their railway expert, Charles Vignoles, were brought in to see the thing through the interminable committee stages in Parliament. When the Act was passed, the smoothy-chops were sacked, and George Stephenson was brought back. The line would be thirty-five miles long and built on the level, all except for an incline down into Liverpool, which would need a stationary winding engine to take the trains to the end of the line.

The biggest engineering problem was the crossing of Chat Moss, a bog between the two towns, which the railway could not avoid. Defoe, in his *Tour of the Whole Island of* 1724, said of it that 'The surface at a distance looks black and dirty, and it is indeed frightful to think of, for it will bear horse nor man.'

Since no one could stand on the Moss, it seemed ridiculous that Stephenson aimed to build a railway across the thing. He ended up floating his railway on mats of hurdle interwoven with heather, a technique he borrowed from the Yorkshire road builder, John Metcalf. On this floating foundation he laid gravel and then sleepers and rails.

Having seen that their railway was crossing Chat Moss, and was thus close to completion, the railway company had to decide between stationary or locomotive steam engines for pulling the trains. Stationary steam engines were proven technology; locomotives were new, and the running of them on the Stockton and Darlington had not been without problems. The directors decided to offer a £500 prize to find a steam locomotive which showed 'a decided improvement on those in use'. This decision led to the famous Rainhill Trials, which were held in 1829. A one-and-a-half-mile course was laid out, halfway between Liverpool and Manchester. The engines had to pull a train back and forth along the course, so that both speed and strength could be tested.

Only three serious contenders were in the Trials. Braithwaite's elegant *Novelty*, which the crowd of 10,000 spectators liked, but which kept exploding at inconvenient times; Hackworth's *San Pareil*, which couldn't get going until the last day, when it belched hot coals all over the crowd before also blowing up; and Stephenson's *Rocket*, which chugged merrily up and down between the markers for a total of sixty miles, pulling a ten-ton train at an average speed of 14 mph. It was a shoo-in, such a convincing one that the directors decided to make their line exclusively powered by steam locomotives. A few weeks after the Trials, and shortly before the railway was due to open, George Stephenson, 'his face fine, though careworn', took the delectable Fanny Kemble, the most feted and glamorous young actress of her age, out for a bit of a spin. George was always one for the lasses. Fanny Kemble's account of the trip on the footplate of *Rocket* is the first modern experience of speed. George, keen to impress, had got up to 35 mph. Miss Kemble wrote: 'When I closed my eyes, this feeling of flying was delightful and strange beyond description; yet strange as it was, I had not the slightest fear.'

The opening of the Liverpool and Manchester Railway was set for 15 September 1830. The company had run out of money during the building of the project, and the Exchequer had coughed up to the tune of £100,000. The state was therefore involved in the building of modern railways from the moment of their birth. The government wished to see the enterprise succeed, and no less a figure than the Prime Minister, the Duke of Wellington, was to attend the opening. This proved so popular that seven trains had been laid on, the first of them, the Duke's train, pulled by Robert Stephenson's latest locomotive, the *Northumbrian*. Seventeen miles out of Liverpool, this leading train stopped for water. The idea was that the other trains would pass by the Duke in solemn procession. The train stopped, and some of the passengers got out to stretch their legs. Among them was William Huskisson, MP for Liverpool, and newly resigned from Wellington's Cabinet as President of the Board of Trade. Huskisson was the leader of the liberal Tories in the Commons, and Wellington needed his support. A meeting was arranged. Huskisson approached the Duke's carriage, but they had forgotten that whilst the lead train was stationary, the others were moving past for the Duke's inspection. As Huskisson tried to climb into the Duke's carriage, he was struck by *Rocket*, driven by Stephenson's assistant, Joseph Locke, which was pulling the fourth train. As he fell under the train, Huskisson cried, 'I have met my death.'

Which he would, later in the day, but not before Stephenson tried to save him. Uncoupling the *Northumbrian*, Stephenson drove the engine into Eccles, the nearest town, at the unprecedented speed of 36 mph. It was this which stunned the contemporary audience, more than poor Huskisson's death. As Stephenson's biographer, Samuel Smiles, wrote in the 1850s, 'This incredible speed burst upon the world with the effect of a new and unlooked for phenomena.'

There seemed nothing to do but continue the journey to Manchester. It was pointed out to the Duke that thousands of spectators were waiting in Manchester to greet their Prime Minister, and that it wouldn't look good if the journey was not completed. The Duke agreed. What he had foolishly overlooked was that the people of Manchester were waiting to greet the mastermind of the Peterloo Massacre, only eleven years before. The mob had taken over the Manchester end of the railway, and the Duke's arrival was greeted by a riot. Once again, emergency action was necessary; the Duke stayed in his coach, which was pulled back to Eccles, where it was found that William Huskisson had died, to embark on his posthumous career as a pub quiz question: Who was the first person to be killed in a railway accident? The train finally arrived back in Liverpool at 11 p.m., the passengers tired, dirty and severely delayed. Unlike Virgin customers arriving in Liverpool now, of course . . .

The following day, 140 passengers were waiting for the first scheduled train to Manchester. Eleven years after Peterloo and two years before the Reform Bill, modernity had been born. Henry Booth, the Company's Treasurer, and the man who had ordered the Rainhill Trials, saw what had happened.

Perhaps the most striking result produced by the completion of this Railway, is the sudden and marvellous change which has been effected in our ideas of time and space. Notions which we have received from our ancestors and verified by our experience are overthrown in a day, and a new standard erected, by which to form our ideas for the future.

Ideas of time and space . . . time and space . . . time and space . . . 'What?' said Johnny.

'Sorry?'

'You were saying . . . you felt weird.'

'Yeah. A bit. Shall we go and get a beer?'

Johnny agreed that this would be best, that I had been acting strangely all morning, that a beer or two would be just the thing.

In the evening, when we had sobered up, Johnny drove me out into the hills to see some tramways. I wanted to visit Whaley Bridge and Bugsworth. Luckily, Johnny is on surer ground out here, in the hills south of Manchester, and we only got lost twice.

'I've got a map, John.'

'I don't need a map! I've been to Whaley Bridge a hundred times.'

I'm sure this is true. Unfortunately, however, Johnny enjoys a quiet cannabis cigarette after dinner. Also after lunch, and after breakfast. He is seriously stoned, has been for a quarter of a century. He may well have been to Whaley Bridge a hundred times. It is pretty, and only ten miles at the most from his house. The problem is, after each time he goes anywhere, he forgets the way.

Whaley Bridge was the terminus of the High Peak Tramway, the longest and most ambitious of the old wagonways. As it crosses the Derbyshire Peaks, it was difficult for its engineers to keep it flat. They overcame differences in level by the use of inclined planes; great banks that the trains of wagons were hauled up or lowered down by stationary steam engines or horse-powered capstans. The car park at Whaley Bridge was built on the old trans-shipment wharf between the tramway and the Peak Forest Canal. Here, goods that had been carried up the River Trent and the Erewash and Cromford Canals, and then hauled over the high hills by teams of horses and winding engines, were loaded on to boats for their onward journey to Manchester or Liverpool via the Bridgewater Canal. The journey from Nottingham to Liverpool via this route would take over ten days.

We turned our backs on the canal and crossed an iron bridge which had once carried the tramway over the River Goyt. A few minutes' walk took us to the foot of the first of the old inclined planes. Rising at about one in ten, Johnny and I climbed to the top. It is a public walkway now, a nice place for the people of Whaley Bridge to walk their dogs.

At the top of the incline, we found the remains of the old horse capstans which were used to pull wagons up the incline. Horses were used on this last incline right up until the line's closure in 1952. I would have liked to have seen a team of horses pulling a train of mineral wagons up to the top of the incline and lowering them down the long slope towards the canal.

We got into the car, to go for dinner at the Navigation Inn at Buxworth. Johnny is practically a local in this pub, which is just three miles from Whaley Bridge, so it only took us half an hour to find. What confuses Johnny is the fact that the village has changed its name from Bugsworth to Buxworth, because it felt that Bugsworth was rude. Can't see it myself. Bug has never really been a rude word. If it had been called Arseworth, then maybe.

Whatever it's called, Bugsworth Basin would be a great place to run a restored tramway. You could have a horse train, and a beam engine hauling wagons attached to cables up one of the inclined planes. You could have boats waiting in the basin. As a day out with the kiddies, I think it would prove highly popular – horses, steam engines, boat rides. There is a maze of canal basins, each served by a tramway. You can follow the courses of these old tramways; there are granite sleepers still in place, and you can walk up them away from the canal and into the hills. And then you could go for a bite at the Navigation, which was once owned by Pat Phoenix, aka Elsie Tanner. The pub looks over the topmost of the canal basins. You can't get there by boat, yet. The basins are linked to the Peak Forest Canal, which is happily still in use, and they have recently been restored to their original state. Boats can't get here because the restorers have discovered why the basins fell into disuse in the first place; all the water keeps running out of them, and no one quite knows why.

We drove back to Johnny's house, where I fell into a blameless stupor. In the morning, I was off to spend the day in Crewe. I woke up early and snuck out of the house. It was Sunday, and Johnny does not like to see daylight. He prefers to get up, make himself a cup of tea and have his first spliff of the day at about the time *Antiques Roadshow* is coming on. I left him a note, and walked the few hundred yards to

Stockport station. It was in the throes of major engineering works. There were no trains to anywhere, nor did there seem to be a replacement bus service, at least not one going to Crewe. I went back to Johnny's and hammered on the door. After fifteen minutes of shouting and banging, Johnny came down and opened it.

'What?'

'Take us to Crewe, John, willya? There's no trains.'

Johnny sighed, and squinted at the sun.

'All right. I'll skin up.' He's a good lad.

Two hours later, I managed to persuade him that it was time to go. I got him into the car and we set off.

'I think it's left here, Johnny . . .'

Too late. We were heading north on the M6 towards Warrington. Warrington, as a railway town, is not without interest. It was from a junction close by that the Grand Junction Railway, second of the great trunk routes, left the Liverpool and Manchester and stretched south towards Birmingham and, at last, London Euston. But I didn't want to go to Warrington.

We turned round at the next junction and headed south towards Crewe.

'Sorry,' said Johnny. 'I thought I was going to Ikea.'

He dropped me off outside Crewe station. I thanked him for the lift, and for putting up with me for the night. We shook hands, and he drove off. The last I saw of him, he was bound for Shrewsbury.

Crewe. The very name sends thrills down the railway enthusiast's spine. York is awe-inspiring, Derby fascinating, Swindon steeped in history; but Crewe is the spotter's spiritual home. All human life passes through Crewe. It was here that the Grand Junction Railway had its headquarters. Crewe grew from a tiny hamlet in 1837 to a town of 40,000 sixty years later, when lines from Chester and Manchester were authorized to meet the Grand Junction nearby. A quarter of the population worked in the locomotive works; many more in other capacities on the railway. Crewe Locomotive Works built about 8,000 engines in the years between 1843 and 1990. That's about one a week, over a period of almost 150 years. In the 1890s, a thousand trains a day passed through Crewe. The town was owned and designed first by the Grand Junction and then by its successor company, the London and North Western. There is no other town in England that is as pure a railway town as Crewe. All the others had some prior existence, like Derby, or some other purpose, like Middlesbrough. Crewe was the railway's baby.

No wonder the enthusiasts like it. It is choo-choo city. Trains are masculine; the engines are never referred to as 'she'. The enthusiasts are almost exclusively masculine, too. From the 1930s until into the 1960s, this is what boys did. They met down at the sidings to spot trains. They stood on bridges and were enveloped in clouds of steam. They ticked off the numbers in specially printed little books, called *abc Guides*, published since 1943 by Ian Allen. Every engine has a number, yes, but it is not really the numbers themselves that they are interested in. According to enthusiast lore, each engine has a soul of its own. Steam engines came in a multiplicity of shapes and sizes, each dependent on the job that it was designed for. All your average spotter is trying to do is to see as many different kinds and classes of steam engine as he can. Ticking off the numbers, for most of the lads, is really an *aide-mémoire*.

Of course, there are a few people who are trying to tick off every number in their Ian Allen *abc Guide*, just for the sake of it. Then there are the enthusiasts who don't 'spot' at all. In railway enthusiasm, as in everything else in human existence, there is a hierarchy, or a series of hierarchies. At the bottom you have 'the rivet counters'. These gentlemen are the ones who are most likely to want all the numbers. They know every detail of their favourite engines down to the last nut and bolt. They know, in short, just how many rivets there are in *Mallard*. 'Rivet counter' is a pejorative phrase in the world of the spotter, applied to anyone who is prone to be over-zealous on the technical details of any railway-related subject, whether they count or not. According to spotters, it is the rivet counters who have given them a bad name. Who do rivet counters look down on? Bus enthusiasts.

Next up on the heap you have your common-or-garden railway enthusiast. He likes watching the trains go by. He takes photos of the trains, and has a camcorder to film them too. He probably likes steam trains more than diesels, and diesels more than the modern trains. He is most likely to be over forty. He goes on steam excursions at the weekend and may work as a volunteer on one of the restored lines. If he is dedicated, he might work his way up to become a driver of steam trains on his chosen line. Almost certainly, he is a modeller, or has at least had a go at one time or another. Although he will always note down the engine details of any train he is travelling on, he is unlikely to be slavish about the numbers thing.

At the top of the tree, you have the bashers. Bashing means travelling in a train behind an engine. They are secretive men, bashers, like Masons up to the thirty-third degree. Sometimes they buy tickets, but a real basher needs to cover a lot of miles, and trains must be bunked. It would be irresponsible of me to reveal their techniques, so I would happily do so if I knew what they were in any detail. Mostly, the bashers cover a lot of ground for nothing because they are railway experts. They know when the ticket collectors come round, when to hide, or to get on to another train. They know what to say if they are caught without a ticket. Top bashers, like 'Bob', are well known to the railway authorities.

'It's too hard, now,' 'Bob' told me. 'I can't get away with nowt. They all know me now.'

There are bashers and bashers, of course. Most of them, like 'Bob', try to travel as far as possible behind a particular type of locomotive. 'Bob' likes Class 37 diesels.

'I did ten thousand mile behind Class 37,' he said. 'It were all I cared about, that and the football.'

But then you have the line basher, who is trying to travel over every inch of the system. You see him travelling around, incomprehensible railway atlas on his lap, crossing off all the lines he has covered in a particular day, or in a lifetime. Intimacy with the timetables is the line basher's ruling vice. And then there are the stop-watch bashers. Armed with stop-watches, calculators and even, these days, satellite positioning equipment, the stop-watch basher leans eagerly from the window, counting wayside markers, working out how fast the train is going, where it is, and how much work it is doing. To them, what they do is serious research. They have a club, the Railway Performance Society, whose members sit on trains making the TOCs' lives a misery by subjecting them to a permanent amateur time-and-motion study. If you called a stop-watch basher a trainspotter, he would be deeply offended. That is child's play; this is the business of a man.

On this particular trip, I wanted to visit Crewe's railway museum, the Railway Age. I had been to the NRM and seen the best railway collection in the world. I had been to the Manchester Museum of Science and Technology and seen the world's oldest railway station. What would Crewe, the railway enthusiast's Mecca, have to offer? As you leave the town heading north, you will see the Railway Age to your left. There is the rotting hulk of the Advanced Passenger Train (APT), a white elephant from the 1980s which was supposed to revolutionize train travel by tilting the carriages. Like the passenger on a motorbike who leans with the driver as the bike goes around a corner, tilting trains mean that the thing can go much faster, theoretically, reaching speeds of up to 140 mph. The APT didn't work. All it did was to spill everybody's drink. Now the APT is green with lichen, a symbol of over-investment in daft trains and under-investment in the actual rails themselves. I've looked at this vision of the future a hundred times, and I know that it's just by the station, so the entrance must be around there too . . . somewhere.

Is it bollocks. It's miles away, a long hike past red brick terraces, almost the only legacy of Crewe's past which still remains. Then you double-back on yourself and head towards the station. Eventually, I arrived at Safeway's. Outside the store there was a tank engine, painted like Thomas the Tank Engine, for the children to play on. In the corner of Safeway's car park, I could see the entrance to the Railway Age.

It bills itself as 'The Railway Age – The Family Destination', but I'd only really advise it as a day out for Mum and Dad, Grandma and Grandad, and the little ones if you have a very strange family. When I presented myself at the entrance, there was nobody there to take my money. I wandered through the gates. I was alone . . . quite alone.

'Hello, love.' An old lady had appeared. She had her knitting under her arm and was followed by a fat black and white cat.

I jumped. 'Oh, hello.'

'Sorry I weren't here to take your money. I had to see to something int' exhibition hall.'

'That's all right. It's a walk from the station, isn't it? I thought it was next door.'

'It is, love. Look, there's the end of the platform, just over there. There's no way through from the station to here. You have to come right round . . Three pound, please. You never walked, did yer?'

I gave the old lady my money; she smiled, unlocked the hut at the entrance, and went in to carry on with her knitting. The cat followed her.

I walked across the site. There was an Exhibition Hall, with not much of an exhibition in it. In the yard there were some steam locomotives, mostly in various states of decay. I realized to my horror that there was no café. There was a miniature train for the kiddies, but it wasn't running. Probably because there were no kiddies. There was a man on a ladder washing lichen from the side of the APT; it looked as though some kind of restoration might be under way. Other than this geezer, there was just me. It was a ghost museum. In front of me, I could see signs pointing me to the North Junction signal-box. There was nothing else to do, so I followed the signs.

The North Junction signal-box looked to have been built some time in the 1930s; it reminded me, in a way, of the De La Warr Pavilion in Bexhill, or one of the Piccadilly Line Underground stations – Arnos Grove, perhaps. I went in. On the ground floor there was a display explaining the history of railway signalling, which is long and complex, and you've been so good sitting through the early history of railways that I'm not going to go right into it here. There were also banks and banks of valves and electrical relays, linked to a control room above. I climbed the steps. An elderly gentleman was sitting in a chair in the old control room. A large display map of Crewe station, and all the lines into and out of it, was covered in little red lights. It was like something out of one of those information films from the 1950s, with white-coated technicians sitting in front of futuristic equipment, while a voiceover says, 'Here we are in a world of free clean energy; and they call it nuclear fission.'

The elderly gentleman leaped to his feet. Staggered, more like.

'Ah, hello, sir,' he croaked. 'Let me show you how to bring a train into the station. This board is a representation of the signals around Crewe in 1955. Now, on this line here, these lights represent the 16.27 Irish Mail, which as you can see is coming into platform seven. Now, I need to set the road. See that lever, sir? If you'd be good enough to help? That's it, that one, pull it over . . .' I complied.

I think the best description of these then modern but now already obsolete boxes is to be found in Arthur Groom's description of Billy and Betty's railway holiday in *The Book of Railways*.

> *'I hope you will like our newest signal-box, children,' said the important official. 'It's one of the most up-to-date in the whole world.'*
>
> *Billy and Betty gulped their thanks, and finally, walking in the wake of their father and another railwayman, they were on their way towards the long new signal-box which was just outside the station. It was a truly wonderful sight, everything being so clean that one could have eaten a meal off the floor, and rows of small levers, over three hundred of them, which looked like bright toys. They were arranged at the level of a man's waist and each was on a green base.*
>
> *'But I thought . . .' began Billy.*
>
> *The guide interrupted him with a laugh.*
>
> *'I know,' he said, 'you thought we still used big heavy levers. Well, you can see that they are only about nine inches long; it is no harder to pull one than it is to pull on the handbrake of a car.'*

Crewe North Junction was built after the same model. The old signal-boxes used to have huge great levers which were attached by steel cable to remote points and signals. To change the signal, or to switch the points, you had to exert physical force to pull on the cable, using the old brass levers. With these new boxes, the electrical relays that I had seen downstairs did the hard work. All you had to do was pull the levers in the right order. The signalman is not just in charge of seeing that a train does not enter a stretch of line which already has another train on it, he is also effectively steering the train by his manipulation of the points. Train drivers choose how fast to go, and they are in charge of stopping, but it is the signalman who decides where the trains are going to go.

The old gentleman in the signal-box gave me a complete demonstration of how the system worked, and then insisted that I have a go myself. I pulled the levers in the correct order, and watched the lights come on in sequence, as my virtual train pulled into Crewe, dropped off some trucks, and retreated to the sidings.

There was not really such a train, you must understand. The old guy and I were just pretending. We were playing trains. But at least we could look out of the window at the tracks once controlled from this box. He was very friendly, my signalling mentor, but it felt strange to be outnumbered by the staff. Who gets out of the station at Crewe? That's the problem. I chatted to the old signalman. He was a volunteer. He had been an electrical engineer, first in the Navy just after the war, and then for a firm in Manchester. He lived out Alderley Edge way now, and every weekend he came to the Railway Age to show the few interested parties who come through the museum the subtleties of signalling.

I left the North Junction box and followed the signs to the only attraction at the Railway Age that I hadn't seen; the Exeter West signal-box. Clearly, this place was more The Signalling Age – The Eccentrics' Destination than The Railway Age – The Family Destination. There was a newly cindered path past the unloved steam engines, and at the end of it were two signal-boxes. The first, I think you'd call the bog-standard signal-box. It was the size and shape of a signal-box. It looked like an Airfix model of a signal-box. It was a platonic signal-box. There was no one in it. I mounted the steps and looked through the window. It had a dozen or so brass levers, just like you'd expect in a signal-box.

This wasn't Exeter West, however. Exeter West was next door. Exeter West is a whopper, a long, high signal-box designed to overlook an important junction; one which, as you might imagine, used to sit to the west of Exeter. I pushed open the door into the ground floor. Here were the frames which were operated by the levers upstairs, which in turn pulled the steel cables that made the distant signals drop into place, which changed the points and set the road, to ensure that traffic wouldn't go off on to the wrong line, and perhaps into an oncoming train. On the walls were photographs showing Exeter West in its heyday, Exeter West being dismantled and moved to the Railway Age, Exeter West restored, thanks to the efforts of volunteers. The ground floor was badly lit, and it was difficult to see the photographs. At the far end of the long box were some wooden stairs. I climbed them into the light clerestory of the box. Two gentlemen in late middle age sat on rickety old chairs, eating sandwiches from greaseproof paper, with flasks and cups of tea on a wooden table.

'Hello,' I said.

They looked at me and smiled through the corned beef and pickle.

'Hello, son. Why don't yer come back in half an hour? We'll be working again by then. We're just 'avin' our lunch.'

So I walked from the light back down the stairs into the gloom, and out again, past the old steam engines. I wasn't quite sure what the sandwich-eating gentlemen were going to be doing, but it seemed as though it might be worth going back for. Still there was nobody about in the Railway Age, except the guy on the ladder cleaning lichen from the APT. Although the place was deserted, and although I had looked earlier, I still could not conceive of a visitor attraction without its attendant tea room. No, I looked again; there really was no café. The lady in the hut was knitting. Her cat was sitting beside her on the ticket counter.

'I'm just popping out for a drink,' I said. 'Will I be able to get back in?'

'You're all right, love,' said the lady.

I walked across the car park and into Safeway's, where there was a coffee shop. I had brown liquid of some kind, and a thing covered in sandpaper which had been advertised as a doughnut. Then I walked back through the car park into the Railway Age, and past the lady in the hut.

'You all right, love?'

'Yes, thanks.'

'Did you have a nice cup of tea?'

'Yes, thanks. You're quiet today.'

'Aye. It might pick up later int' year.'

I walked past the locos, up the cinderpath and back up the steps into Exeter West signal-box. Only one of the gentleman remained.

'Ah, hello, son. Glad you came back. We've started working again . . .'

A bell clanged urgently.

The signalman rang the bell himself, pulled at two of the thirty or more brass levers, and then rang the bell again twice.

'There we are. That's the local for Paignton through . . . if you'll just excuse me . . .' I was standing by the wooden table which had held their flasks. I moved aside, and the gentleman started to write in a large ledger on the table.

'I can keep up with the trains, but it's the paperwork that kills me.'

'What are you writing?'

'We're running a Sunday timetable, just as it would have been at Exeter in 1960. We keep all the records, just as the signalman would have.'

'I see. Even though there's no one here to watch?'

'No, that doesn't bother us. And you're here. Like to have a go?'

'Rather!' My eyes lit up like Billy and Betty's.

A bell clanged.

'Right. That's a fast goods for Penzance. First you need to set the road . . .'

He clanged the bell in reply. I pulled at the heavy brass levers he indicated. I looked out of the window of the signal-box. There were no railway lines outside. Our fantasy was even further removed from reality than the one I had shared with the man at Crewe North Junction. At least he had the actual railway lines to look at. The view from the window of Exeter West was a portacabin. In this hut, my signalman's friend sat clanging the bells which were linked to the box. As we completed each task successfully, more bells clanged. As a train left the station, the man in the hut activated a train whistle, to show that the thing had been done correctly. Once, things got a bit hairy when my signalman forgot to clang confirmation to his mate that the line was clear. There was a hurried telephone call to the adjacent hut, and the problem was sorted.

My signalman smiled. 'That was a relief. The next train is the 15.37 London express. We'd get the sack if we held that up.'

I didn't want to get the sack. I was glad that, due to our efforts, the ghost of the 15.37 London express would be able to continue unhindered. It was a spirit journey for a long-gone spirit train, but I'm glad the two guys playing trains didn't have their afternoon spoiled by me slowing its passage. I stayed in Exeter West for an hour, pulling levers, clanging bells. No one else came in to spoil our fun. My friend was called Brian. He had worked in engineering all his life, but now he was retired, he could devote most of his spare time to his hobby.

'I've always been interested in signalling,' he said. 'When I was a lad, the old signalman used to let me up into the box with him.'

His childhood had been spent in the north-east; now he lived on Anglesey and hacked across to Crewe most weekends, to keep the timetable running. The trains have gone; only the timetable is left.

'Do you come to Crewe by train?' I said, pulling a brass lever and setting a distant-in-space-and-time signal to caution.

'No, the trains now don't interest me. They've got no romance. I drive, I'm afraid.'

I told the old signal fan that it was time for me to catch my train back down to London. We shook hands, and I walked through the empty museum site.

'Tara, love,' said the lady in the ticket office. 'Come again.'

Back at Crewe station, the platform was rammed. Bad-tempered passengers with mountains of luggage glowered at information boards which regretfully informed them that their train was twenty-five (two-five) minutes late. When the train pulled in, it was packed too, and I watched my fellow passengers scramble for a seat.

Not I. I was hungry and tired, and I couldn't face sitting outside the loo all the way to Euston. So I got a Weekend Upgrade. These cost £15 and are worth every penny. If you are tired, you get a seat, a nice comfortable seat. This is the new democracy of money; first class no longer guarantees you the company of doctors and QCs, but it saves you having to sit outside the bog next to students called Gareth who shit on about how much they had to drink last night to their mate Darren on the mobile. You sit in comfort, basking in the glow of the human misery that has been left behind in standard class. And you get free refreshments. I hadn't eaten all day. They brought the trolley round three times on the trip from Crewe to Euston. I had three packets of peanuts, three ploughman's sandwiches, three raspberry flapjacks and three cups of coffee. By the time we got back into London I felt sick as a dog, but I reckon I got at least eighteen quid's worth of railway buffet scram, thus making me three quid ahead on the deal.

At the end of their railway holiday, Billy and Betty's father asks them if they have had fun.

'Rather, Daddy,' they chorus. 'Thank you ever, EVER so much.'

I'd had fun too, too much fun perhaps. The time had come for a harder challenge, for me to undertake a serious bit of line-bashing. On the trip back to London, between sandwiches, I looked at the most lucid of all railway maps, designed by Harry Beck for the London Underground. It called to me. I started to plot a route. There was a Jam song in my head as I walked up the platform at Euston.

'I'm going Underground . . .'

Twilight Zone Six

I knew that I wanted to try my hand at bashing, and I felt instinctively that I was by both inclination and disposition a line basher at heart. I did not want to travel for 1,000 miles behind a Class 37 Diesel. I did not want to sit on a train with a stop-watch and a calculator trying to work out how fast it was going. I did want to colour in a map. I like the idea of colouring in maps. Much more than actually going places. When I am old, I don't want to say to my grandchildren, smiling up at me with Vaseline eyes, 'Look, children. Here are all the places I've been. Here are the sketches I made of all the wonderful people I met along the way.' I don't want all that Werthers Originals shit.

I want to say, 'Look, children. Here are all the maps I've coloured in. And I didn't cheat; I really had to go to those places before I was allowed to colour them in. Well, pass through them anyway.'

Line-bashing is not travel in any accepted sense. It is one thing to travel to Samarkand by sand yacht, and then, upon your return, to pore over the old maps and relive the experience. It is another entirely to wish to travel on every railway line, just so that you have travelled on every railway line and can therefore colour in the map. But, that's what I want. Sod excitement, I wanted to find a map that I could colour in, and the Underground map seemed the obvious choice.

Oh, and I wanted to do it in a day.

When I told people that I intended to travel round the whole of the London Underground in a day, they inevitably asked me, 'Why?'

To which I could only answer, 'Because it's there.'

Then they said, 'It can't be done. It's simply not possible.'

'Nonsense,' I replied. 'It's been done before. It's only 257 miles long. It would take about three hours to go that far on an InterCity train, and the system is open for eighteen hours. Nothing to it.' As for it having been done before, people compete to do it in the shortest possible time; the record has just been broken again. Record breakers have to be photographed at every station. But I don't mean to get off at every station. I just intend to cover every inch of every line on the map. The map is the thing. If it's in colour on the Underground map, then I'm going there. Except the Docklands Light Railway, which is too much to ask. Then someone enquired, 'What will you *do* while you're on the train?'

'Look out the window. Read.'

Oh yes, it all seemed so carefree as I said it. It was not until the thing was over that I realized what it meant to sit on the Underground for eighteen hours, looking out the window and reading.

The fun of this kind of futile exercise is much more in the planning than in the execution. I bought special 'get through the Underground quickly' maps so that I knew which carriage to sit in to expedite fast line changes. I had a wall-sized version of the Underground map with movable tape on pins. I traced parts of the Metropolitan Railway into my *A–Z*. I sat with copies of timetables and a stop-watch. Let me talk you through some of the conundrums I would have to face on the day. If you have an Underground map of your own, I'm sure it would help you to follow my thinking.

I realized that my main problem would be the Fairlop Loop, which is right at the far eastern end of the Central Line. There are no trains beyond Hainault after 8 p.m., so to cover the whole thing, I would have to be there well before that time. I was sure that I could do it. I managed to convince myself that I would be on target to catch the last train round the Loop, changing at Woodford for Epping. The other fly in my ointment, I felt, was Shoreditch, at the northern end of the East London Line. Trains don't run that far after 7 p.m., but, again, I was sure that my chosen route would give me time to get there and back without too much difficulty, as long as I got lucky on the line from Earl's Court to Olympia, earlier in the day.

I thought of nothing else, spoke of nothing else. My friends offered to sponsor me, if only I would shut up. I thought that would spoil the authenticity of the experience. Bashers don't bash for cash, Dad. Especially not for charity. They need their money for fines.

I was to take the first train out of Highbury and Islington north to Walthamstow, on the Victoria Line, which leaves at 5.47 a.m., so I packed my bag and, to the relief of my flatmates, went early to bed.

In the morning, I would be born again as a line basher.

My girlfriend made me a packed lunch. Railway enthusiasts are nothing without their packed lunches, and I imagine a legion of wives and girlfriends making sandwiches, grateful at the prospect of a bit of peace as they send their men-folk out for a day of harmless fun. No one has made me a packed lunch since my mum in 1973. I should point out that I am perfectly capable of making my own lunch, but it seemed somehow much more appropriate for my girlfriend to do it for me. More spotterly, somehow. She took some persuading, but she saw the force of my argument in the end.

As well as a packed lunch, I was taking *The Railway Traveller's Handy Book*, *Notes on the Underground* by Rosalind Williams, a bunch of copies of the excellent *Lines on the Underground* series, published by London Underground, each booklet an anthology for travellers on a particular line, and Paul Theroux's *Great Railway Bazaar*, which tells of his journey by train across Europe into Asia, and back again on the Trans-Siberian Express. That seemed appropriate, too.

A poor start to the day. I'd set the alarm for five, but I slept through it, and didn't get out of the house until 5.47, the exact moment at which I should have been getting on to my first train. This was especially annoying in view of the fact that *The Railway Traveller's Handy Book* is explicit in its instructions on waking up to catch your train. It suggests that the best way to get up in time is to ask a policeman to call you at the proper hour by throwing some gravel at your bedroom window. The book says that you should chalk the hour at which you wish to be woken on the door, so that the policeman will not forget his instructions while he is on his beat. The last time I was woken up by a policeman was during Operation Julie in 1977, an experience I had no wish to repeat, so I had trusted in my alarm; a mistake, quite clearly.

I bought my ticket, an All Zones All Day Travelcard, and made it to the northbound platform for 6.15, half an hour late. This could prove a serious problem when it came to making the Fairlop Loop on time, but

I pressed on regardless. There was no one else on the platform, and when the train drew in, it was almost empty, Here and there, sunk in misery, a handful of broken souls were scattered over the seats. It was a freezing January morning, and we were heading for Walthamstow. God knows, I felt like crap, and I was doing it for fun. The few passengers on the first train looked like cleaners or canteen workers, off to prepare for the day. I felt as though I was intruding on their grief.

At 6.27 we arrived at Walthamstow, and everyone got off, except me. As the southbound passengers got on, I picked up a copy of *Metro*, the free morning newspaper, which had been left by one of the disembarked cleaners. *Metro* is sponsored by London Underground, and it is full of murder, horror, Hear Say, Mariah Carey and double-dealing politicians, as well as carrying a whole page about how great the Tube is. This paper will be abandoned all over the Tube network as the day goes on. There were many more passengers heading south towards the City than there were on the way up. Lots of the passengers were construction workers. We headed south for Brixton.

By the time we got back to Highbury and Islington, it was standing room only, even that early in the day, and no one was talking. Hardly anyone does on the Tube. If you could filter out the noise of the trains and the voices of the platform announcers, it would be almost entirely silent down there. Certainly in the morning, all you would hear would be footsteps, coughs and the sussuration of artificial fibre on artificial fibre. By Victoria, the train emptied out, and the copies of *Metro* were piled up like drifting snow. I looked out of the window. There is a nice tile panel at Vauxhall, a faux William Morris representation of leaves and flowers commemorating the old Vauxhall Pleasure Gardens. Mostly, though, there's not much to see from the window, just tunnels. I opened my book.

We arrived in Brixton, and I hurried across to the northbound platform. The trains were filling fast, even though it was still only 7.15. I hopped off at Stockwell to change for the southbound Northern Line. Stockwell station smelled of hot buttered toast. Why this is, I can't imagine, but it did. It can't be that all the passengers have been eating toast for breakfast, or all the stations would smell the same. There was an experiment a few years back in which perfume was sprayed down the tunnels to try to keep everyone calm, but all it did was make people feel ill; perhaps this buttery smell is a new attempt. The train, when it came, was full. I was trying to follow Theroux's adventures on the Orient Express to Istanbul, while jammed between two sweaty builders. Theroux was heading for the Blue Mosque, I was heading for Morden. I felt a twinge of jealousy.

At Morden station the train came out from the Tube into the open, and I popped out for a quick fag, losing myself precious minutes. The station has four platforms, each thronged with passengers who had disgorged from buses outside. It was 7.50, and the sun was starting to rise. Morden derives its name from Old English, and means the hill in the fens, but the hill and the fens were concreted over years ago, and the place reminded me rather of Mordred, morbidity, betrayal and death. I finished my fag, and got on to a train heading north for High Barnet, via Charing Cross.

It filled up at once; any passengers who got on at subsequent stations would have to stand as they read their copy of *Metro*. The builders and cleaners had gone now, to be replaced by office workers packed silently together. The train was jammed solid until Embankment, when most of the office workers got out, leaving behind a carriage half full of young creatives on their way to the West End and Camden. Each line has a different dress code. The Central is all suits, heading for the City; the Hammersmith and City and the Bakerloo are much hipper, as every day is dress-down Friday for the workers in television and the media; but the Northern is the hippest of all; it's full of would-be crusties heading for the advertising studio. And there was me, dressed in a green beanie hat and a donkey jacket, with a large bag containing my packed lunch, notebooks and pencils, looking pretty much the complete railway enthusiast.

By Camden the train was almost empty again, and I nipped around collecting discarded newspapers. Both the *Sun* and the *Star* led with stories about *Coronation Street*; both had pictures of Mariah Carey semi-naked on the cover. Both papers had stories about how poor Mariah was recovering from a suicide attempt, and to help her through it, both papers published long-lens paparazzi pictures of her arse. The *Mirror* had its slimmer of the year on the cover, wearing not much more than

Mariah, only less pretty. This is part of the *Mirror*'s makeover since 9/11; shows it's got a bit of class, nice homely lass in a bathing costume on the cover, not some mega-star in a bikini. In the whole paper, only Jonathan Cainer's astrology column made any sense to me. The *Guardian* was po-faced and hypocritical, the *Mail* was psychotic and mystical, the *Express* was pointless, *The Times* teetered on the brink of insanity, the *Telegraph* was drooling with early-onset senile dementia (except the sports pages), and the *Independent* was worthy but dull.

So no change there.

None of the City types had left an *FT*; that's how you get rich, I guess, by hanging on to what you've got. My review of the press was interrupted by a pleasant surprise; between Highgate and East Finchley, the train popped out of the Tube and into bright winter sunshine. The run from Morden to this point is the longest continuous underground run on the system, at seventeen miles, and it was good to be out in the open, and to see the white hoar-frost shining on the roofs of suburban houses.

The train was almost empty now. A flabby-faced and depressed-looking salesman lugged his samples case out on to the icy platform at Totteridge and Whetstone. I was alone in the carriage for the final part of the trip to High Barnet. When the train stopped, perhaps ten people got off. I went out of the station for another fag and discovered a kiosk selling coffee near to the entrance. It was 9.10, and the coffee was like nectar, my first for over three hours.

Back on the southbound train there were stragglers heading into the office. Two of them were talking to each other, the first conversation I'd heard all morning. A tired-looking Frenchwoman was explaining to her colleague about her child's special-needs teacher, but after a few minutes, they buried their heads in *Metro*. All the other passengers were reading *Metro* too, except for an Indian woman reading an Andy McNab novel. I can't remember having seen a woman reading Andy McNab before, but there you are.

I hopped off at Finchley Central to wait for a train going up the branch line to Mill Hill East. The sign said that there was a twelve-minute wait for the train; again, I nipped out for a fag and a wander.

I got back on the train for Mill Hill East, on the least underground part of the Underground, carried high on embankments and viaducts across North London. I can remember reading once that lots of taxi drivers live in Mill Hill East, but I have no idea if this is true, or, if it is true, why it should be the case. But I loved the place, because it is one of the tiny handful of stations which boasts a fully functioning Gents. The train back didn't go for another eight minutes; I had time to examine the local map which all London Underground stations have in their entrances. The one at Trafalgar Square shows you how to find Nelson's Column, Admiralty Arch and the National Gallery. The one at Mill Hill East shows you how to find the gas works, the allotments and the Frith Grange Scout Camp. I can't help feeling that it must be a wee bit of an anti-climax, if you are a scout, to be taken camping in Mill Hill East, but I suppose that if you get homesick, at least it would be easy to find a taxi to take you back to Mum and Dad. I got on the train, and ate a ham sandwich.

I changed at Camden for the Edgware branch. There was a lone talker on the platform, an elderly gentleman in a checked trilby, carrying a huge shopping bag. He shook his head in exaggerated annoyance at something, and attempted to strike up a conversation with a white-haired lady, who obviously didn't share his exasperation. It is simply not done to try to talk to strangers on the Tube; she smiled, but did not take the bait. At Golders Green we came out again into the sun, and the old gentleman got out, still shaking his head. Now we were rattling through the northern suburbs; Brent Cross, Hendon, Colindale. These northern suburbs, Edgware in particular, I felt, were a parody of the true Metro-Land, away to the west. I didn't expect great things.

I arrived in Edgware at 10.55, and I was beginning to suspect that I was not going to make it round the map. I'd still only done the Victoria Line and three-quarters of the Northern, and if I didn't stop for a coffee and a fag soon, I was going to top myself. I liked Edgware. In the winter sun, the brick-built parade of 1930s neo-Georgian shops and the matching station opposite warmed the air, and I sat in a café, amending my itinerary. If I was to come anywhere close, I was going to have to grasp the nettle that is the Fairlop Loop. I must do it next. I got back on a train, Morden via the City Branch, and worked out my new route. Just at this point in *The Great Railway Bazaar*, Theroux amended his itinerary too, and decides to go north through Afghanistan, rather than through the war in Baluchistan, so I felt some affinity with him. I got off at Bank, a little after twelve, and headed for the Waterloo and City Line, which I decided I might as well get out of the way while I was passing. Also, because there would be a Gents at Waterloo.

The Waterloo and City is the shortest line and one of the oldest parts of the Tube system. Regular passengers call it the Drain, and you can see why. The journey is very short; there are just two stations, Bank and Waterloo. It was almost empty; there was a South-West train strike, and hardly any trains were leaving Waterloo. So no one was going to Waterloo on the Waterloo. The great curving terminus was almost deserted, but at an information desk an irate passenger was shouting at two ill-used railway employees. He was the kind of guy that I hate most in the world, a posh hippy. Peace and love, maaaaaan, except for the working classes, who exist only to serve. He had long hair tied back in a pony-tail and a spacky little goatee. He was wearing a black hooded top and carrying a back-pack. He screamed, 'Well, if there are no trains to Putney, why did that facking moron sell me a facking ticket?' in THAT voice, cut glass, expecting the world to run according to his wishes, a spoiled public schoolboy too privileged to bother growing up. The information guy replied quietly, calmly – couldn't hear what he said. The rich hippy screamed again, I don't WANT to go on the facking Tube! You are a hopeless facking idiot! and stormed off. I followed him down into the Underground, hoping to get a chance to trip him up, but he went through the Bakerloo barrier, and I was heading back to Bank on the Drain train. You get to ride on the excellent travellator at Bank station on the way up from the Waterloo and City Line. It's a kind of sloping escalator, and I recommend it highly. Escalator fans should also try the one at Angel. It's Europe's longest, and well worth a detour. Why not try it next time you're commuting to work? I'm sure a sympathetic boss would understand. I didn't have time for such fol-de-rol. I was off, out into Zone 6, to find the Fairlop Loop. I boarded a Central Line train at Bank, heading east; it was 12.43 p.m.

London's transport system is banded into zones; Zone One at the centre, spreading out to Zone Six around the edge. Space is different in Zone Six. It is like spreading ripples in reverse. Zone 1 is big, Zone 2 slightly smaller, Zone 3 smaller yet, and so on, until you reach the tiny outer band that is Zone 6, skimming the edge of London like a faint aura. It is mysterious out there. Londoners may go to Reykjavik for the weekend, or to Vietnam for their summer holidays, but precious few of them have ever been to Theydon Bois or Ickenham.

Beyond Snaresbrook, it was clear that London was coming to an end, and we were out into the country by the time we got to Woodford. There were fields on either side of the line now, badly cared for. This was the year after foot and mouth. Were these abandoned pastures? Or was it blighted land waiting for the developers to swoop? Somewhere between Buckhurst Hill and Loughton we passed into Zone Six; I celebrated with a cheese-and-pickle sandwich.

They speak a different language out here. Take Theydon Bois. How would you pronounce it? As we pulled into the pretty station, I felt that I would have to ask a fellow passenger, but a taped announcement from the platform revealed that it's 'Boys' rather than 'Bwa'. I'd like to get off one day and have a poke around Theydon Bois proper, but time was my enemy, and I had to press on to Epping.

Epping station is everything a station should be, a Gothic cottage with roses round the door and bright plantings of flowers in summer. The train stops here, but the line goes on, to North Weald and Ongar. Opened in 1865 and closed as recently as 1994, it is what the enthusiasts call a ghost line. On older metal Underground maps still in use on the deep-level stations of Zone One you can see where strips have been screwed over the old stations, air-brushing them out of history. Epping to Ongar is the Trotsky of Underground lines. It was always the poor relation; electrification didn't arrive until 1957, making it the last part of the system to use steam trains. London Underground closed it because it was a loss-maker. So what? Couldn't the system support a couple of miles of subsidized line? Does it make any sense whatever to close railway lines any more? Lord Beeching, who closed thousands of miles of British railway lines in the 1960s, was a criminal; he should be dug up, and his head impaled on London Bridge.

The line to Ongar snakes out of Epping station around a leafy corner, rusty but intact. It is like a red rag to a bull for the train buffs, and there are moves afoot to restore the line and re-open it for steam traffic. If it was on the map, I would happily go to Ongar still, by steam or electric. But it is not on the map, and I got back on the train. At Theydon Bwa, sorry, Boys, three white-trash youths got on to the train, their baseball caps resolutely turned around the wrong way. They were talking to one another, only the second conversation I had heard all day, but unfortunately I could not make out a word they said. I gained the impression they were talking about a fight; they seemed to understand one another, but they might have been discussing the best way to make trifle, for all that I could make out. I did notice that they used the 'shh' sound which has appeared in London over the last few years, as in 'shtrait', or 'shtupid'. Where did that first manifest? I think it was that woman on *EastEnders* with no nose, but I can't be sure. I was pleased to get off at Woodford, but depressed to find that I had a twenty-minute wait for a train to take me around the Fairlop Loop. I walked outside the station for a fag.

A car had broken down in the middle of the High Street. People were hooting. One girl was steering, another was pushing, and two big guys were standing at the side of the road, ignoring them. The guys were talking about industrial carpet cleaners. I crossed the road and helped the girls push the car a short distance into the station car park. There was a baby in the back.

An Underground official hurried across. 'You can't leave that here, mate. This is a staff-only car park.' He addressed his remarks to me. Car equals bloke.

'They've broken down. They're calling for help. They won't be long. There's a baby in the back.' And I swear this is true, but he pushed back his hat, scratched his forehead and said, 'You can't leave that here, mate. This is a staff-only car park.'

'But they've broken down. They're calling for help. They won't be long. There's a baby in the back.'

I thought this could go on for hours, but the driver had been on her mobile phone, her husband was coming, thank you. I walked back into

Woodford station, feeling very much as I imagine Paul Theroux must have, emerging from a scrape along the line on the Trans-Manchurian.

When the Fairlop Loop train came, there was only me and a Scottish lass who got on. I knew she was Scottish because one of the Underground guys was Scottish too, and he'd been talking to her. She was going to visit a friend in Chigwell. At 2.05 p.m. we set off, and at last I was on the Loop. It was rather pretty. No one got on at Roding Valley; at Chigwell the Scottish lass got off, and for the first time in the day, I was completely alone on a train. We entered a wintry cutting, its sides covered with so much frost that it was indistinguishable from snow. At Grange Hill (there really is such a place) a passenger was waiting, and my brief period of solitude was over. We were out in subtopian country. There were fields divided by icy dykes and broken-down hedges, but in the distance, blocks of flats and rows of council houses. Just before Hainault there was a vast depot for Central Line trains. At each of the stations, Fairlop, Barkingside, Newbury Park, more and more passengers got on, and we dived into a tunnel for a time. An old nutter got on at Newbury Park; he muttered to himself and ceaselessly searched his pockets. He got off at Leytonstone, where the train re-emerged into the light, and an access father got on with a five-year-old daughter. They were clearly thrilled to be together again and were talking about what they were going to do with their afternoon. It was 2.30, and this was only the third conversation I had heard all day.

At 2.50 I was back at Bank, and it was quite clear that I was not going to be able to do the whole map in a day. This was depressing, but I carried on anyway, in that British way, regardless of success or failure, into the valley of death rode the six hundred, Dunkirk spirit, etc., etc. I decided to see how far I could get. How much of the map I could colour in. Perhaps, given this realization, I should have got off at Elephant and Castle, but I was driven by a kind of madness, and I went one stop further to Kennington, so that at least I had covered the whole of the Northern Line. That must count for something.

All over the Underground, people deface posters which depict women. I noticed it again, coming out of the lift at Kennington. They draw on them, they put stickers and chewing gum on their faces, on their breasts, but they don't do it to pictures of men. It would be nice to imagine that it is feminist action at work, but I don't think so. I think it's men who do it, but why, I'm not at all sure. Fear, probably. It's certainly not a romantic impulse.

Romance is hardly to be found on the Underground. In its place, you have over-sexualization. Passengers are crammed into tunnels like sperm in a fallopian tube. Posters depicting giant women with vice-like thighs and ballooning breasts leer down from the walls. The sight of a well-turned ankle climbing on to a train still fills the male passenger with enough fluttering excitement to last all eight hours in the office. The Underground is horny.

Realization struck reading Rosalind Williams' excellent *Notes on the Underground* as to why there is no romance on the Underground, and never really can be. The Romantic ideal proposes a chemical wedding between man, nature and the transcendent. But, as Williams argues, 'The defining characteristic of the subterranean environment is the exclusion of nature.' There can be no romance that is divorced from nature. Romanticism aimed to bring authenticity, as represented by Nature, back into the over-rationalized and artificial human world, to re-introduce Nature to the human realm. But as Williams says, 'Subterranean surroundings furnish a model of an artificial environment from which nature has been effectively banished.' They 'take to an extreme the ecological simplification of modern cities, where it seems that humans, rats, insects and microbes are the only remaining form of wildlife'. If nature has been banished, so has high romance.

What you get instead is cool. Underground railways are the only cool railways. Hip media professionals of my acquaintance go on open days to Neasden Depot, or the London Transport Museum, and they would die if you called them trainspotters. They see themselves primarily as ironists. London Underground is the only ironic railway. Simon Patterson's *Great Bear*, a print which utilizes the Underground map, but which changes the names of the stations to those of philosophers, composers and footballers, is the supreme emblem of the ironic railway. It hangs on a lot of North London walls. You can buy a copy from the London Transport Museum.

London Underground has always utilized good design as a central part of its marketing strategy. Girls wear 'Angel' T-shirts, 'Angel' being the sign from the Underground station. It would take a brave lass to wear a T-shirt which said 'Biggleswade Model Railway Club', or which celebrated the 175th anniversary of the opening of the Stockton and Darlington railway. The Underground publish interesting, well-made and well-designed books, which sell to young professionals who would never dream of owning another railway book. Who probably don't think they *do* own any railway books. 'It's about design, darling.'

Back up the Northern Line one stop to Elephant and Castle, and I climbed on to a Bakerloo Line train for Queen's Park. There was an elderly postman opposite me, trying hard to keep his eyes open; I felt like sleeping too, and dozed over *The Great Railway Bazaar*. There were very few passengers about, and those that were looked tired. It was that time of the day, about half-three in the afternoon, when civilized people should be asleep. I noticed that north of Oxford Street, the passengers were mostly elegant ladies of a certain age, laden with shopping from the West End; and that they got off at Warwick Avenue or Maida Vale. At Queen's Park, the train terminated, and I waited on the freezing platform for the train to Harrow and Wealdstone. It was 3.50, and the January light was fading.

When the train came into the station, it gave a little toot. I was glad to get into the warm carriage. I was sitting opposite a pretty girl, and when her mobile rang, she answered in Russian. They are a recent phenomenon, the Russians in London, and it is always thrilling to hear them talk, especially for old Eighties types like me. Back in the Eighties, we expected all-out thermo-nuclear heck at any moment; we never imagined Russian commuters on the Bakerloo. At Stonebridge Park a lady got on and sat next to me. She pulled a religious tract from her bag and offered it to the Russian lass, who took it with a sombre thank you, read it, and put it in her bag. The missionary ignored me; perhaps she felt that I was beyond redemption.

The line from Queen's Park to Harrow and Wealdstone is the bumpiest and rattliest part of the whole Underground. Paul Theroux almost jumped out of my hand. But it is thrilling railway country.

InterCity 125s screamed past on the adjacent West Coast main line; great cranes ablaze with light straddled the tracks at the Willesden Junction Yard, and just past Queen's Park, the line went through a little shed. Such excitements are the very stuff of bashing.

The train reached Harrow and Wealdstone at 4.15, and I got out and started walking to Harrow-on-the-Hill station, on the Metropolitan Line. I had my *A–Z*, but just to check my bearings, I asked a lady if I was heading in the right direction.

'Harrow-on-the-Hill? Oh, that's a good long walk. It's at least half a mile,' she said pityingly. I assured her that, despite my appearance, I was probably still just about up to the trek. This is not a pretty part of London. It was dark now as I walked along a main road lined with insurance offices, kebab houses and furniture shops. There was one called 'Beds R Uzzzzzzzzzzz'.

It had been a long day, and a packed lunch can only go so far. If I'd thought I had any chance of making it round the map, I would have soldiered on, but since it was quite clear that I was nowhere close, I stopped and had an all-day breakfast in a café. At the next table, there was a man doing a thing you rarely see; he was openly reading a copy of the *Daily Sport*. I had always thought of the *Sport* as a solitary pleasure, but this guy clearly felt no embarrassment whatsoever, as his eyes lingered for much longer than was decent over a picture of Linsey Dawn MacKenzie. I ate my all-day breakfast as quickly as I could, found Harrow-on-the-Hill station, and by 5.02 I was back on the Underground, on a fast train for Amersham.

This is the Metropolitan Railway, the oldest Underground railway in the world, and it is central to the poetry of Sir John Betjeman.

Betjeman was born in 1906, in Highgate. His blank-verse autobiography, *Summoned by Bells*, tells of his childhood, watching as the suburbs spread around him. He described his 'topographical predilections' as being for 'suburbs and gaslights'. From 1972 until his death in 1984, Betjeman was Poet Laureate, the best loved since Tennyson. He was a deeply funny and approachable man, and one of the greatest broadcasters, which no doubt accounts for much of his popularity, as does his metrical, usually rhyming verse. But it is in his subject matter that he most appeals.

He writes of ordinary failure and disappointment, of small-town love, of the life of the suburbs. He was the master of bathos.

> *Early Electric! With what radiant hope*
> *Men formed this many-branched electrolier,*
> *Twisted the flex around the iron rope*
> *And let the dazzling vacuum globes hang clear,*
> *And then with hearts the rich contrivance fill'd*
> *Of copper, beaten by the Bromsgrove Guild.*
>
> *Early Electric! Sit you down and see,*
> *Mid this fine woodwork and a smell of dinner,*
> *A stained-glass windmill and a pot of tea,*
> *And sepia views of leafy lanes in PINNER, –*
> *Then visualize, far down the shining lines,*
> *Your parents' homestead set in murmuring pines.*
>
> *Smoothly from HARROW, passing PRESTON ROAD,*
> *They saw the last green fields and misty sky,*
> *At NEASDEN watched a workmen's train unload,*
> *And, with the morning villas sliding by,*
> *They felt so sure on their electric trip*
> *That Youth and Progress were in partnership.*
>
> *And all that day in murky London Wall*
> *The thought of RUISLIP kept him warm inside:*
> *At FARRINGDON that lunch hour at a stall*
> *He bought a dozen plants of London Pride:*
> *While she, in arc-lit Oxford Street adrift,*
>
> *Soared through the sales by safe hydraulic lift.*
> *Early Electric! Maybe even here*
> *They met that evening at six-fifteen*
> *Beneath the hearts of this electrolier*
> *And caught the first non-stop to WILLESDEN GREEN*

Then out and on, through rural RAYNER'S LANE
To autumn-scented Middlesex again.

Cancer has killed him. Heart is killing her.
The trees are down. An Odeon flashes fire
Where stood their villa by the murmuring fir
When 'they would for their children's good conspire'.
Of all their loves and hopes on hurrying feet
Thou art the worn memorial, Baker Street.

('The Metropolitan Railway:
Baker Street Station Buffet')

Betjeman's best-known television work is *Metroland*, the kind of television essay using archive footage, music and commentary which is not made any longer. In it, he both celebrates and mourns the coming of the city to 'autumn-scented Middlesex'. This part of London owes its existence to the Metropolitan Railway. While the Metropolitan was building its branches out into what was then unspoilt countryside in the 1890s, the company was forced to buy a lot of land next to the railway, in order to secure its route. After the First World War, and Lloyd George's demand that Britain be made 'fit for heroes', the company decided that it should develop this land. In 1919, it set up Metropolitan Country Estates Ltd, in order to exploit the potential for suburb-building alongside the line. It published, from 1915 until 1932, an annual booklet, called *Metro-Land*, extolling the virtues of the line. The first few editions deal with the benefits that could be obtained by walkers and cyclists from exploring rural Middlesex. After 1919, the booklet (price 2d) eulogized the benefits of living on a new estate in a rural community. The company itself did not build many houses, but laid down roads and services, and then sold plots of land to builders or private individuals. Hugh Casson described *Metro-Land* as 'that strange Arcady that was the product of a partnership between the Metropolitan Railway and the speculative builder'. The scheme introduced the concept of owner-occupation to the new middle classes, who had previously rented their homes. Ninety-five per cent mortgages were available. The land, which had been marketed as a rural idyll, was swallowed in housing development. Rayner's Lane station had been built in 1906 to allow access to two local sewage farms. One of the suburban developments, the Harrow Garden Village, was sited there in 1930. In 1931, Rayner's Lane station carried 22,000 passengers per year. By 1938, the number had risen to 4 million. The suburbs had arrived; and the beautiful county of Middlesex had disappeared, buried beneath pavements laid by the Metropolitan Railway.

The train was full, but not packed. No one was standing: it was too early for the rush hour to have spread this far. A mobile phone rang, and everyone went for their bags and pockets, me included. I smiled at the woman sitting opposite as we both realized that the call was not for us, and she looked away. Smiling at people on the Underground is almost as bad as talking. We both had to sit with our legs turned slightly to one side so that our knees didn't touch. As the train stopped at selected stations, it began to empty out. Four pissed lasses piled out at Chalfont and Latimer, shouting and giggling, and there was plenty of room left in the carriage. The woman opposite and I were faced with one of the central dilemmas of train travel. Do we move into one of the empty seats, thus making ourselves much more comfortable, but somehow implying that there is something wrong with our travelling companion, or do we stay scrunched up where we are, uncomfortable, but safe from the embarrassment of making total strangers think they have a personal hygiene problem? Even the *Railway Traveller's Handy Book*, usually so eloquent on all matters of train etiquette, has nothing to say on this one. We stayed where we were, noses in books.

At Amersham, the highest point above sea level on the Underground, I stayed on the train and headed back for Chalfont and Latimer, where I could change for the branch to Chesham. At Chalfont I waited for twenty minutes, the longest wait of the day. Proper trains from Marylebone to Aylesbury use this station too. The Metropolitan used to get that far, once, but the suburbs never spread beyond here. There was a large car park next to the station, almost empty, and the attendant was chatting to a driver who had come to collect his car.

'I hate the little shits,' he was saying, 'they run through here, banging on the cars.' I don't know who they were, but I hated them too. I imagined them as clones of the youths in Essex, identikit proles, with nothing in their heads except baseball caps, lager and fighting. I'm getting old. Wasn't I a hoolie, back in the Seventies, following Brighton around the country? Didn't we sit in the luggage racks drinking cider, didn't we smash phone boxes, and terrorize old ladies? Well, yes, but hypocrisy is one of the undoubted pleasures of middle age.

When the train to Chesham came, it was full of suits coming back from the City to the Buckinghamshire countryside. There was even one old gentleman wearing a bowler hat, surely the last in London. In its heyday, the Met must have been full of bowler-hatted men heading home after a hard day; now there is just the one, and he faces extinction, like the sole survivor of a once-flourishing species of parrot who wanders through the Amazon, calling plaintively for a mate. Perhaps one day, a hundred years into the future, there will be one old get on the train wearing the last baseball cap on earth. I shan't live to see that day, but I have faith that it will come.

So it was 6.05, and there I was in Ultima Thule, the end of all lines, Chesham, the final destination on the Underground. I wasn't even in London any more, but Buckinghamshire; the buses outside the station were going to High Wycombe and Milton Keynes. I was tired and dispirited. It was strange to be right out here when, in central London, the rush hour was still throbbing away.

I must carry on . . . must . . . carry . . . on . . .

At least the next train out of Chesham was heading back into London, and I wouldn't have to change at Chalfont and Latimer again. Just at Moor Park for the Watford branch. Because, although I knew that I couldn't get round the whole map, I had to keep going. Giving up in the face of hopeless, one might even say pointless, odds is just not the done thing. Would Theroux have gone home, just because he got a bit fed up? Would Captain Scott? No. But, like Scott, I was moved to write in my notebook at Moor Park, 'Great God! This is an awful place.' And it was. The train for Watford arrived, and I got on. I regretted that all-day breakfast in Harrow; indigestion is one of the prices that the middle-aged pay for their hypocrisy.

I'd been to Watford before, on a Steam on the Met day, with my ex, the trainspotter. At the time, I found it difficult to get my head around the fascination with locomotives. It really doesn't make all that much difference what kind of engine is pulling the train. It's fun at journey's end to hop off and see the engine, but while the train is moving, it's actually impossible to tell whether it's a steam engine, or a diesel, or an electric that's pulling the thing. No, what fascinates me is the p-way, the permanent way, the line itself, the building of it, the way it curves invitingly out of the station, with its promise of things unknown, just around the bend. That's why I'm a line basher. So the biggest thrill on that Steam on the Met day was going round the Rickmansworth Curve. There will be railway enthusiasts reading this, sucking air through their teeth. 'Lucky pig,' they will say. 'I've never been round the Rickmansworth Curve. Why can't I go round the Rickmansworth Curve?'

It's not even marked on the map, but it's there, if you look, after Moor Park and before you get to Croxley. It links the Watford branch with the Amersham branch. It's just a curve, which is used for moving trains about from one station to another. Passenger trains seldom use it. But it was the highlight of our trip.

For the Map-in-a-Day attempt, there had been no opportunity to go round the Rickmansworth Curve. I just bashed up to Watford from Moor Park. I didn't get off at Watford. I stayed sitting, and waited for the train to head back to Harrow-on-the-bloody-Hill.

My mobile chortled. It was my girlfriend.

'Hello?'

'Hello, darling. Where are you?'

'I'm on the train.' This seemed so funny that I almost wet my pants.

'Yes dear, of course you are. But where?'

I tried to stop laughing, but I was so knackered and Tube-lagged that I couldn't. I had become hysterical, The other passengers who were sitting on the southbound train, waiting for it to go, were giving me what my mum calls 'old-fashioned looks'. I caught my breath and tried to get a grip.

'Watford.' This started me off again. I was bent double, tears of laughter rolling down my cheeks. 'Watford', quite simply, was the funniest thing I'd ever said.

'Come home, dear. Give it up.'

'I can't . . . I . . . I . . . I've got to go TO UXBRIDGE!' I screamed into the phone, helpless, a gibbering fool. She hung up.

The train pulled out of Watford, and I hid behind Theroux, trying not to catch the eyes of the other passengers. God knows, they were happy enough not to look at me, after the scene I'd just made.

Back at Harrow-on-the-Hill, waiting for the Uxbridge train, I took my life into my hands and had a go on the chocolate machine. It is a well-known fact that these things take your money, but never give you sweeties in return. I've been taken in by their promise a thousand times, but, like a gambler who thinks that just one more go on the one-armed bandit might be the one to hit paydirt, I can never quite give it up. My first selection, a Fruit and Nut, was unavailable. Unsurprising, this; it is the most popular choice in Underground vending machines. I looked again at the menu, and it came into my head, I know not why, for the first time in many years, that a packet of Snack Biscuits might be sustaining. This time, I was lucky; there was a thud, a series of thuds. The little screen instructed me to collect my item. And, knock me down, there in the drawer were my Snack Biscuits, AND a Fruit and Nut, AND, from somewhere, a Picnic. Paydirt indeed. I couldn't believe my luck. I hid the goodies in my pocket and got on the train for Uxbridge.

At Eastcote, described in the *Metro-Land* booklet of 1922 as 'a charming hamlet', there was freezing fog, and a palm tree on the platform. At Ruislip and Ruislip Manor, I was saddened by the fact that I wouldn't be able to get round the Tube in a day, so I wouldn't be visiting South Ruislip, Ruislip Gardens or West Ruislip. I'd looked forward to that. Saddened, too, on behalf of the hard-done-by residents of North and East Ruislip, who have no Tube station they can call their own. Unlike those fortunate souls who live in Acton, who have six railway stations to choose from.

Ickenham is yet another station on the Metropolitan Line with literary connections; Wodehouse's Uncle Fred is, of course, the Earl of Ickenham. I imagined Wodehouse, sitting in upstate New York, looking with nostalgia at the Tube map and picking a name which struck him as funny. If you were picking names at random from the Tube map, of course, the name you would be most likely to pick would be Acton, with Ruislip a close second.

Hillingdon is a fantastic station, but it looks better driving past up the A40. The really modern stations are mostly to be found on the Jubilee Line, but Hillingdon is a *tour de force*, silver, gleaming in the light. If anyone ever tells you that railway architecture is not what it used to be, show them Hillingdon. It used to be called Hillingdon Swakeleys, and it still has Swakeleys in tiny brackets on the station sign. But it just sounds inappropriate, somehow, a little bit of Yorkshire transplanted into West London. Ayup, lass, stop yer mither-in' and I'll tek thee t' Swakeleys. Swakeleys is just not a London word.

Seven thirty-five p.m. Uxbridge. Must have a beer. I'd been going for thirteen hours or more, and I was losing it. If I didn't have a beer . . . well, I don't know what. But I had to have a beer before I got on another Tube train. This continual need for breaks is what ruined my scheme, as much as anything. I still feel that the Tube system can be traversed in a day, but that it needs a non-smoker with a vacuum flask and a strong bladder. I liked Uxbridge station, which even has a sign for the buffet, unique as far as I'm aware on the whole of the Underground, but I liked the Three Tuns, just outside the station, even more. Good beer, too, Marstons, from Burton, which at one time would have been trans-shipped into St Pancras. Now it comes by road. But I felt fortified, and I headed back to the station. I had hoped to get a Piccadilly Line train, but there were none at this time of the day, so I got another Met train, and changed at Rayner's Lane.

There was a twelve-minute wait till the next Piccadilly Line train, so I went out of the station for a fag. Opposite, there was a wonderful old Thirties cinema in High Art Deco. Mostly, these suburban cinemas have been turned into bingo halls, but not this one. No, it has been turned into the London Zoroastrian Centre. Zoroastrians flock from all over London to come here to worship. It is against the Zoroastrian faith to be buried at death; rather, their bodies are left on the top of 'Towers of Silence', where vultures strip their bones. At least, that's what happens in India; I looked, but I could see no vultures in Rayner's Lane.

A couple of estate agents, yes, but surely even they have to draw the line somewhere. Perhaps the roof of the old cinema is covered in dead bodies. Perhaps Freddie Mercury is up there, being pecked at by pigeons. He was a Zoroastrian, by birth at least. Thunderbolt and lightning! Very, very frightening!

The Piccadilly Line train left Rayner's Lane at 8.10 p.m. and entered a twilight zone of floodlit car parks, carpet warehouses, superstores and shopping centres. The train was far from full, and I would have liked to read the *Standard*, to complete my press review of the day. But there were none; there had been none all evening, and throughout the course of the rest of my journey, I would not see one. Since I had found and read all the rest of the papers, except the *FT*, this struck me as very odd. People obviously cherish their copies. I was bored, bored of looking out of the window and reading; bored to the point of stark staring madness. I looked at the Underground map and tried to write my own Betjemanesque poem; but I have no talent for poetry, and could get no further than rhyming 'Northwick Park' with 'data-input clerk'. The train stopped and started; the beer was lulling me into sleep. The stations were badly lit, and it was difficult to read the signs. I should have given up hours ago.

At last we lurched into Acton Town, and I was sorely tempted to stay on the train and go home. But the gods of bashing urged me on, and I got off and stood waiting on the freezing platform for the next train to Heathrow. When it came, it was the first full train that I'd been on since the morning rush hour, and for the first time since the Northern Line south to Morden, I was forced to stand. I had thought that the evening trains might be a bit chattier, but no; they were as silent as the grave, and a more than usually miserable bunch this lot were, too, as though they had been witness to some nameless horror just before arriving at Acton Town.

I have worked out a rule of thumb. During the morning, trains into London are silent because everyone's depressed at going to work; in the evening trains out of London are silent because everyone's depressed about going home. Any chatting is most likely to happen on evening trains heading INTO town, as friends go out for the night. But there's precious little of that, either. I kept expecting the silent, gloomy passengers to get off at the frequent stations, but they didn't; at South Ealing and Northfields, no one stirred; at Osterley and Boston Manor, only a handful got off. Where were all these people going? A few of them had luggage, and were clearly off to Heathrow, but that can't account for a full train. The answer soon presented itself; they all got off at Hounslow. No wonder they were so miserable.

Half the air travellers got off at Terminal Four, the rest at Terminals One, Two, Three. If I was anywhere close to achieving my whole-map-in-a-day ambition, I would have stayed on and gone back to Acton Town, from where I would have started my peregrination on the District Line. But I was nowhere close, and if there's one thing I can never resist, it's airports. After a day in which the departure board had nothing more exotic to offer than Cockfosters or Wimbledon, I felt that a visit to the airport might bring some much needed relief. After all, what I'd come to investigate was the relationship between romance and reality on the railway, and all I had done was prove that the Underground can never really be romantic; only cool. It would be good to see departure boards for Samarkand and Timbuktu. So I detrained.

The airport was fairly empty, and I couldn't really see any departure boards. There was an Air Namibia flight to Windhoek, but I can't say I fancied it. I grabbed a latte in the Departure Lounge, and reflected on the difference between an airport and a station. A station feels like a destination. When you arrive at Manchester Piccadilly, you have arrived in Manchester. A station is somewhere. But an airport is an in-between place, neither here nor there. When you arrive at Manchester Airport, you have in fact been dumped in the middle of the Cheshire countryside. It is as genuinely Mancunian as Man U, forced into the outskirts by the respectable citizens who support their local team, who are called Manchester City. An airport, like Man U, belongs to nobody and nowhere. A station belongs; it has identity. Airports are part of a soggy, lowest-common-denominator world culture, like Man U, Oirish pubs or Starbucks. Apologies to the residents of Trafford here, incidentally, though if I were you, I'd support Altrincham.

On my way back to the Underground station, I noticed a sign for the

Heathrow Express, the ultra-modern train which runs fast from Paddington out to the airport. It said that the train is free between Terminals Three and Four. It sure as hell isn't on the map, but I determined to have a ride. The station was fantastic. A series of escalators carrying passengers down from the airport stretched through a cavernous vestibule, grey, well lit and modernistic. I loved the train when it came in. The biggest disappointment of the Millennium was that we woke up, not to a bright new tomorrow, but to the same old England, moaning, drizzly and creaking under the strain. This was not how it was supposed to be, according to *Tomorrow's World* back in the Sixties. We were supposed to be riding in hover cars and wearing silver catsuits. The Heathrow Express train is one of the tiny handful of artefacts which look truly modern. Midnight blue, with black windows, it looks like it should be ferrying agents around the Roswell Air Force base. The seats are insanely comfortable, and the ride is the smoothest I have ever experienced on a railway. There was even an on-train TV, which was playing some truly horrible Enya-esque neo-plainchant stuff, with an accompanying video depicting deprived inner-city children struggling against the odds to better themselves. As we approached Terminal Four, a cheerful talking head, dressed as a Heathrow Express stewardess, came on the screen to thank us for travelling with them. She urged us to mind the gap between the platform and the train, and there were pictures of the gap, with little arrows, showing us where it is. Only a geisha with the tiniest conceivable stilettos could stand in the slightest risk of getting into this gap, but I guess you can never be too careful.

I made my back to the Piccadilly Line, and headed back to town. It was 9.45 p.m. The other passengers seemed to be solitary back-packers. Bags were piled in the corridor. No one had come to meet them.

There was no doubt at all now that I couldn't come anywhere close to doing the Tube in a day. The train was in no hurry and sat waiting for a path outside North Acton station. I changed my itinerary again, to try to get in as much as I could before 12.30. One of the passengers who had got on at Heathrow was pacing nervously about the carriage, looking again and again at the central London Tube map. I wondered what waited for him at the other end. Had he flown halfway round the world to meet an estranged lover, to attempt a reconciliation? Or had he come to work in an Aussie theme bar in Earl's Court?

I felt miserable and stupid for trying to do this pointless thing. So did Paul Theroux, hacking back across Russia on the Trans-Siberian. He quotes the nineteenth-century traveller Henry de Windt, who wrote a book called *From Pekin to Calais by Land* (and I wonder if he visited the hypermarket when he got there, to stock up on fags and booze?). De Windt says, 'I can only trust this book may deter others from following my example.'

Theroux concurred with this advice, and so do I. If I have put anybody off trying to go round the Tube in a day, then my work will not have been in vain.

I stayed on the Piccadilly Line, heading for Green Park. The silence was growing oppressive. I was getting the fear. Those of us left on the train were tired. The pacing man got off at South Kensington. A drunk grasping his tinnie got on at Knightsbridge. And at 10.55 I got off at Green Park station, heading for the Jubilee Line. There was a man running on the platform.

You see quite a few running people on the Tube, and I'd love to know what they are running for. You get to the station, buy your ticket, and someone comes sprinting past you, runs down the escalator, and disappears round the corner. You walk quietly, arrive on the platform a good thirty seconds after they have, to find them pacing nervously up and down. Then you both get on to the same train. I long to take them aside and explain, 'So, you're late for work? Will it get you there any quicker by running through the station? Not really. But let's imagine that it does; that you catch a train which leaves two minutes earlier than the one you would have caught if you hadn't run for it. What are you going to do with those two minutes? Will it really annoy your boss that much if you are two minutes late? Then hand in your resignation. Life is a railway trip whose destination is the grave. Walk through stations, my friend, and enjoy the journey! The train will come soon enough. Read a book. Meditate. Railway travel is like carp-fishing. It demands patience.' The last time I ran for a train was in

1974, at Newhaven Town station. I missed it, and the porter on the platform (because there were such creatures in those days) said to me, 'Son, let me give you some advice. There are two things in life you never run after, a train and a woman. Because there will always be another one along in a minute.'

I have followed half of this advice for almost thirty years, with happy results.

Those Jubilee Line trains have doors on the platforms as well as the trains, to stop people from throwing themselves on to the line. Odd, really, because if you were that desperate, you could just walk through the tunnel and throw yourself under a Piccadilly Line train instead. My Tube-spotting ex-girlfriend took me on the Jubilee when it first opened; we got off at all the stations, and they really are wonderful. Canary Wharf station is the best Underground building in London, and is well worth a trip if you've never seen it. Tonight, I got off at Canada Water, and waited for a train to take me up the East London Line to Whitechapel.

It's an unassuming little line, the East London. Next to the Waterloo and City, it's the shortest. It only has nine stations, two of which, New Cross and New Cross Gate, are practically next to one another, and another, Shoreditch, which is closed for much of the day. But it plays unwitting host to one of the great miracles of nineteenth-century engineering, between Rotherhithe and Wapping – Marc and Isambard Brunel's Thames Tunnel.

It's not much to see now. It looks no different from any other stretch of Tube, but it isn't the same at all. If you could get out, if you could silence the train, you would hear the sound of ships' propellers passing in the river overhead. The band of the Coldstream Guards played down here, Brunel swam through this tunnel, a rope tied to his waist. As the train pulled out of Wapping, I started to feel paranoid, as though someone was sitting behind me. A ghost of one of Brunel's dead navvies, maybe? Whatever it was, I felt really uncomfortable as we got into Whitechapel, and I hurried up into the night air for a fag. The fear was taking over. The photo-booth was talking, for some reason, explaining that you should draw the curtains and adjust the height of the stool, and it made me jumpier yet. As I was rolling one in the station entrance, a guy approached me and asked me for some tobacco. When you are having the fear and are gripped by horrible foreboding, you don't want to be approached by anyone, least of all in Whitechapel, when you're already thinking about Jack the Ripper. But I gave the guy a couple of roll-ups' worth of bacca and a few skins.

'Chiz, pal. Yore a lifesaver.'

'I bet you won't say that when you get emphysema.'

'Ha ha ha. Dead right, pal.'

'Don't sue me . . .'

Now I was really getting paranoid. I made my way back to the platform, past the possessed photo-booth, down badly lit stairs, and down and down the dark escalators, aware now that I was entering an Underworld, the Chthonic world, below the earth and beyond it. This is the world of the dead, the ancestral, the demonic. One of the early critics of the building of Underground railways, a Dr Cuming, said, 'The forthcoming end of the world would be hastened by the construction of underground railways burrowing into the infernal regions and thereby disturbing the devil.'

I feel the Light Bringer's presence in these echoing tunnels. Spare me, oh great Lucifer! I remembered the countless ghost stories of Underground lore: the screaming spectre of Farringdon, the Black Nun at Bank, the ghost trains at South Kensington. Nature has been excluded, so too should be the Human. We are not welcome here, in these endless, pitiless tunnels, knocking on the doors of Hades. There are rumours of a terrible race of mutants who live in these tunnels, descended from workers who were trapped down here when the railways were being built. Now, after a hundred years, the mutants grab unsuspecting passengers and gnaw their bones. They have lost the power of speech, all but one chilling phrase that strikes terror into their victims' hearts – 'MIND THE DOORS! MIND THE DOORS!'

Rosalind Williams says that 'Narratives about journeys to the underworld are inherently sacred'; I muttered a prayer, crossed my fingers, and kept my eyes resolutely ahead.

My teeth were aching from the Fruit and Nut, Snack Biscuits and

Picnic, and back on the platform for a westbound District Line train, the feeling of fear refused to go away. Theroux says that all travel writing starts off breezy and ends up confessional, and I was beginning to see his point. At half-eleven, an empty Tube train came sparking round the corner, and it lurched its way to Victoria with me on board. It squealed and protested. So did my head. Enough already.

One last time, I came up for air, at Victoria. The concourse was full of parents meeting teenage children getting off the Gatwick Express. I bought a cup of Ritazza coffee from a sandwich bar, and leaned on a display stand to drink it. During the day, this stand was obviously used to demonstrate mandolines (the vegetable slicer, not the musical instrument). There were pictures showing the various uses that mandolines can be put to, and, in capital letters, the proud assertion that 'THIS INVENTION IS ENJOYED AND VALUED WORLD-WIDE'. Valued, perhaps, but enjoyed? Mind you, it takes all sorts.

What I would really like to have done was go outside the station and catch the 38 bus again. But somehow, I drew on my last reserves of strength and courage, and at five past midnight, I caught my last train, north on the Victoria Line. The train was full of youths? In, like, baseball caps? At least they were talking; but in the interrogative? This last train is the most talkative of the day, English tongues finally loosened by drink? But why do they have to talk like Australians? I finished Theroux, and sat with my bag on my lap, waiting for the last stop.

It was 12.15. I arrived back at Highbury and Islington. A guy asked me for my Travelcard, but I refused. We'd been too far together. Besides, who would get the use of it? The trains only ran for another twenty minutes or so, and you can hardly get anywhere in twenty minutes, as who knows better than I?

They could wait till the morning and buy their own Travelcards; the first train was leaving in five and a half hours. I would be asleep by then, dreaming of the Underworld.

The Titfield Thunderbolt

Me and Perry Venus go back to 1976. We met at a Freshers' disco in the Students' Union at St David's University College, Lampeter. We were both eighteen. We didn't know one another, but we didn't know anyone else there either. Neither of us had the courage to speak to women, or the inclination to dance about on our own to records that disgusted us. So we had three choices: we could sit like lemons, staring longingly at the girls we knew we'd never cop off with; we could go back to our different sets of wonky first-six-weeks-at-college mates who spent the evenings sitting in their rooms drinking tea, listening to Vaughan Williams and discussing the influence of the poetry of Gerard Manley Hopkins on the modern Church in Wales; or we could talk to each other.

We fell to talking. We quickly realized that we had three shared ambitions; three great goals that we wished to achieve during our time at university. These were: to be in a band, to lose our virginity and to take drugs, in no particular order.

The band was easy. This was the autumn of 1976, so it was obvious that we had to have a punk band, and before you could say 'Eddie and the Hot Rods', we did. I sang, and Perry played bass. Within a year, ours was the hardest, grittiest, indeed only, English-speaking punk band in the whole of north/central Dyfed. I believe we even got into west Powys on one occasion. We changed our names to punk ones. Mr Perry Venus is in the peculiar position of being a middle-aged man whose punk name has stuck. I was called Nat West; and later, after the birth of my eldest daughter, Terry Nappies. Luckily my names didn't stick.

Losing our virginity was less easy than changing our names and learning to play 'Sweet Jane', but we stuck at it, and we got there eventually. I'm sure you'd prefer it if I drew a veil, so I will.

Drugs were harder to come by than you might imagine. It took weeks in those days, rather than the ten minutes it takes now. But when we did get drugs, we found we liked them. They became a solace and a haven for us. Away from home for the first time, missing our mums, and lured from the path of tea and Gerard Manley Hopkins by evil hippy pushers, we took comfort in the arms of hash, grass, speed, acid, mushrooms, Pro Plus, Dodos, and that old student favourite, strong drink. We preferred quantity to quality, though we didn't mind quality when it was to be had. We liked the naughtiness, too. Those were the days when drugs were straightforwardly illegal as well as difficult to get, not like now. It was wicked, in every sense, and we liked that. I suppose this is one way it is perfectly possible that President-for-Life Blair could have been in a Seventies rock band and not have taken drugs, just as he claims. They might have simply been too hard to get. He might just not have met the right people. Seems unlikely, but we must admit the possibility.

No, I am certain that the man has never taken drugs. Look at him; it's something about his ears. That is the crucial difference in our careers. I was in a band, had sex and took drugs, which made me decide I wanted to be a pop star and have lots of fun. As is perhaps obvious, I didn't become a pop star, but trying to be one was a laugh, a gas, a hoot. But Mr Blair, who played in a band and who one would imagine had various sexual experiences of some kind, but who *didn't* take drugs, decided that being a pop star was nothing like half so much fun as being a lawyer, a Party apparatchik, and, eventually, President-for-Life. Drugs made all the difference, clearly. That and the public school thing. And yet can we say who is the better man, Mr Blair or I? Perhaps he had a hoot too; perhaps that was his idea of fun. Or perhaps funny isn't the highest good; perhaps there is more to life than just enjoying it.

Perry and I stopped playing music together at the end of the Seventies, though we went on to play with others. Sex, to be frank, has been both fraught and sporadic for both of us, but we have continued to enjoy mild intoxicants together on a fairly regular basis ever since. So when I asked Perry if he would like to come on a bash with me, and take some photographs of the Great Little Trains of Wales, it seemed clear to me that we should do it gonzo.

Of course.

It was obvious.

It would be like *Fear and Loathing in Blaenau Ffestiniog*. I would be Hunter S. Thompson, Venus would be Ralph Steadman. We would cut through the bullshit, and discover deeper realities. It would, I felt, give us a unique way into the heart of what we mean by 'train'. Perhaps we would become, in some sense, at one with the train; maybe, somehow, we would really *be* the train.

Not high-octane gonzo at our stage of life, obviously – no ether-soaked towels on the carriage floor. Slow steam-hauled gonzo, that's what we wanted, i.e. a little spliff, and a couple of pints of Felinfoel. But still worth a try. Probably no one has smoked a spliff and then gone on the Great Little Trains ever before. And the bye-laws are plain; *The Railway Traveller's Handy Book* had warned us what we might expect.

Any person found in a carriage or station in a state of intoxication, or committing any nuisance, or otherwise wilfully interfering with the comfort of other passengers, is hereby subjected to a penalty not exceeding forty shillings; and shall, in addition to incurring the aforesaid penalty, be immediately, or, if travelling, at the first opportunity, removed from the Company's premises.

Forty bob! We were up for that. We were punks once, you know. Oh yes. To hell with the Company. Let them fine us if they would. If you can't do the time, don't do the crime, friends. That's just the kind of guys we are, I guess. Mine's a pint of mild and a piece of hash fudge!

Good people of Towyn, lock up your daughters!

Alas – I had forgotten that we are middle-aged, 'bald and fat and full of sin'. If you know how much forty bob is, you should be watching Denis Norden TV shows and organizing beetle drives, not titting about with your pals. So it didn't quite come off, not in the fullest sense that I had hoped for. But we did eat some nice cakes.

And I did fall in love with a railway, a real romantic railway, and I did meet lots of people who were much more in love with that railway than I was; crazy, head-over-heels love-sick fools. This beautiful, brave, funny, pretty, clever railway is called the Tal-y-Llyn. It is great, little, and in Wales. It was saved from closure after ninety years of obscurity and thrown for a time into the nation's consciousness by a man called L. T. C. 'Tom' Rolt.

Tom Rolt was one of the most important figures in the twentieth-century rural conservation movement. He was one of the first of the Greens, and an early proto-hippy. He empowered local communities to take charge of at least part of their environment. He was concerned with scale; he was anti globalization. He disliked American corporate culture, which he saw as threatening an 'authentic' English culture. He was a writer, on canals, on topography, on railway disasters, on industrial archaeology and engineering history. His biographies of Telford, the Stephensons and Brunel are still the most readable. An engineer by training, in his philosophical writings he attempted to reconcile God, Men and Machines. And for all that, it is for his first book, *Narrow Boat*, that he is probably best loved and best remembered. It was certainly a work that would have far-reaching consequences.

In the summer of 1939 Tom Rolt and his first wife, Angela, set out on an elegaic voyage through England's canal system. Rolt was an unemployed gentleman car mechanic, who had served his apprenticeship in steam engines. He had been part-owner of a garage outside Andover which had gone bust, through no fault of his own. Now he had married the beautiful and wilfull Angela. Angela was a blue-blood, the real thing; her aristocratic family disowned her when she married Rolt. They needed somewhere to live. Rolt wanted to try his hand as a professional writer. He'd had a few ghost stories published in the 1930s, and the signs were encouraging. But they would need to live cheap. Rolt, a lifelong lover of the English canals, suggested converting an old canal boat, a seventy-foot-long, seven-foot-wide wooden-hulled narrowboat which had been used by his family for holidays. Angela agreed; the boat was bought and converted. The newly-weds set out on their maiden voyage in 'that fateful summer', watching as the last of old England came under the shadow of war.

Rolt wrote the journey up as they went, as what he hoped would be his first published book.

The war came, and no one was interested in books about canals. Tom and Angela still lived on their boat, *Cressy*, but it was permanently moored at Tardebigge, outside Birmingham, in which city Rolt worked for the duration as a factory inspector. He had never given up his ambitions as a writer. He had a few things published in *Horizon*, the officially sanctioned literary magazine run by Cyril Connolly as his contribution to the war effort. Most importantly, Rolt began a correspondence with another influential ruralist, the writer H. J. Massingham. Massingham asked to see Rolt's manuscript. Rolt dug it out from a suitcase under his bed on board *Cressy*, and Massingham saw its worth. It was published late in 1944.

It is a remarkable book. It deals with that journey taken over the English canals in the summer and autumn of 1939, and it celebrates a lost pastoral England of market towns and farmhouse cheeses, tinkers on the roads and horse fairs and nut-brown ale. Above all, it tells the tale of the 'Number Ones', the handful of families who still struggled to survive in horse-drawn boats by transporting coal over the almost lost canals of England. Rolt argued persuasively that the canals should be preserved, not as holiday destinations, but as working transport arteries. It was an argument that he lost, with a great deal of bitterness.

Narrow Boat was one of those end-of-war books, like *Brideshead Revisited*, which pandered to a nostalgic feeling, sprung from war exhaustion, for a bygone and clearly lost-forever England. The book seemed to tap into that vanished Arcadia, and it was a huge success. Many of its readers felt that 'something should be done' about the state of the canals. Rolt was approached, meetings were held, and in 1946, the Inland Waterways Association (IWA) was founded to do something. Rolt was elected secretary, and was set up as a figurehead and campaign organizer for the new movement.

The IWA may not sound as though it could be a cauldron of boiling passions, but in its early days it certainly was. Rolt wanted to preserve a way of life, that of the travelling canal community. He attracted a small band of like-minded idealists to his cause, but they were very much in the minority. The pragmatists in the IWA saw that the canals could only be kept open at the expense of the dwindling freight traffic; that the post-war boom in long-distance lorry transport spelled the end for canal transport. The only way to keep the canals open was to let the pleasure boats in. The two wings of the new movement moved on to a war footing. Rolt's idealist wing led campaigns over some of Britain's finest canals – the Stratford, the Llangollen, the Huddersfield Narrow. But he was politically naive, and the pragmatists wanted him out. Time has proved them largely correct, but Rolt took his defeat in the in-fighting very badly.

It was 1950. Rolt had been thrown out of the IWA. His marriage to Angela was in ruins. *Cressy* was still his home, but her condition was now so bad that he knew he would have to give her up. His writing career had not really taken off after the success of *Narrow Boat*. His book of philosophy, *High Horse Riderless*, had found only a handful of readers. He was depressed and full of self-pity. Then he got a phone call from some friends based in Banbury. A retired Welsh MP, Sir Henry Haydn Jones, had died. And Rolt was about to get a new lease of life.

The Tal-y-Llyn Railway had been opened in 1867. Built to a narrow gauge, it was six and a half miles long, running from slate quarries outside the village of Abergynolwen to a junction with the Cambrian Railways Line at Towyn. Built primarily to carry slate, it had obtained Parliamentary assent to carry a few passengers from Abergynolwen to Towyn and back. It had two locomotives, *Talyllyn* and *Dolgoch*, and just one four-wheeled passenger carriage. Her Majesty's Inspectorate of Railways sent an inspector. His recommendations stated that, as long as trains didn't exceed 10 mph, the thing was probably safe. *Talyllyn* and *Dolgoch* started to beat up and down the line, carrying slate and occasional passengers – more in summer. Three more carriages were obtained. Then the world forgot it was there. The Railway Inspectorate forgot it was there; after their first visit, they didn't inspect the line again until 1951.

Traffic declined over the first decade of the twentieth century, and the original owners sold the line to the local MP, Sir Henry Haydn Jones, in 1911. Through the First World War, labour drifted away from the dangerous slate mines the line had been built to serve. The railway became increasingly reliant on the summer trade. *Talyllyn* and *Dolgoch* pulled such summer traffic up and down the line every year through the First World War, through the 1920s and the 1930s. There were three staff who worked on the railway. One of these was Edward Thomas, general manager, accountant, ticket seller and train guard. The other two staff members were a driver and a fireman, who also doubled as the track maintenance staff. Sir Haydn refused to invest the capital needed to maintain the railway, but Edward Thomas somehow kept the thing running right through the Second World War.

That was when Rolt had first discovered the line, in 1943. He had been staying by Lake Talyllyn (three miles above Abergynolwen; the train never went there, and no one is really sure why the railway is named after it). He heard that two trains a day were still being run, on Mondays, Wednesdays and Fridays. So he caught a bus down to Towyn, hoping to catch a train most of the way back. He was disappointed; at Towyn Wharf station he found only a handwritten notice, 'No Trains Today'. He started to walk back up the line towards Abergynolwen. He found someone trying to mend *Dolgoch* with a hammer; that was why there were no trains. Then he walked back the length of the line. He described it as being more like a country lane than a railway. In places, the rails were almost overgrown with turf. Gorse and rhododendron crowded the line and obscured the platforms of the little halts. He didn't catch the train, but he remembered the line.

In 1948 Rolt, still at that time secretary of the IWA, was reading the draft of the Transport Bill which would nationalize all Britain's railways, canals and road hauliers. He took delight in spotting the most unlikely railway and canal companies that were to be nationalized. The Tal-y-Llyn wasn't on the list. Everyone had simply forgotten that it was there. As it became clear that Rolt could not hang on as secretary of the IWA, he began to take an increasing interest in the little line. He took some friends to visit, and managed at last to ride behind *Dolgoch*, six years after his walk up the line. They met the elderly Sir Haydn, who told them that although he was willing to see the railway continue during his lifetime, he was sure that at his death, his executors would wish to close the line down. It was already marked as closed on the Ordnance Survey Map. Rolt and his friends began to lay some plans. He wrote a letter to the national press, calling for ideas. In 1950 the call came. Sir Haydn was dead, and the line carrying the two elderly engines was bound to be closed.

Rolt called a public meeting in September 1950, in Birmingham. He knew how to drum up public support; he had done it with the canals, and he knew what might be achieved with courage and intelligence. He and his two friends, supported by Edward Thomas, then approaching seventy, proposed the formation of the Tal-y-Llyn Railway Preservation Society. The meeting agreed, and negotiations were undertaken with Sir Haydn's executors. The Society agreed to take over the running of the railway from the summer of 1951. It was the world's first preserved steam railway. And Rolt, with his engineering and campaigning background, seemed the ideal person to run it. In the first season after the Society took over, Rolt gave up more of his precious writing time, and moved to Towyn to take up the post of general manager on expenses of £30 per month. He found that *Talyllyn* was useless, and *Dolgoch* in need of extensive repairs. He'd never run a railway before, but he got through that first summer. In 1952, he again took up his post, this time accompanied by his second wife, Sonia. As from that date, the Society went from strength to strength, and the line is now safer and better run than in the whole of its existence. Rolt eventually became its chairman, and in 1991, seventeen years after his death, the Society named its seventh and newest locomotive *Tom Rolt*.

There is one more episode in the story of the railway to tell. In 1952 Rolt was approached by Ealing Film Studios. They had heard of the Tal-y-Llyn's struggle for survival, and had decided that it would be a good subject for a comedy. Rolt was happy to help, and the result is *The Titfield Thunderbolt*, one of Ealing's minor gems, which deserves rewatching.

A local railway is under threat. A group of locals, led by an excellent railway clergyman, struggle to take the railway under their control in the teeth of opposition from the local bus company, aided by a young steam-roller-driving Sid James in the days before he got to play funny roles. Stanley Holloway plays Mr Valentine, the local businessman who helps keep the line open, once he has been assured that there will be a refreshment car where he will be able to drink out of hours. However folksy it looks now, in 1952 *The Titfield Thunderbolt* was pungent social comedy, another clarion call from Ealing on behalf of the little guy who does things for himself.

The interest generated by the saving of the Tal-y-Llyn, and the widespread publicity generated by the film, meant that other groups trying to save other railways came into existence; first, just up the coast at the Ffestiniog Railway, and then in Sussex, at the Bluebell, which had been ignored for the first ninety years of its existence. A spark was lit at the Tal-y-Llyn, a spark which has ignited a hundred thousand days out with the kids on wet Bank Holiday weekends. It was here, thanks to the courage and campaigning ability of one man, that the preserved railway movement was born.

Something of the *volkisch* spirit of Rolt lives on in the Tal-y-Llyn. It still goes to exactly the same place it has always gone. *Dolgoch* and *Talyllyn* still occasionally pull the original carriages. The canal preservation movement, real ale, folk-song and custom, all seemed like symbols of a vital but threatened culture to the English ruralists like Rolt and Massingham; out of their ideas came moves towards self-sufficiency and the hippy rural idealism of the 1960s and 1970s. Rolt was a folk romantic, and it is in this atmosphere that the story of the saving of the Tal-y-Llyn needs to be understood.

Or, of course, you could just get stoned, like me and Perry planned to.

Aberystwyth, as well as being a British Rail station, is also the starting point for the Vale of Rheidol Railway, yet another of the Great Little Railways of Wales. It climbs into the mountains and ends at Devil's Bridge, high above a spectacular gorge. This used to be how we filled quiet weekday afternoons as students: to get stoned, we'd drive the twenty-five miles or so from Lampeter to Devil's Bridge, and then catch the train down into Aberystwyth and back. We always did the trip gonzo, and of all the Great Little Trains, it was the only one me and Perry were a bit bored with. We've been there, and I'm happy to report that we didn't go on to buy the T-shirt. Or the key-ring, or the souvenir mug. So on this trip I wanted to see, first, the Tal-y-Llyn, and then, the next day, the Ffestiniog Railway, known to aficionados as the Fessy.

But the Vale of Rheidol is worth a visit. Until privatization, it was the only steam-hauled line still operated by British Rail, and Aberystwyth is one of the very few stations where you get a regular opportunity to see steam-hauled narrow-gauge railways alongside modern characterless trains. Anyone who fancies a weekend playing on trains should start in Aberystwyth. The standard-gauge run from Shrewsbury is very attractive; then you could go up the Vale of Rheidol; and then you could do as Perry and I planned, to catch the Cambrian Coast Line north for Towyn and the Tal-y-Llyn, and then on to Porthmadog for the Fessy.

Waiting for the train at Aberystwyth, we thought we might go across to the pub for a couple of pints, get the gonzo thing going. So we looked into the pub outside the station, but we both admitted that we couldn't quite face it that early in the day, so we went to the station buffet for a cup of Ritazza coffee and a biscuit instead. A disappointing start, but perhaps if we found a sexy enough biscuit, that would give us a sugar kick which would mean we wouldn't need alcohol; and God knows, Ritazza coffee gets the heart pumping under any circumstances. But sexy biscuits are not to be had, in Aberystwyth or elsewhere.

I have a chum called Big Doctor Dave, and when he was a boy, his mother always used to buy dull, unappetizing biscuits on the grounds that 'they didn't get eaten'. This annoyed Big Doctor Dave, and he swore that if he ever had kids, he would buy nice biscuits. I can now tell the world that Big Doctor Dave's mum is the chief biscuit buyer for the various catering companies that serve refreshments the length of Britain's railways; or, if she isn't, her biscuit-buying philosophy has somehow spread throughout the entire network.

Coffee has always been bad on the railway. The proprietors of the refreshment room at Swindon took offence in 1845 when it was reported to them that Brunel had complained about the badly roasted coffee, so he wrote a letter to put their minds at rest.

Dear Sir,

I assure you that Mr Player was wrong in supposing that I thought you purchased inferior coffee. I thought I said to him I was surprised you should buy such bad roasted corn. I did not believe you had such a thing as coffee in the place; I am certain I never tasted any. I have long ceased to make complaints at Swindon. I avoid taking anything there when I can help it.

Yours faithfully,

I. K. Brunel.

Dickens described railway coffee as 'brown hot water stiffened with flour', but I think that both Dickens and Brunel would be impressed by Ritazza. The social historian, G. M. Trevelyan, called the railways 'Britain's great gift to the world', and he may have had a point, but he was writing in the days before Ritazza coffee, and I can't help wondering if a few cups of this extraordinary substance might have dimmed his enthusiasm somewhat.

British rail sandwiches have been the butt of jokes for as long as I can remember, but it is the coffee that sticks in the craw. Ritazza coffee is the great drink of institutional Britain. You find it not just in station buffets, but in hospital and university canteens the length and breadth of this once great nation. Why this should be so defies the imagination. It is hot, and brown, but so is dog shit, and you would hardly describe it as coffee. The stuff sits in big flasks on the back of the counter, stewing. When the catering outlet operative depresses the nozzle, your paper cup is filled with coffee that was freshly brewed only last week in a depot outside Hounslow. It is thin as Michael Howard's smile, with only the faintest hint of bitter coffee flavour, but by Christ, it gets you going. It is worth putting up with the disgusting taste to get the unrivalled caffeine buzz that a large Ritazza delivers; just as well, since there is no other kind of coffee available on British stations. A note to incontinent passengers, however. The ordinary diuretic properties of coffee are multiplied ten-fold in a cup of Ritazza; you do not want to be caught short on a suburban train whose lavatories are closed due to vandalism after a couple of shots taken in a moment of madness at the station.

Perry and I were most certainly buzzing by the time our train came, much more than we would have been after a pint of Felinfoel. It was not a direct train. We had to change at Dovey Junction for the Cambrian Coast Line to Towyn and Porthmadog.

'Where's Dovey Junction?' asked Perry. 'I've lived in Wales for twenty-five years, and I've never heard of Dovey Junction.' (He's a long-time car driver, as you have to be if you live in rural Wales, and has never taken the train from Aberystwyth to Shrewsbury.)

'Between Borth and Maccynlleth. I thought we could smoke a spliff there while we wait for the connection.'

Perry is paranoid at the best of times. He thinks MI5 bug his phone and have a special recording device which kicks in when he says 'pot'. He thinks that there are sniffer dogs everywhere.

'Do we have to? It's still a bit early for me. Anyway, won't the other passengers notice?'

'Yes, we do have to. You're supposed to be Steadman. He was Welsh.'

'Oh, all right. But we'll have to be careful about the other passengers.'

Yes, well. What I haven't told him is that in twenty-five years of taking the Aber to Shrewsbury Line, I have never once seen anyone get on or off at Dovey Junction. That's why I want to go there.

It's a short run from Aber to Dovey Junction; we got off the train in a rainstorm, a rainstorm with a dash of hail. Hail is not good for bald men. We started to run towards the platform shelter, but we were instantly soaked to the skin. I decided that this was not the moment to tell him that we could have changed at Maccynlleth, the next station up the line and one of the nicest towns in mid-Wales, at one time a candidate for the siting of the Welsh Assembly.

'You can change in Maccynlleth, lads,' said the guard.

'No, we're fine here, thanks,' I said.

'Fucking hell,' said Perry. 'You really are mad, aren't you?'

Dovey Junction is where the line to Shrewsbury meets the Cambrian Coast Line. There are two platforms and two shelters, sitting in the middle of a windswept marshland. There are no houses to be seen. We huddled together in the shelter, and I sparked up.

'You see. Safe as houses. Not a soul in sight. And as far as I have been able to ascertain, Dovey Junction is one of only three stations in Britain which can only be reached by rail. It has no road connection. No passing sniffer dogs to worry about. No one can catch us.'

'Until the train comes.'

'Yes, but we'll be finished by then. Here.'

We smoked the spliff in an open-sided train shelter in the pissing rain and howling wind in the middle of a Welsh estuarine marsh.

'It's like *Trainspotting*, isn't it?' I said.

'Shut up.'

'Why don't you take some pictures?'

'Shut up.'

After twenty minutes huddling in the shelter, the train came. Regular passengers stood up to watch somebody get on at Dovey Junction. It would be something to tell their grandchildren.

They probably thought we were on drugs.

Perry said he had a headache; I nodded off. He shook me as we approached Towyn; I wiped drool from the shoulder of my jacket and came to full attention. There are two stations in Towyn: one for the Cambrian Coast Line; the other is Towyn Wharf, terminus and headquarters of the Tal-y-Llyn. The rain had stopped, or been left behind at Dovey Junction. We walked through the town from the regular station to the Wharf. I suggested to Perry that we have another jay in the car park, but he didn't seem too enthusiastic, so instead we went for a cup of tea and several pieces of cake in the café at the Tal-y-Llyn. And there at last were the fat cheerful ladies, the china cups, the scones and the white tablecloths that we'd been hoping for in a station refreshment room.

These ladies are not volunteers; it wasn't fair to keep asking them to make the sandwiches while their men-folk played on trains, so all the buffet staff are paid. Besides, the Tal-y-Llyn appeals to women too. Its newsletter is edited by a woman; and when our train pulled into the station, we were delighted to see that the guard was a teenage girl. What's more, it was clearly her first trip as a fully fledged guard, as at least four members of her family had come to ride the train. They stood watching her with the kind of pride Mr Beckham Sr has in his eyes while watching the boy David. There are more women enthusiasts than you might imagine, spread around the many restored lines. Not hundreds, admittedly, but certainly more than a handful.

Perry and I were strangely hungry; we ate two pieces of cake each, and then went for a wander around the site. We bought our tickets (Edmundson's, natch), and got chatting to the booking-office clerk. His name was Chris, and he couldn't have been more friendly or helpful. He has been a volunteer since 1964. After he was made redundant, back at the end of the Nineties, he moved from Brum to Towyn, to work full-time, or spend as much time as he can, on the railway. In his holidays he goes to Argentina, where he drives steam trains for a fortnight.

He took us for a guided tour around the tiny marshalling yard. There were the skeletons of a couple of old engines; we looked into the honeycomb-like boiler of one of them. Chris showed us the tiny slate wagons with rusting wheels which had, after all, been the reason for building the line. Back in the 1920s and 1930s, these slate wagons would on occasion be left at Abergynolwen for picnicking trippers who wanted to come back to Towyn after the last train. The line is on a gradient for the whole of its course from Abergynolwen to Towyn; all the returning picnickers had to do was get into the slate wagon, take off the brake, and roll back down to the Wharf station. Chris told us that he had tested this a few years back, and confirmed that it was possible. He showed us the unique wagon turn-tables on the trans-shipment platform where the narrow-gauge line comes down to meet the standard. Did Hunter S. Thompson get this kind of treatment? I think not.

I asked Chris about Rolt; he made a face.

'Well . . . sometimes the talent for starting things doesn't translate into a talent for keeping things going. We're very proud of him and what he achieved. We named our newest engine after him. But he wasn't a committee man, you know.'

One of the things I like about experts is the way they assume that everyone else is an expert in the same subject. This happens to secondhand booksellers all the time. Somebody will come into the shop and say, 'Have you gat a copy of Ernest Morris?'

'I'm sorry, I don't know. What did he write?'

'Ernest Morris? You don't know Ernest Morris? Call yourself a bookseller? *The History and Art of Change Ringing*! That Ernest Morris! Good God, man, it's the standard work!'

Chris was like that. As I hope is obvious, I do know a fair bit about trains, but Chris launched into a diatribe about the technical specifications of steam trains in Argentina which left me completely in the dark.

'They're light years ahead of us in steam-train technology over there,' he assured me when he had finished, and I was happy to take his word for it.

We wandered into the gift shop, where I cast an expert eye over the T-shirts, mugs, novelty rubbers and key-rings. I should also add that it has the best selection of secondhand railway books in any railway gift shop, though it is run a close second by the shop at Hythe, on the Romney, Hythe and Dymchurch Railway.

We got talking to the shop manageress, another salaried employee. She is married to a 125 high-speed train driver, who works for Virgin but lives in Towyn so that he can be near to the Tal-y-Llyn.

'Is your house full of trains?' I asked.

'Let's put it this way; apart from the InterCity 125 phone, the bedroom is the only railway-free room in the house. It's the only room I've managed to keep the trains out of.'

'Except for the InterCity 125 phone?'

She laughed. 'I had to let him have that. I bought it for him for Christmas.'

It's the thin end of the wedge. *Flying Scotsman* bedspreads can't be far behind. And then it's powerful steam engines thrusting into dark tunnels, isn't it? You be Trevor Howard, I'll be Celia Johnson.

People were starting to get into the antique carriages. The doors only open on one side, for safety reasons. The guard was clearly getting a bit anxious, and keen to check the passengers' tickets, so we got in too.

There was a couple sitting in the seats in front of us. The guy was in his fifties. He had grey hair, an easy tan, white teeth, a Fair Isle sweater, jeans and Timberland boots. Perry and I disliked him at once. Hate good-looking men. Always have. Me and Perry, we're as ugly as sin; it's more honest, somehow – as you see us, so we are. Good-looking men are like secondhand car salesman, not entirely to be trusted. His companion was rather pretty, Perry and I came to realize in the course of the trip. Later on, we'd even find out her name.

The bloke was making what I have come to think of as Asperger's jokes. Asperger's Syndrome is one that people like to trot out when talking about trainspotters. Which shows what an astounding attitude we have towards mental health and cognitive disablement, as much as anything; it's still funny. We still like to go to Bedlam for a bit of a laugh. But you know the kind of jokes; literal ones.

So when the teenage ticket collector came up to them and said, 'Can I see your ticket?', old Handsome 101 said very loudly, in that John Major voice that people put on when they're impersonating nerds and anoraks, 'Not unless you've got X-ray vision. Otherwise, I'll have to get it out of my pocket before you can see it!!'

How he laughed. The ticket collector, Perry and I all shrank a little in horror. A ghost of a polite smile crossed his female companion's thin mouth (neither Perry nor I, it later transpired, cared to think of her as his girlfriend). But he roared.

And then he repeated it, his mirth turning to annoyance. 'Not unless you've got X-ray vision, eh? You see? It's in my pocket! So you can't see it unless I get it out? Oh . . . too clever again. Do I have to explain everything? Chuh!' clicking his tongue against the roof of his mouth.

There are several kinds of people who repeat jokes. Professional comedians do it for a living. It's not always a bad thing. But this is the most difficult kind of joke repeater to deal with. Someone has made a shit gag, and no one laughs. The person who has made the shit gag thinks it's a right old hoot, and that he's up there with Oscar. He thinks his audience is stupid, unsophisticated, has an undeveloped sense of humour. So he retells it, explains it, and when no one laughs again, he attacks them for their stupidity. Why was that pretty lady keeping company with that schmiel?

There was a grandad in the carriage, a proper craggy-faced, unsmiling grandad with a cloth cap and a scarf. He had two teenage grandsons with him; proper teenagers, with gameboys and baseball caps worn backwards. He had obviously brought them out for the day, from Birmingham way. He was explaining to his elder grandson about the difficulties of reboring a cylinder on an underpowered lathe. Grandpa and the lads had clearly been going on trips like this for years; clearly the boys had in the past enjoyed these days out very much. But now they were well into the sulky years, and it was obvious that they were not interested in reboring. They were not listening any more; not interested in anything much right now. But when the old guy finished his story, his elder grandson began to explain twelve-digit code, and analogue/digital interface, and now it was the old boy's turn to be bored beyond distraction.

This is clearly one of the things that explains how an interest in trains has become nerdy; we have lost interest in mechanical engineering. Old granddad spent his life working in engineering workshops in the Black Country, and like most boys of his generation, he was thrilled by mechanical power; it was cutting-edge technology. His skills are not needed in the same degree any more; his grandson will work in microprocessors or in a call-centre or at KFC. Technology becomes obsolete, and so do the men who built the technologies. But whereas steam train technology has evolved slowly since *Rocket*, modern technologies fall into obsolescence at a much higher rate. In the Museum of Science and Technology in Manchester, I saw a mainframe computer. It comes from Manchester University; it is huge, and grey, and when it was installed in 1985, it was one of the most powerful in the world. Now, seventeen years later, it sits in the basement, awaiting display in the museum, a relic.

The engine driver and the fireman were standing by the engine, waiting for the off. I was thrilled to see that the engine was *Dolgoch*, as old as the line. Unlike the crew. The driver was in his late twenties, the fireman was maybe twenty-two, but both clearly revelled in the idea of being much older. They were wearing blue overalls and shiny peaked caps, and the driver was quite unselfconsciously smoking a pipe. I can't swear to it, but I bet they play bowls. I like young men who try to look much older than they really are; so much more preferable than old men who try to look young. Or middle-aged men who still sneak spliff on railway stations.

The teenage guard blew her whistle, and with a answering poop poop, the plucky little engine chuffed its little beating heart against the weight of the carriages. Shades of thrice-cursed Thomas the Wank Engine, I admit, but it really felt like that. If any engine has a personality, it is *Dolgoch*, which has been pulling trains up this line for so long. We drew away from the platform, beginning the eight-mile climb to Abergynolwyn.

People smiled and waved at the train as it came through the town and into the country. They were pleased to see it pass, as it has every year since 1867. The train squeezed through bridges and between new-laid hedges. At each little halt it stopped, and the fireman picked up a staff at the tiny signal-box which gave him permission to proceed. He looked up and down the train, and called 'Right away' to the driver. They followed the safety routines slavishly, although there were no other trains running on the line and almost everyone stayed on until the end of the ride, save a few walkers who scrambled off at Dolgoch Falls.

The line climbed perceptibly as it wound into the hills. Through pastures at first, where a few sheep who were closest to the line moved half-heartedly away as the engine came steaming past at 15 mph. They were not really scared; they are too familiar with *Dolgoch*. And then the line was carried through forests, and the ground to the left started to fall away. Suddenly, we crossed a short but high viaduct over a series of waterfalls. It was enough to make even bored grandson look up from his gameboy, though not enough to stop old handsome shitface from crapping on about something to his desperate-looking, increasingly pretty, speccy and blonde, same-age-as-me-and-Perry female companion. Perry wanted to kill him, I could tell. I felt less aggressive, and found myself looking forward to a scone in the tea room.

The railway clung to the side of steep hills, and I realized that it would be almost as good without the train; that there is a strange magic in watching the line curl away around the bends in front of us. Nothing attracts us more than corners; we are drawn to them like moths to a flame. What's around the next one? And the next? Just one more corner, then we'll turn around for home. I can imagine Rolt on his walk in 1943 when he first came across the almost derelict line, wanting to see around the next corner . . .

All our journeys should be taken at 15 mph. We all know it's true; that speed kills. Mind you, for Perry and me, it felt slower still; the twenty-minute journey seemed to last for an age. Cake filled my head. At last, we pulled into Abergynolwyn station, and all the passengers piled out from the carriages and into the tea room, Perry and I in the vanguard. Time dragged, but at least we were at the front of the queue.

'A pot of tea for two, four scones, a slice of coffee cake and a macaroon, please. What would you like, Perry?'

'Same, thanks. Got any peanuts?'

We sat down and wolfed the cake. Just remember, kids; smoking spliff makes you fat.

Sitting at the table behind us were a young couple with a very young baby, and we got talking to them. I'd noticed them sitting on the station at Towyn Wharf, waiting for the train. They had been laughing and joking with the driver and the guard while we waited for the off. They clearly knew them well; I had guessed that the couple were volunteers who had come for a trip even when they weren't volunteering, and now my guess proved right.

'His name's Daniel, and it's his first trip,' they said of the baby.

'How old is he?'

'Twelve weeks.'

We admired the trainee train buff, and I asked, 'How many trips have you made?'

The husband laughed; his wife smiled and rolled her eyes to heaven, indulgent of her partner's other passion.

'I started coming when I was fifteen, and I spent all my summer holidays here, working as a volunteer. So God knows how many times I've been up and down the line.'

'That's how we met,' said his wife. 'He used to come and stay with us every summer holiday. My mother was his landlady.'

'That's so romantic,' I said, 'marrying the landlady's daughter.'

They smiled at each other.

'So you're clearly a lifelong enthusiast,' I said to the guy, 'but what about you?' to the wife. 'Do you mind, or do you get bored?'

'I haven't had much choice, have I? If I didn't put up with the railway, I wouldn't have got him, would I? Besides, I've come to love this railway too. Who couldn't?'

I often find this about the wives of rail enthusiasts, resignation coupled with some degree of empathy; spiced with a pinch of relief. I guess it could be so much worse; if, for example, your husband was a drummer in a thrash metal band, or spent all his spare time restoring antique concrete mixers in the garden (I have met a guy who did this). Or if he was a noxious rugby-playing boor, off with his shouty mates every Saturday night trying to pull, and expecting his kit to be washed on a Sunday. No, with railway enthusiasm, at least wives know their husbands are hanging around at stations trying to nab numbers, rather than hanging around in bars trying to knob pissed-up gullible girls.

'Are you a driver?' I asked.

'Oh yes indeed,' our new friend, Dave, said proudly. 'You start at fifteen as an engine cleaner, and if you do all right at that, you start training as a fireman. And if you do OK as a fireman, eventually you start learning how to drive.'

'But that's not all, is it? I mean, you get to stay in a hostel with loads of other people of your age, all having a laugh, all interested in the same things, going down the pub to drink beer; there's a real friendly atmosphere here,' said his wife, Karen.

'And families too. That's why we've brought him for his first trip. He might be a driver one day too. You see Martin, who's the fireman today? Well, both his father and grandfather were drivers. Still are, in fact.'

These people were so fucking nice that I was deeply ashamed of the gonzo thing. These guys form lifelong friendships through trains, just like Perry and I have through sex, drugs, rock and roll, etc. and they are not interested in cool; or, at any rate, it is not their prime motivation, as it was ours. And we are so not cool. I envied them, this clean, young, attractive, loving family. They didn't need two stoned old hippies like us drooling over their baby. We should have slunk away from all this goodness at once, but of course we couldn't, as decadence is always attracted to innocence. If you can call me and Perry decadent, which is questionable. Put it this way; up Old Compton Street, we are as vanilla as they come; in Brighton we are sad old middle-aged has-beens; but on the Great Little Trains of Wales we are Verlaine and Huysmans rolled into one, trailing clouds of opium smoke, a copy of *The Yellow Book* sticking out from the pockets of our silk smoking jackets.

Dave worked in the railways, as do many of the volunteers on the Great Little Trains. I find it reassuring that there are people working in the modern rail industry who have cut their teeth on the Tal-y-Llyn; who, from age fifteen, have been dealing with maintenance, signalling, safety and customer care. I can think of no better training. What a shame that it didn't occur to Railtrack until after Hatfield that it might be useful to have anyone who knew anything about running railways at the highest level of the company. They should come and spend a couple of summers in Towyn to see how it should be done.

Dave told us that he was a computer engineer, working in a two-man operation in Manchester, modelling the action of new carriage designs on different sections of the track.

'If it wasn't for privatization, I wouldn't have a job. All these kinds of research used to be done at the British Rail research centre in Derby. Now they've been contracted out.'

'Couldn't you have worked there?'

'Who wants to live in Derby?'

'Yes, but surely it was a huge mistake to break up the one centre of excellence and blue-sky research in the whole of British Rail into tiny fragments?'

'Yeah, it was, but who wants to live in Derby?'

He is the only person I've met who thought privatization a good thing, apart from the suits who stand to make a quick buck. Is Derby so very grim?

The guard announced that the train was due to leave Abergynolwen in five minutes for Towyn Wharf, so we polished off our scones and prepared to get back on the train. We were so crazy with spliff, tea and cake that it came into our heads that we should splash out the extra 50p and travel back in the only first-class carriage. The guard blew her whistle, and we hopped into the little carriage, to find ourselves trapped with the handsome bastard with the joke problem and his thin-lipped female companion.

'Hello!' he said.

We found faint smiles from somewhere and said hello in return.

'This is fun, isn't it?' he said.

'Yes, rather,' I said.

'One of the best we've been on, isn't it, Bronny?'

A rueful smile crossed her face. 'Yes.'

'We always go on them, wherever we are, don't we, Bronny?'

She sighed, and looked pleadingly into my eyes. 'Yes.'

'Oh yes, wherever we are, when we see one of those little brown signs with a steam train on, we always make a detour, don't we, Bronny?'

'Yes.'

I started to devise a plan of rescue, involving kicking him out of the carriage at 15 mph.

'Of course, we're not trainspotters, are we? We're not geeks. We don't talk in that John Major voice that nerds and anoraks use, do we?' He tried to impersonate this voice at that point, but what he clearly failed to realize was that THAT WAS EXACTLY HOW HE TALKED ANYWAY. He really didn't know that he was impersonating his own voice. It was hugely embarrassing, and poor, ill-used Bronny sank back into her seat. I can be masterful in these situations, so I started talking to Bronny about what she did. She was a nurse, a district nurse, who lived in Chichester. She hated Chichester, drove a Land Rover, and wanted to live in the country. She didn't live with Mr Handsome, I quickly established. It was clear to me that I had made a hit with her, so I told her why Perry and I were on the train taking photographs. I told her about this book, and you could see that she was impressed. I spoke to her of the romance of the railway that I was in search of, and I could almost see the noble heart knocking under her red North Face anorak. I gave her the address of my website, and when we got to Towyn Wharf and said goodbye to her and her dreary companion, I felt as though the little spark that had passed between us had brightened up her day immeasurably. To my surprise, I found that Perry thought she had fancied him. He was convinced that it had been his little jokes that she had laughed at rather than mine and, what is more, he'd given her his card with the address of his website on it, so that she could look at some of his snaps. He has no idea about women, sometimes. I've often thought that. But, in spite of this misunderstanding on his part, he did at least agree with me that Bronny couldn't be the bore's girlfriend. What other relationship there could be between them, however, we could not account for.

We walked back through Towyn for our train north. We agreed that it had been a great day out, so much so that when the Cambrian Coast Line train for Porthmadog arrived, we took it in turns to go to the loo on the train to smoke our second spliff of the day. There is no doubt that this time it livened us up a little, and we passed a pleasant journey discussing the merits and otherwise of the disestablishment of the Church of England. I am a passionate believer in the idea, whereas Perry, though broadly in favour, took time to argue out some points about the difficulties involved. He illustrated his case with some examples from the post-disestablishment condition of the modern Church in Wales.

'Of course,' I said, 'Gerard Manley Hopkins read theology in Wales, and even learned Welsh.'

'Did he?' said Perry. 'Look; here comes the trolley; shall we treat ourselves to a cup of tea and a cake?'

'Let's.'

That wise old bird, the unknown author of *The Railway Traveller's Handy Book*, would urge caution upon us: 'Do not engage in discussions whether political or theological; there is no knowing what tender chord may be touched, or what pain we may give to others in maintaining some pet theory or dogma,' and I'm sure he knew what he was about when he wrote it, but I am just as sure that neither Perry nor I touched any tender chords amongst our fellow passengers. In fact, I'm sure they benefited from our discussion.

My mobile chuckled. It was my girlfriend.

'Hello, darling,' I said.

'Where are you?'

'I'm on the train with Perry.'

'Have you been smoking weed?'

'No, darling. We've been eating cake and talking about God.'

'But you haven't been smoking weed?'

'Well, a bit.'

'How old are you again?'

I mumbled a reply, but the train went into a tunnel and we were cut off.

Me and Perry relaxed as the train headed north into the twilight. If you are not moved by the beauty of the Barmouth Railway Bridge over the Mawddach estuary as the sun sets in Cardigan Bay, while four teenagers shout at one another in Welsh just behind your ear, why, then you will never see what is great about the railway. We certainly enjoyed the ride up to Porthmadog. It was seven when we arrived, and dark. We hadn't bothered about finding anywhere to stay, we just thought we'd phone around. Who comes to Porthmadog in February?

Almost everybody, apparently.

We called B and Bs, hotels, pubs, caravan parks, self-catering apartment blocks, the lot. Packed, all of 'em. So we started casting our net a little wider, and the only place we could find that could put us up was called the Old Priory, about five miles away.

'We'll just have a spot of dinner, then we'll get a taxi out. We'll be with you about nine, nine-thirty,' I said to the lady over the phone.

'That's fine,' she said.

She could have warned us. There are nine pubs, bistros and restaurants which offer an evening meal in Porthmadog, and all of them were rammed with diners. I know, because we visited them all, and they all said the same thing: 'We might have a table about nine, nine-thirty.' What was going on in Porthmadog that night? It was 7.30 and we were hungry. The cake which had seen us so admirably through the earlier part of the day was wearing off. So we trooped all around town; and in the end, we found the address of a Little Chef about half a mile out on the Penrhyndeudfaeth road. We were so hungry after the walk out there that when we arrived, we shared an Hors d'Oeuvre Platter, as well as tucking into a nice Early Starter apiece. We even split a half-bottle of Little Chef house red. But what with wandering around Porthmadog looking for somewhere to eat, and walking out for our disgusting slap-up feed, it was a quarter to ten by the time the taxi dropped us off at the Old Priory.

We were met by the owner, and she was not pleased that we were so late. 'But I'm used to it. That's what my shitty fucking life is like. Trying to keep this shithole going all on my own, I haven't got much choice but to take who I get.'

She asked us why we had come to Porthmadog, and when we told her, she growled, 'Bloody trainspotters.'

She showed us to our room, outside the main house in a little motel-style chalet, with two single beds about six inches apart. It was freezing cold, with a tiny electric blow-heater. We climbed into our beds, shared our third spliff in twelve hours while watching *Match of the Day*, and fell into a blameless sleep.

And that's how you do trains gonzo. If you're middle-aged.

We were up early in the morning to catch the first train out of Porthmadog for Blaenau Ffestiniog. Our landlady gave us a reluctant breakfast, and sat down with us to explain how much she hated Wales, the Welsh, holiday-makers, gay men (I suspect that she suspected that Perry and I fell into this last category); almost everybody really, especially children.

'A good smacking, that's what they want. I always smacked mine, and it only did them good.'

'Where do they live?'

'My daughter lives in Dubai, and my son runs a car-hire place in California.'

If the proprietoress of the Old Priory was my mum, even Mars would be too close.

The taxi came and delivered us to the Porthmadog terminal of the Fessy. At once, we could feel the changed atmosphere from our ride of the day before. Where the Tal-y-Llyn is like a family, marinated in the ruralist idealism of Rolt and his contemporaries, the Ffestiniog Railway feels much more corporate. It is also, it must be admitted, much more spectacular. It has several unique engines, the Fairlie Double Headers, which can be driven from either end. The history of the line is similar to that of the Tal-y-Llyn; an old slate line, which also carried passengers in summer. But the Fessy didn't survive the Second World War. The passenger service stopped in September 1939. The slate traffic finished in 1946, and the owners effectively walked away from the railway, leaving engines, carriages, signalling exposed to the gales coming in from the Irish Sea. It was not until 1951 that a group of enthusiasts, inspired by Rolt and the Tal-y-Llyn, started the long process of restoration.

The line leaves Porthmadog over the sea wall, the Cob. The only other thing in Porthmadog that people have heard of, other than the railway, is Cob Records, named after the same sea wall, one of the greatest secondhand record shops in Britain. Later on in the day, after our trip, Perry and I will go into Cob, where I will give way to a long-held desire for a Carpenters' Greatest Hits CD. Not very Hunter S. Thompson I admit, but this was our non-gonzo day. You could argue that buying Carpenters' CDs is exactly the kind of thing that can happen if you *don't* take drugs.

We had arrived on a gala day, when almost all the Fessy's engines were out for a spin. Coming into Penrhyn, where the Fessy owns and runs a hostel for its volunteers, we saw an engine without a train, getting up steam, which was driven and fired by a sweating woman in her thirties. I'm sure the male drivers would make more of a fuss if they didn't have a fireman with them.

There are places where the road crosses the railway, and at one of them there was a proper level crossing, manned by yet another volunteer. There was a family of scousers sitting behind us, who were clearly struggling with the voluntary principle.

'This is all run by volunteers,' said Dad.

'This is all run by volunteers?' queried Mum.

'This is all run by volunteers?' asked Gran.

'Yeah. This is all run by volunteers,' said Dad.

'Why?' said Mum.

'I dunno,' said Dad. 'I suppose they get a kick out of it.' This was the only time they spoke to one another over the whole trip. The legendary Liverpudlian wit in action.

Although we felt ashamed after our tea and cake exploits of the day before, and resolved to take it much easier, we could not resist the refreshments on offer on the train. A camp steward came and took our order. He asked if we would like any biscuits. We asked what kind he had. He rattled off a long list of biscuits; a considerable feat of memory, but every last one of the biscuits on offer could have been purposely designed by Big Doctor Dave's Mum. We just went for the tea, which we sipped as the scenery slipped past. Through hanging woods, clinging to the side of the hill, the train climbed towards Blaenau Ffestiniog. One of the halts was called 'Campbell's Platform', and there was an enthusiast filming the train as it passed. This had been a private station, where passengers for Campbell's Manor could get off to spend a weekend shooting and fishing with Major Campbell. Major Campbell was one of the earliest benefactors of the revived line, and it is a good thing that his private platform still survives.

The Fessy saves its most spectacular sights for the last few miles into Blaenau Ffestiniog. The line is carried over itself on Britain's only railway spiral at Ddualt, before the Moelwyn tunnel and the last mile into Blaenau past the reservoir at Tanygrisiau. This would be a remarkable stretch of line under any circumstance, but what is particularly notable about the last few miles is that they were not restored, but are a new construction.

In 1954 the then British Electricity Authority announced a scheme to build a pumped-water storage facility, which would enable supply to be boosted at peak times. Unfortunately this would involve submerging the last few miles of the line. The volunteers who had just taken over the running of the railway objected, but the Authority saw them as a bunch of crazed amateurs, and ignored them. So the volunteers came up with the idea of the Great Deviation. The line would be carried up to a new level by the Ddualt spiral (thus taking the sting out of the gradient), through a new tunnel, and would then skirt the reservoir on a newly built line. If you look, you can see where the old line left Ddualt station, and you can follow its route right up to the reservoir. Work started in 1965 and was finally completed in 1982. This top section of line is the largest and most ambitious engineering work that has ever been undertaken by voluntary labour.

I don't like Blaenau Ffestiniog, and neither would you if you had been there. It is a dirty, grey old town lurking under the dirty, grey old slate quarries which justify its existence. Perry and I couldn't face cake at the tea room, so we wandered off into the town to find somewhere to eat. We found a chippie, and had cod 'n' chips with the greenest mushy peas I've ever seen.

'More colouring in your peas, Dai?'

'Oh yes please, Glyn. I love a bit of food colouring, me.'

We asked the chip shop man where there might be a loo. He laughed.

'You're kidding, aren't you? There's nothing like that in Blaenau. Most people use the alley next to the bank.' On the way back to the station we passed the Kingdom Hall, where somebody had spray-painted Mebyon Glyndwr graffiti. If you lived in Blaenau, if you weren't a Jehovah's Witness, you'd have to be an extreme Welsh Nationalist; no other approach could make sense. We were both glad to get back on to the train for the run back to Porthmadog.

We tried to avoid the hilarious scousers for the return trip, and we sat behind a family from Birmingham; Mum, Dad and two small girls. They ended up annoying me even more than the Handsome Bloke with Bronny. All the way back, the little girls asked bright, interested questions.

'Mum, what's that? Why does the train go round a big loop?'

'Dad, look at that steam engine! It looks like two stuck together.'

'Dad, what does F.R. stand for?', pointing to a carriage in the Boston Manor railway yard. (If you ever read this one day, little girl, it stands for Ffestiniog Railway. Not a tough question under the circumstances.)

But at no time did those people even try to answer these questions. They simply blanked their children out, and talked about some technical difficulty regarding the installation of their new immersion heater. At no point did they acknowledge the little girls' existence. I hope their immersion heater explodes.

Back at Porthmadog, Perry and I had shopping to do. In the Fessy gift shop, I bought a copy of *The Titfield Thunderbolt* on video, and then we got ourselves over to Cob Records. Then we caught the Cambrian Coast Line south for Aberystwyth. This time we changed at Maccynlleth for Aber, and drove back to Perry's house for some dinner.

After dinner, we had a couple of spliffs, and watched the film. *The Titfield Thunderbolt* is the funniest film ever made, of that there can be no doubt. Certainly Perry and I were wetting ourselves. Stanley Holloway as Mr Valentine is one of the best amiable drunks in British cinema history. He was so permanently and beautifuly intoxicated on the line that he most certainly should have been fined forty shillings. Which was a lot of money in those days.

With Palin to Kyle

When I was eleven, I went for a week with my dad to La Baule on the French Atlantic coast. The following year I went for a fortnight's camping in Italy with my mother and brother and stepfather. I went on a school trip to Switzerland, on a school exchange to Germany, and in 1973, on a school cruise around the Baltic. And that was it for foreign travel and me for the next twenty-five years. Then, in 1997 my trainspotting ex took me on the Eurostar to Paris for three nights. In 1999 I drove my parents through Northern France and Belgium for four days, looking for my great-uncle Harvey's war grave. In 2001 I went to a wedding in Madrid with my girlfriend. We were there for five nights. I make it that in my forty-five years, I've spent a total of twelve weeks outside the British Isles.

Nothing against abroad, mind you. All in favour of it. It looks very nice on the television. All my friends have been there, and they tell me I should go. The weather's great, the bazaars are colourful, and they have marvellous cheeses/tropical fruit. It's just that money, time and inclination have never really come together at the same time. It doesn't mean I haven't travelled. I've travelled a lot around Britain. I could get from Abergavenny to Basingstoke, and on to Zeal Monachorum, without a map. I could tell you the best place to get a hairdo in Grimsby, where to find a decent upholsterer in Gainsborough, and the secret knock you need to be admitted to an illegal gambling den in Godalming. I'm a local in the British Isles. I like it here.

Anyway, it takes longer than a lifetime to see your back garden. And as for meeting strange new people? The old ones are strange enough. My neighbours are difficult to understand, my friends are baffling, my family are strangers and my lover a mystery. I'm bewildered by my own behaviour. What need do I have to go poncing off across the globe to gawp at indigenous people, when there are plenty of indigenous people right here at home just begging to be gawped at?

And then there's Michael Palin.

Michael Palin goes abroad for me.

He's been to the Poles for me, he's been Around the World in Eighty Days on my behalf. He's rimmed the Pacific and crossed the Sahara, all so that I could feel that I had really been there, and still get over to the pub for lasties. Michael Palin is just much better at going abroad than I am.

But it would be nice, sometimes, to get out a bit more. To go on an epic adventure, to follow in Palin's footsteps. Maybe one day. Then I remembered *Great Railway Journeys*, a popular travel series that led to at least two follow-ups. In the first series there was Ludovic Kennedy going coast to coast in the US, Miles Kington climbing the Andes on steam trains; and Michael Palin bashing up to Kyle of Lochalsh on the West Coast of Scotland. I could do that.

I wouldn't need special equipment. I wouldn't have to stand, open-necked and tanned, in the prow of small fishing vessels. I could just throw a few things in a bag, get down to Euston with my credit card, and go. It didn't need much planning. I didn't have to set up a Hotmail account so that people could contact me while I was away. I could set off on one of the *Great Railway Journeys* on Thursday night, and still be back in time for *Antiques Roadshow*. I booked the ticket. The first part of the journey, from Euston to Inverness, was to be on a sleeper.

As soon as you tell people that you are going to Scotland on a sleeper, their eyes mist over. 'How romantic,' they say, 'I've always wanted to do that.' If there is romance to be had on the railway, surely a sleeper is the place. It's like living in the set of *Murder on the Orient Express*. Gouts of steam spouting from the locomotive hide the spy on the night mail from the plucky British agent. A mysterious *femme fatale*, half glimpsed by gaslight, boards the first-class Pullman, accompanied by her mulatto maid and a Pomeranian, which she carries under her arm. You share cocktails in the dining car; later she breaks your balls and then squeezes the juice from your heart, when she tells you that her love is saved only for Poupouliana. That's the Pomeranian, yeah? An ancient

Chinaman with a long white beard and an opium pipe throws the yarrow stalks for you, and comes up with Hexagram 23, Breaking Apart.

'Beware, my friend,' he croaks, raising a bony finger. 'Beware!' If only the reality were half as good as the romance, you couldn't keep people off the things.

I'd only ever been on a sleeper once before, and that was from what was then Leningrad to Moscow. It was part of the school cruise around the Baltic. We were in the fourth year, so I must have been fourteen going on fifteen. The trip cost a hundred quid, which was a lot of money in those days. My school used to organize a cruise like this one every year; my parents felt it would be educational.

We sailed from Southampton, on the SS *Uganda*, and made landfall in Copenhagen thirty-six hours later. Educational things that happened to me there included my first visit to a porn shop, and my first Slush Puppy, in the Tivoli Gardens. Then we sailed to Leningrad where, as I say, we entrained for Moscow. I wish I could tell you more about it, but I can't. Ours was a mixed school, and for all the educational benefit we gained, we might as well have had a fortnight in Bexhill-on-Sea. All me and my mates cared about was Jackie Sinclair, whose secondary sexual characteristics had continued to develop spectacularly since our geography field trips. Our ride through Russia by night, our visit to the Kremlin, to St Basil's Cathedral, our return to Leningrad, the visit to the Hermitage, my impressions of the Soviet era, all have been lost. The sting of Jackie's hand on my face, the contempt in her eyes, those have stayed with me. Perhaps, this time, romance would not prove so elusive.

So there I was at Euston, so excited that I'd turned up two hours early. The train was due to depart just after nine, and by seven I was pacing around the station, desperate for the off. I think I got there early so that I could keep an eye open for spies, *femmes fatales* and sinister Chinese soothsayers. There was one man with a beard and a Homburg hat who looked promising. A spy if ever I'd seen one. I followed him, discreetly, but he got on the 19.27 for Milton Keynes Central. Which is not to say that he wasn't a spy, of course. Probably there are lots of spies living in MK. I decided to have a Ritazza coffee while I waited.

I'd brought *The Railway Traveller's Handy Book*, but for once it was little help, as it was written before the sleeper carriage was conceived. To keep me occupied, I had Christian Wolmar's *Broken Rails: How Privatisation Wrecked Britain's Railways*. Nothing could be less romantic, or more terrifying.

My trip was taking place a week after Stephen Byers, the then Transport Secretary, had published another of the government's marvellous new plans for the railways. Transport Secretary is not regarded as an important or interesting job by politicians. Sorting out Britain's ancient transport infrastructure will take both courage and long-term vision, characteristics which politicians singularly lack. They like short-term profit and self-aggrandizement, and Transport Secretary hardly ever leads to either. So the post gets passed about from one second-rank careerist hack to another, each of whom comes up with a new crackpot scheme. Byers then, Darling today, somebody else tomorrow.

Take the last Railway Modernization Plan, which happened in 1954. Millions of pounds were poured into the railway, whose management spent it on vast new marshalling yards for freight traffic which never materialized, and lots and lots of lovely steam engines, which were scrapped within a decade. And then Ernest Marples became Transport Secretary – the last one anyone really remembers – and he liked motorways, not horrid old trains. So he made Dr Beeching chairman of BR, and he didn't like railways, either. So he decimated Britain's railway system, only five years after the investment of the Modernization Plan. So what hope for Mr Prescott/Byers/Darling/ (insert name here)? The plan is a nonsense, with billions of pounds going into largely unnecessary safety upgrades. The Strategic Rail Authority has recently admitted that this money is nothing like enough. Real investment is negligible. All Western politicians are scared of car drivers, and don't give a stuff about nonsense like the Kyoto Accord, and if they thought that there were votes in it, they'd sell their grandmothers and shut down every inch of line they could get their sticky fingers on.

Ritazza coffee gets the old adrenalin pumping, and I was wound up.

Luckily, Mark Lawson wandered past, bellowing into his mobile phone, so I decided to follow him about and see if he looked like getting on the sleeper. I liked the look of him. He was much bigger than on the telly; big, bald, fat and speccy, and he was wearing black jeans, brown shoes and a donkey jacket. In short, he looked like me. Perhaps, if he gets on the sleeper, I'll have a chance to point this out to him, I thought. He didn't; he entrained for Wolverhampton.

There was no one who looked even vaguely like a *femme fatale*, either. There was a very old lady with dropsy, a tam-o'-shanter and a moustache who got carried up the platform on one of those golf carts that the Queen Mum used to use. It beeped, and is one of the things that makes me think it can't be so bad getting old. I was met at the door to my sleeper by Violet, my hostess. At once I was on my guard. The last time I spent with a hostess . . . but that's a different story. Violet was mumsy. She showed me to my compartment; there were two bunk beds and a sink. The compartment was about the size of a mobile phone.

'Will I be sharing?' I asked.

'Well, noo. Let's have a wee look . . . aye, you're sharing with a Mr Mackenzie.'

Oh. Still, I suppose that's the stuff of sleeper legend. Perhaps he'd be a spy. Perhaps he'd have some vital document that has to be carried, for some reason, to Inverness. Then, perhaps he'd be poisoned by agents of SMERSH, and I'd have to get the document to safety, helped only by Elizabeth Hurley in a rubber leotard. Perhaps.

I went for a stroll up the platform. This is a long train, at sixteen coaches, the longest scheduled train there is in Britain, bar the Eurostar. This means the engine has to be very powerful to pull the thing. The trip from London to Inverness has some of the steepest gradients the network has to offer. So the engine has to be very powerful indeed, at least for the first part of the journey, before it splits into three, just after Edinburgh. One bit goes to Inverness, one to Aberdeen, and the third to Fort William. They tried to stop this last service a few years back. It's the so called Deer-stalker Express. It's not used by very many people, but the people who do use it are largely rich and powerful people going up to the Highlands for a shoot. So the Deer-stalker Express was saved.

Well, the locomotive certainly looked powerful. I made a decision, and for the first, and, hopefully last time, I jotted down its number. It was on hire from EWS, the freight company, and its number was 90035. There. That wasn't so bad. I felt shifty, dirty, secretive; emotions that are widely shared in the strange world of railway enthusiasts. I smoked a few tabs and strolled up and down the platform. I stopped and chatted with Violet.

'I'm looking for romance on the train, Violet. You know . . . spies. *Femmes fatales*.'

'Well, you do get people spending the night in one another's compartments. They meet in the lounge car and have a few drinks, and one thing leads to another. I don't know if any of them lead on to anything. I think they usually just say goodbye in the morning.'

'Well, I really meant romance in a somewhat wider sense . . .'

She looked at me as though I was mad, and at this point Mr Mackenzie turned up.

'Good evening, Mr Mackenzie,' said Violet. 'You'll be sharing with Mr Marchant here . . .' He looked about as thrilled to see me as I was to see him. He was skinny, in his late twenties, and we exchanged watery smiles. He went off to the kennel in which we were to sleep, while I sashayed up to the lounge car for a drink and a fag. There was only a couple in their sixties in there, drinking tea. They certainly looked like deer-stalkers. She wore a calf-length A-line tartan skirt and a twin set; he, one of those little sportmen's waistcoats that Jack Hargreaves used to wear, with lots of pockets to keep trout flies and shotgun cartridges in. Who's Jack Hargreaves? A guy who used to present fishing and shooting shows in the Sixties and Seventies, the good old days when animals were for catching and killing. He had a beard.

As the train pulled out of Euston, I was childishly thrilled, bowled over with excitement. I have been on this line a hundred times, but it had never felt like this. The steward approached me. He was Blakey from *On the Buses*. Clearly, since most of the newly privatized train companies are now owned by bus companies, the staff had been moved from one form of transport to another, and Blakey was now the steward on the sleeper.

'Hggo, swr. Whit cnnu gttyu?' he said through his moustache.

I smiled. 'I'm sorry?' I said.

'Wld ewe lka drnk?' The man was a mumbler, a very bad one, so I adopted a technique I picked up from the 'Dear Mary' column in the *Spectator*.

'I'm sorry,' I said. 'I'm a little deaf. Could you speak up?' This never fails; he tried again, and it transpired that he had been asking me what I would like to drink.

'A scotch and water, please. And are you serving food?'

He handed me the menu and said gloomily (I'll drop the mumbling, though he very much kept it up), 'There's everything on the menu except the chicken tikka marsala. And the venison pâté.' He paused. 'We haven't had the venison pâté for months.'

I chose the haggis, neeps and tatties. Well, what would you choose on the sleeper to Inverness?

Mr Mackenzie came into the lounge, sat down at the table next to mine and ordered a Coke. He was reading an Andy McNab book.

'I hope I won't keep you awake,' I said brightly.' My girlfriend says I snore like a pig!'

He gave me another wintry smile. 'I've got my personal stereo,' he said.

'Good,' I said. Shit, I meant. Did that mean I'd have to lie there all night listening to a faint shhhhhh from the bunk above? He returned to his Andy McNab, and I to Christian Wolmar and his analysis of the Southall train crash, which he says would not have happened but for privatization. Wolmar makes the point, a very good one, that private companies do not exist to run trains on time, or efficiently, or safely. Like any company, they exist to make profit for their shareholders. The badly trained, ill-informed drivers and the astoundingly cavalier attitude to sharing safety information which led to the crash can all can be directly attributed to privatization. They are things which could not happen with an integrated system.

With the hastily botched-together privatization that we got, every possible function on the railway was hived off to a different private company, all of whom exist to make profit. And there's no profit to be had from doing things properly. The TOCs do not even own the trains; they lease them from a company which owns the rolling stock. They don't own the track; that is owned, or was, by the complacent mothers at Railtrack. All the TOCs own are time slots, the right to run trains at a certain time over a certain length of track. Railtrack got its money from selling these slots to the TOCs. In return, you might imagine, Railtrack was responsible for safety and maintenence. Well, ha ha ha. Yes, they were still responsible for signalling, but maintenance is contracted to yet another set of companies, all of whom are determined to make another buck at the expense of our old friends the tax-payer and the travelling public. Network Rail, the new not-for-profit company that has taken over the system, simply has to be better than Liartrack, one of the most irresponsible companies ever to have their fingers in your pocket.

As for safety: there was a small crash, nothing terribly serious, nobody hurt, at Royal Oak just outside Paddington, in 1995. The inquiry into the crash made fourteen recommendations. A safety review group looked at these recommendations, and accepted nine of them. Railtrack proceeded with just two. Why? Three of the recommendations became the responsibility of Peter Wiseman, Railtrack's business development manager. He didn't implement them because he didn't find out that they were his responsibility until *after* the Ladbroke Grove crash, when thirteen people were killed and 425 were injured. And as Wolmar points out, 'business development', which presumably involves thinking up ways to make money, is hardly compatible with safety responsibilities, which inevitably cost money, and for no return. Oh, except saving lives, obviously. But who cares about namby-pamby stuff like that when your bonuses are on the line?

As we rattled through Berkhamsted, Blakey brought my haggis, and Mr Mackenzie headed off for our cupboard. He didn't say goodnight, which hurt. The haggis was rather good, served hot 'n' fresh from the microwave. Blakey told me a humorous story about haggis, of which I didn't catch one word.

We were passing through Tring. I washed my haggis down with a cafetière of tea. I suppose teatière sounds stupid. This railway line is so familiar, probably the most familiar line to the most people. Anyone who's been to Birmingham, Manchester, Liverpool, Holyhead for Ireland, the Lake District or Glasgow by train will have used this line. The familiar place names rattle past: Berkhamsted, Milton Keynes, Rugby. It is hard to remember, in this ordinary and familiar landscape, that between 1833 and 1838 the building of this railway was, to quote Tom Rolt, 'the greatest task that any civil engineer had undertaken'. Between 12,000 and 20,000 men worked on the line at any one time. The French engineer Leconte said of the work, 'Never since the building of the pyramids had the world witnessed such an undertaking on so gigantic a scale.'

The line's engineer was Robert Stephenson, who, when the job began, had not yet turned thirty. After the railway was completed, Stephenson estimated that he had walked its 112 miles at least fifteen times. Like Brunel, he smoked heavily to help with the stress of the undertaking, and there is some suggestion that he used laudanum. He wrote during construction. 'My courage at times almost fails me, and I fear that some fine morning my reputation may break under me like an eggshell.'

If you watch from the window, you will see some of the problems that Stephenson had to deal with: the massive cuttings at Tring and Blisworth, the embankment and viaduct crossing the Great Ouse at Wolverton. The 2,400-yard-long Kilsby Tunnel was the longest railway tunnel attempted up until that date. Sceptics thought that passengers would be suffocated in its Stygian depths, and Stephenson wasn't so sure they were wrong. He built two huge ventilation shafts to keep travellers breathing; they look like miniature castles if you drive by them on the A5 today. The hill at Kilsby turned out to be full of liquid subterranean quicksand. It took thirteen pumps working for nineteen months to clear the muck from the tunnel workings. When Kilsby was completed after four years of struggle, on 21 June 1838, the London and Birmingham Railway was declared open throughout its length. The railway had arrived in London. The earliest terminus was at

Chalk Farm. This station was demolished during the construction of what is now the North London Line, but it stood pretty much on the site where Chalk Farm station is today.

The evolutionary philosopher Herbert Spencer, the man who coined the phrase 'the survival of the fittest', worked in his youth as an engineer on the London and Birmingham Railway. He was based at Chalk Farm station, and was one of the first people to travel by train through the raw new finished defile of the Tring cutting. He was based in London for almost six months, during which time he 'visited no places of amusement'. Instead he spent his spare time solving conic sections and making drawings of steam engines. In his fantastically pompous *Autobiography*, published after his death in 1903, he said of the experience that he felt it gave him 'valuable opportunities of obtaining information and undergoing discipline'. He was seventeen at the time. That's how much the world has changed.

The section of line that Spencer was working on was the 'Extension', from Chalk Farm to the classical terminus building at Euston. From Camden to the chosen site of the terminus, 'a vacant piece of ground in a place called Euston Square', trains would have to be lowered by stationary engines. In the site where Euston stands were market gardens, dairy farms and London's fireworks manufacturers. It was here, thirty years previously, that Robert Trevithick had demonstrated the 'Catch Me Who Can' to a largely indifferent public. Now that trunk railways had arrived, society would be changed beyond recognition. Dr Thomas Arnold, headmaster of Rugby School, rejoiced in the coming of the railway, declaring that 'Feudality was gone forever'.

The last gasp of the Middle Ages was lost in a puff of steam.

Feudality might be on the wane, but poverty and degradation were proving to be as popular as ever. That certainly summed up the life of a navvy, the men who built the line using muscle power and shovels. They had 'navigated' the canals, and now, for most of the rest of the nineteenth century, they would move on to build the railways too. Few of them had settled homes; they followed the work, terrifying the communities in which they landed, more despised than the gypsies. The Northamptonshire village of Kilsby, after four years of regular rioting outside the village pub on pay-day, was particularly pleased to see them go.

They died by the hundred, in accidents, from alcohol, from physical exhaustion. There are no records of how many men were lost during the building of the London and Birmingham, because no one ever bothered to count the bodies. Eighty per cent of them were English, but they didn't belong anywhere. Most of them were only known by their nicknames. They lived in communal huts, called shants, which were run by old women whose job was to feed the men and look after the beer. The shants were places of unimaginable filth and degradation. The navvies were relatively well paid throughout the Railway Mania of the 1840s – as much as twenty-two shillings a week in 1846, when an agricultural labourer could expect ten shillings. By 1851, after the disgrace of George Hudson, the railway bubble had burst, and such navvies who could find work could only command fourteen shillings. This was when they were paid in cash. Otherwise they were often paid under the so-called Truck system, in which they received their wages as coupons which could only be redeemed in mean 'tommy shops' owned and run by the contractors. Beer was their main requirement, and the tommy shops made sure that they had plenty to sell. Very few navvies came out of the good years with any savings. Without getting shit-faced every night, the work could not be contemplated. Millions of cubic feet of muck had to be dug from the cuttings and tunnels, removed by horses pulling wagons on temporary railway, and tipped on to the site of embankments. It was back-breaking, brutal and soul-destroying work. We should remember these men, I think, these thousands of dead men, before we close any more lines. The least we owe them is to look after the system they built, and the landscape they transformed with nothing more than muscle.

The sleeper train is not a fast train; it's too heavy for that. It can get up to 100 mph, but tends to average 80. This would be a long night. At Stafford, I guessed that I felt tired enough to attempt sleep. I squeezed along the narrow corridor of the sleeper carriages, and couldn't help noticing that most of the compartments were empty. In fact, Violet told me that there were only sixteen passengers on our part of the train. So why were Mr Mackenzie and I forced together against our joint will? Presumably, it saves time and money at the turn-round in Inverness, but it didn't make me feel any better about sharing with Mr M.

I got to our compartment and tried the door. Mr Mackenzie had locked it. I rattled the handle and he let me in. Now I had to get undressed, and if there's one thing that British men don't like, it's getting undressed in front of other men. In point of fact, I always feel some nervousness about getting undressed in front of women, too. It still makes my girlfriend laugh when she sees me naked. I don't blame her for this, but I do think that after all these years, at least some of the comic potential of my body should have begun to wear a little thin.

Mr Mackenzie had the top bunk, so if I stood next to the beds to strip off, inevitably, given the size of the compartment, he was going to be able to have a fairly intimate look, unless he kept his eyes shut tight. I decided the best thing would be to get undressed lying on my bed. Not easy, this; it's how it must feel for vampires, trying to get dressed lying in a coffin. It makes you wonder how vampires always look so great, especially since they can't check their appearance by looking in a mirror. I grunted and struggled my way out of my jeans, and what Mr Mackenzie thought I was up to, I dread to think. Eventually, I got down to my Y-fronts and T-shirt, slid under the covers, and turned off the bunk light.

I can't say I slept well. The West Coast main line stands in severe need of relaying, and it is bumpy. At Preston, at round about mid-night, I heard several more passengers get on, and they were not quiet. Then, of course, like many men of my age, I had to get up in the night and stagger along to the loo. If I'd been on my own, I'd have used the sink, but I can't imagine Mr Mackenzie would have been too thrilled to wake up and find me having a piss. But I didn't want to blunder about the train in my Y-fronts, so every time I got up I had to struggle into and out of my jeans again. At last, I fell into a kind of doze. I was asleep, but I was also aware of the fact that I was on a train, and that the train was moving. It was one of those sleeps where you are aware of the passage of time; aware, somehow, that you are asleep. I used to have this thing where I would lie awake all night before the alarm clock went off and woke me up, so that I realized I had been asleep the whole time, but dreaming that I was awake. It was like that. Not romantic. And no hint of *femmes fatales*.

When Violet knocked on the door at 7.30, I was instantly awake. She brings you breakfast in bed, continental breakfast, at least. Tea, croissant, jam. Or should that be *thé, croissant et confiture*? When did the continental breakfast first appear in this country? And is having tea truly continental? The bunk above sagged with the weight of Mr Mackenzie's bum, which put me off a bit. I finished my breakfast as quickly as possible, wriggled into my clothes, and headed off to find Blakey in the lounge. At least I could smoke there, which is all the breakfast I find I usually need. Besides, I wanted to be out of the cupboard before Mr Mackenzie swung his hairy legs out of the bunk above me. Perhaps Mr Mackenzie would be one of those frightening people who are not ashamed of their body; perhaps he slept without his pants on; perhaps I would be faced with another man's todger swinging about in front of my nose, which I have never much enjoyed, especially first thing. Sadly, all these thoughts were uppermost in my mind as I got dressed as quickly as possible. I'm glad to report that neither of us saw the slightest hint of each other's pale northern nakedness.

Blakey was not terribly forthcoming, and he was determined not to bring me more tea. He was tidying up and packing his bag, and even though there were at least five people hoping for a hot drink, not one of us got lucky. Looking out from the window, I could see pine forests, sheep and deer, and very few houses. The Highlands are empty of people. The rising sun stained the eastern sky, and beside the line I could see scraps of snow. The passengers who had got on at Preston were also in the dining car, smoking and without tea. They were discussing with the undisguised glee of the true football fan last night's home defeat for Manchester United. Each of them took it in turn to cough, wet, noisy smokers' morning coughs. And they reviewed the press.

'T' *Star*'s best for football,' said one.

'Aye, and Jordan's tits,' said his friend; and, in fairness, they have a point. They tried to laugh, but it only made them cough more.

The sun was getting above the hills as we approached Inverness, and I hurried back to the compartment to get my things together. Mr Mackenzie was just leaving as I arrived.

'Did you sleep well?' I asked.

'Aye, verra well, thank you,' he said.

'I didn't snore then?'

'No.' And that was that. Quite enough intimacy for both of us.

We pulled into Inverness at 8.30, eleven and a half hours after leaving Euston. It is not a pretty town, at least not the part of it that you can see from the station. The station sign is bilingual; Inverness is called Inbhir Nis in Gaelic. I found this sad. It is not like in Wales, where the Welsh language is vital and alive. The Gaelic language is dead, or very nearly. Because the people who spoke it have gone. We see the Highlands as romantic. The run from Inverness to Kyle should be the most romantic rail journey, through all that magnificent emptiness. The Highlands are empty for a reason, which I think today we would have to call ethnic cleansing. Look from the window, and remember the price that was paid for our romantic journeys.

Bonnie Prince Charlie's doomed attempt to reclaim the throne for the Stuart succession came to an end at Culloden, in 1745. After Culloden, the clan chieftains had lost faith in the old way of life. They had lost their powers to raise armies. They lived in draughty castles and could not be considered rich by comparison with their aristocratic cousins in England. They were defeated, and all they wanted to do was make a few bob. The population who owed them fealty in return for low rent were not going to be necessary, now that war was over for good.

The Highlanders who had formed Charlie's army had slunk away in defeat, back to their townships of crofts hidden in remote Highland glens. Here they lived a peasant existence, subsisting on the land, which was rented from sub-tenants of the clan chiefs. They were a different people from the Lowlanders. They were Gaels, speaking in their own language, singing their own songs. They were peaceable and not inclined to hard work. They loved their story-haunted glens, and they loved the whisky they made from the little wheat that they could grow on the poor Highland soil. For eating, they had potatoes. Life was OK. They were like peasant people from all over the world. But from the point of view of their landlords, they didn't pay.

Sheep might pay, if enough land could be found. The few sheep kept by the Highlanders had no value outside their own communities. But if sheep could be raised in great quantities, then the increasingly aristocratic and absent-from-Scotland clan chieftains could rent their vast estates to sheep farmers from the south. In the Lowlands of Scotlands, great fortunes were being made from one particular breed of sheep, the Long Hill, or Great Cheviot. Each sheep needed six acres of mountain pasturage, and access to valley floors in winter. So the people had to go.

A whole culture was driven from its land, as the landlords started to evict their tenants. From the 1780s until the 1850s, tens of thousands of people were forcibly driven from their homes. Often, when the eviction notices came, the tenants were unable to read, or to understand English. So the bailiffs came in, dragging women and children from their crofts, beating the men insensible, setting fire to the peat roofs of the cottages, not caring if there was anybody left inside. The glens began to empty, so that the sheep could appear. Glens that had supported townships of hundreds of people were now inhabited only by the shepherd and his family. The Highlanders were forced down to the coasts, where they had, on occasion, generously been allocated new tenancies by their masters. The evictions would take place in winter, and whole townships would arrive at the coast to find nothing but sand and sea.

Sometimes they were allowed to take the wood from the roofs of their cottages down to the coast, but more often, the landlords burnt it. After all, it belonged to them. Why couldn't they burn it if they liked? Wood is scarce in the Highlands; the crofters would not even be able to build themselves new houses. Sometimes the landlords gave the displaced Highlanders fishing nets, even though they had no real sea-going tradition. The landlords called this improvement.

It certainly improved the lot of the Earls of Stafford, who turned themselves into the Dukes of Sutherland and built themselves a fine castle at Dunrobin, high up on the east coast north of Inverness. They were the largest landowners in the far north of Scotland, and were therefore most deeply sunk in the iniquity of the clearances. One way they had to clear townships was to call upon the loyalty of their tenants and recruit them to fight for the King in the Napoleonic Wars. Then, when all the men were away fighting, it was much easier to throw their wives and children out on to the mountainside. Men returning from the wars came over the brow of a hill to find their glen empty, their families cleared. The Sutherlands did all right out of the Highlands, but they didn't go there often. The sheep had made them fabulously wealthy, and they preferred the company in London. When they did trouble to get up there, they saw things that upset them. The Duchess of Sutherland, on one of her occasional visits to Dunrobin, saw pregnant women and starving children breaking up rocks to build harbours so that the men could try to fish. They were living in unspeakable hovels unfit for swine. No wonder the Sutherlands felt their tenants had needed improving. Whatever had they been like before they were cleared off the land? This was obviously preferable. Anyway, the estate managers always managed to persuade the Duchess that the tenants were comfortable.

Another solution was forcible emigration. From the middle of the eighteenth century until the outbreak of the First World War, the unwanted Highlanders were sent in their tens of thousands to Canada and Australia. They were settled in Prince Edward Island and Nova Scotia. To a Highlander, exile from your glen is exile, whether it be four or four thousand miles. They did not have the skills, and many did not have the will to survive Canadian winters. Hundreds died of starvation and exposure.

Although the forcible clearances were largely over by the 1850s, the few who were left were hardly made welcome, and emigration from the Highlands was still prevalent into the 1940s. The landlords had found deer-stalking an even better way to earn money than sheep-farming. The great sheep walks were converted into sporting estates, a process which began in the middle of the nineteenth century with the coming of the railway. That is why the Highlands are empty of people, but full of deer. If you look carefully from the window of your train, you will see bright squares of green dotted about the glens in the darker bracken and heather. That was where the Highlanders lived. Those were their potato patches. Lowland Scots call those who live in the Highlands today 'teuchters'. They see them as a race apart. But they are not. Most of the people who live in the Highlands of Scotland today are the descendants of Lowlanders brought in from the mid-eighteenth to the mid-nineteenth century to look after the sheep. Most of the people who live in the Highlands are Lowlanders

The Highlanders have gone, and their language and their culture are gone with them.

Still, there you go. No use crying over spilled milk, or even a bit of quiet genocide. The Dukes of Sutherland got to have a nice railway carriage, the one I had seen at the NRM. And the Duchess had her engine. No one seems to mind that the money is the tiniest bit blood-soaked, or else why would a civilized society allow their descendants to hang on to their plunder? Read John Prebble's *Highland Clearances* or David Craig's *On the Crofter's Trail*, and then try to defend the hereditary principle.

I had a train to catch in twenty minutes to the West Coast, through the emptied glens to Kyle of Lochalsh. But looking at the departure board, I very quickly realized that there was no such train. I do wish they'd tell you things like this when you buy your ticket. The train was only going as far as Strathcarron, and the last ten miles or so of the journey would be by bus. I was disappointed, to say the least. If I'd known, I might have gone to Thurso, (next to John 'o' Groats), or chosen another of the *Great Railway Journeys* instead. Ah me.

The dropsical lady who had been carried to the sleeper at Euston on the beeping golf cart was catching this train, but this time she was being pushed in a wheelchair. Perhaps getting old isn't so great after all. Still, no time to worry about the old and infirm, either; I nipped into the station buffet, bought myself a nice hot cup of Ritazza coffee, and settled down on the train for such of the ride that was up and running.

The light was grey, like twilight. Was this because of the cloud cover, or because it was winter, and I was in the far north? The latter, I suspected, even at 8.50 a.m. Certainly the light was different, as though it had been dimmed slightly. The line from Inverness up to Dingwall is shared between the line to Kyle, and the line to Thurso in the far north. It runs along the Beauly Firth, and to my excitement crossed the River Ness and the Caledonian Canal. The river was rough and flowing fast; not at all an English river, this close to the sea. Inverness means the mouth of the roaring water, and you could see why. The Caledonian Canal is a great example of early government subsidy; it has never been used by the coasting ships that were expected, and now it is used mainly for leisure, but you can still see the occasional fishing boat going through the massive locks, in order to cut off the long journey around Cape Wrath and the north of Scotland. I am a canal buff, a canal bore, even, and I had never seen it before, so I was thrilled, but it too has had its part to play in the emptying of the Highlands. Improvements, they called them, remember?

It was wonderful scenery, even here on the sea shore, before the main event of the mountains started. I watched the white tails of small deer bouncing away from the side of the line as the train passed. There are small towns. Muir of Ord, and then Dingwall. A few people got off the train; none got on. Walking through the carriages, there were now only four passengers the length of the two modern cars. Dingwall is called Inbhirpheofharain in the Gaelic; once again, it felt like something which had been laid on for the amusement of visitors. To my utter delight, I spotted the ground of Ross County FC. Scottish football teams are a constant staple of pub quizzes. Where do St Mirren play? Whither St Johnstone? Which team plays in Dumfries? Now I can't wait for 'Where do Ross County have their ground?' Inbhirpheofharain, I shall answer, just to cause the quiz master grief; and to help me remember the time, only perhaps 150 years ago, when English was the minority language in these empty hills. Just to the north of Dingwall, the lines divide. One, straight ahead, is for Thurso and Wick; but ours curved steeply away to the left, for Kyle and Skye.

The scenery was thrilling. Thrilling. The line plunges through gorges, clings to the side of cliffs, rattles through pine forests lined with spindly silver birches. It passes Loch Garve, which in Scottish terms is probably not much of a size, but which to my Sassenach eyes looked huge. But there were no boats on it. You may like utter desolation; I suppose I do under certain circumstances, but I do like to see boats on the water. Does no one come sailing here? Why should they? The people of the glens were driven from their homes long ago. There were some Highland cattle beside the line as we pulled into Garve station; they would have looked very well on a tin of shortbread, with a backdrop of tartan, but I remembered Prebble's closing words in *The Highland Clearances:* 'the tartan is a shroud'.

Two of the passengers got off at Garve, and now it was just me and the dropsical old lady. We were hurrying across the high moors; the tops were skimmed with snow, and the deer were coming down from the heights, driven down by the bad weather; they ran away, startled, as the train passed them. The waterfalls by Loch Luichart were channelled into small hydroelectric stations. I saw one boat, and a tiny pier. There was a small caravan encampment, too; not for holiday-makers, but for intrepid hippies, who know a good thing when they see it. The light was still strange to my southern eyes; like twilight, though it was half-ten in the morning. We passed through a couple of small stations without stopping; why should we stop? Who uses them, out of the shooting season? We passed a couple of huge shooting lodges; arrogant, incongruous, built in ludicrous Scots Gothic. A fast wide river brown with peat flows down Strath Bran, and here and there were occasional abandoned cottages, each with a tiny bright field of green in the brown of the moors.

My mobile stuttered. It was my girlfriend.

'Hello?'

'Hello, darling.'

'What? Hello? Are you there, love?'

'Hello! Can you hear me?'

'I can't hear you. If you can hear me I'll phone you when I get to Kyle.'

'Hello, I can't hear you . . .'

I'm surprised the landlords haven't bunged up a few mobile phone masts out here for the benefit of the fat cats who come shooting. After all, how is one to stay in touch with one's business?

We waited at Achusheen station while an engineering train passed through. I asked the train guard why the last part of the line to Kyle was closed; after all, engineering works usually happen at weekends, and this was only Wednesday. He told me that there had been a landslide where the line runs along the foot of steep cliffs by Loch Carron, and that it had been decided to rebuild it further away from the shore, but Loch Carron is deep, and the rebuild was proving more technically difficult than had been at first imagined. He told me that it was going to cost £4.5 million to re-open the line, but that work was in progress. He thought it should be opened again by early summer 2002. (The line has now been re-opened.) The train moved on.

We passed through an abandoned station, green with plantings of rhododendron and wellingtonia. There was a shooting lodge close to the line, Glencarron Lodge, and this was once its private station. Rhododendron is always a marker in the countryside of the Celtic nations. It shows where the grandees live, or lived. Its roots are poisonous to other native species, and it loves the acid-rich soils of the wilder places; so now it is a weed, spreading out of control, killing the native plants it grows next to. There is an analogy here, somewhere.

The train reached Strathcarron (there is a station, a couple of houses and an hotel), and I hurried across to the twenty-seater bus that was waiting outside. The guard was helping the dropsical old lady from the train to the bus; she walked painfully with the aid of two sticks. Slowly, the guard and the driver helped her on to the bus. She was coming home; she had been visiting her daughter in Bath. I knew this because she and the bus driver were acquaintances. She was very posh; English posh voice, though clearly Scottish in every sense. London is full of the Scottish aristocracy who did so well for themselves after Culloden, and although they may have Scottish names, none of them have posh Scottish accents, not even the legendary Morningside voice, where sex is what you put the rubbish out in. This lady sounded as English as English can be, a voice that we only hear very occasionally now, as the aristos attempt to hide their wealth and power by the adoption of the glottal stop. But I suspected that she would be upset if anyone called her English; that she would feel fiercely Scottish. And the pain that she was in, and the effort of an eighteen-hour train journey from Bath to Strathcarron, showed her commitment to this place. Life cannot always be easy out here, right up in the North-west Highlands.

The bus wound its way along narrow single-track roads. The scenery was breathtaking; high mountains, sea lochs. The road was carried higher above the side of Loch Carron than the railway, which I could see from time to time, following the coast far beneath us. The bus driver pointed out where the line was being built out over the sea. He told me that the landslide was really very small; a political landslide, he called it. It was caused by scrub-cutting on the embankment above the line. As the roots of the scrub were what had been holding the bank together, the landslide was inevitable. I couldn't help feeling that it was yet another example of Railtrack's stupidity and incompetence. If the scrub-cutting had been thought out properly, then maybe the £4.5 million could have been saved. But at least they are spending the money, and not using the landslide as an excuse to close the line. It had taken four years, from 1893 to 1897, to build the last ten miles of it, from Strome Ferry to Kyle of Lochalsh. Mile for mile, it was the most expensive stretch of railway built up until that date. Shame to waste it.

The Kyle Line serves a few tiny but functioning settlements along the edge of Loch Carron. The bus burrowed down single-lane roads to find these hidden villages. At Duirinish, the posh old lady prepared to get out.

'I arranged with Morag that she should leave my car by the station . . . ah, here we are.'

The driver helped her down, and she hobbled across to the car, opened the door and lowered herself in. It was left unlocked, and presumably the keys were inside. I thought of the world where you can leave cars unlocked, with the keys inside, without fear; a world where people are called Morag and can always be relied upon. This is the world I had arrived in, and I was so in love.

At last the bus pulled up outside Kyle of Lochalsh station, I was quite alone in the little bus as I ended my odyssey from Euston; it was

11.30, fourteen and a half hours after I set out. If there is a more spectacular station in Britain, I have yet to see it. A long single-storey bungalow, with a ticket office, a small museum and a seafood restaurant, it is built out into the sea, on a pier, so that passengers from the train could step on to the ferry for Skye. There are no ferries now, but a small coaster was unloading stone on to the quay. There was a work train standing ready; the stone is for the rebuilding of the line. Directly in front of me were the mountains of Skye, cloud-capped and iced with snow. The sea rushed through the narrow strait. Rain was sheeting down. I picked up my bags and wandered through the little village, looking for somewhere to stay.

The Kyle Hotel on Main Street was comfortable and warm; too warm, really, and I lay on the bed and caught up on the bad night's sleep. Very annoying, this; I'd travelled God knows how many miles on one of the *Great Railway Journeys* just for a snooze at the end. But there. Eventually, I woke up and went for a stroll. It was still raining, though not half as badly as when I arrived, so I decided to walk across the Skye Bridge, which links the mainland to Skye. It is perhaps half a mile from the village centre to the toll booth along the edge of the water. The mountains on the other side of the strait screed down to the grey water. I wondered why I lived in London.

The Skye Bridge is a wonderful thing, and built in two parts; the first long and low out to the island of Eilean Bahn, which was the setting for Gavin Maxwell's *Ring of Bright Water*. Maxwell's house has been turned into a visitor centre, and the tiny island into a nature reserve. From Eilean Bahn, the bridge curves in a fine arch over the narrows to Skye. The people of Skye could be proud of their bridge; proud, that is, if it wasn't yet another example of corporate greed and the rank cowardice of politicians. It was built using private money, what Mr Blair would have us call a Public Private Finance Initiative, but what you and I might call blackmail. The contractors who built it were allowed to charge tolls for using it, and they are exorbitantly high. It costs, for example, £5.70 for a car to get on and off the island. Perhaps you could argue a case for this, as long as the contractors had got their money back and made a modest profit; and this, in fact, is what was supposed to happen. After the private investment had been repaid, the tolls were supposed to stop, or at least to come down to a nominal sum. Needless to say, this has not happened; the tolls remain disgustingly high, and the people of Skye are being held to ransom. There is no real alternative to the bridge. The ferry from Kyle stopped on the day they opened it, and although there is a tiny ferry from Glenelg to Skye, it is even more inaccessible than Kyle, and runs only in the summer months. There is a strong local campaign against the bridge tolls; they are trying to organize a boycott, but it is hard, when there are no alternatives. The bridge, so far from improving access to Skye, has cut it off even further.

This does not stop it being a beautiful bridge. Standing on the highest point, I realized what a ridiculous London ponce I'd become. Who else would walk across it in freezing rain and a howling gale wearing suede shoes and no hat? I walked on to the island. I could see a filling station in the distance, and I walked towards it in the hope that they might sell hats. They didn't, but they did sell chunky Kit-Kats, which are the next best thing. I bought the *Highland Free Press* and got talking to the garage owner. I was interested in how many people speak Gaelic out here. I know there are very few out on the East Coast, and hardly a soul in the Central Belt and Borders, but here, surely, the language must still be alive? Not really, according to the garage guy. Yes, there are Gaelic speakers on Skye, he told me, but they are getting fewer and fewer by the year. He couldn't remember the last time anybody came into his garage speaking it. He didn't speak it himself, and blamed the young people, who are not interested. This seemed a bit easy to me; young people are not interested in anything, in my experience, the whole world over, except sex, drugs and baseball caps. You can't blame them for everything, though it might be tempting to try. No, if we need somebody to blame, let's stick with the clan chieftains, who valued sheep above men, and money above everything. I walked back across the bridge and into Kyle.

The following morning the sun had come out, and it had been snowing. It was like a tiny miracle; beyond the bridge, a whole new mountain range had appeared. The mountains of the Applecross peninsula are very old, some of the oldest on earth; they are high, but rounded and smoothed by the passage of unimaginable periods of time. Now they were covered again by new snow, as they have been for countless millions of years, and were shining in the sun. A small fishing boat pulled away from the quay. Another coaster had arrived in the night. Waterfalls tumbled down the now all-white mountains of Skye; it was a wintry Eden.

Oh, and here comes the snake; a grey RAF Nimrod flew low and loud above the water, and a military helicopter came chattering in to land at the military base that lies hidden on the edge of Kyle. Big, big toys for pathetic little boys; bad education, failing health services, and a crumbling transport infrastructure, all accounted for in this mini fly-past. On the door of the ticket office there was a handwritten sign: *'Security Notice: due to bombings in America and threats to Great Britain we have had to withdraw all left luggage facilities and all litter bins.'*

Presumably, it is the proximity of this military base which means that the fall-out from 9/11 had spread even here. And however horrific the events of that day, we should not forget that the number of people who died in the attack on the World Trade Center is about the same as the number who die each year on Britain's roads. On the railways, it currently averages out at about ten dead p.a. Of the new money the government is putting into the railway, some £2 billion is earmarked for safety, which works out at about £3.2 million per life saved. On the roads, ministers are reluctant to spend more than £100,000 per life saved.

I climbed on to the bus waiting by the station. Snow was rolling in, and the mountains of Applecross were hidden again behind a wall of cloud. The only other passengers were a couple of American back-packers.

On the road back to Strathcarron the sun came out, and where yesterday the mountains were brown, today they were all white. In the mouth of Loch Carron, a rainbow curved into the sea. As we came in to the station yard, where the train for Inverness was waiting for us, I felt a deep sadness, as though I was leaving home behind me. I'd never been here before, and I didn't really know if I'd ever be back, but I felt my heart breaking as I turned my back on this wonderful and cruelly empty place.

Rousseau and his late-eighteenth-century contemporaries gave us our modern ideas about natural beauty; they were the progenitors of the romantic ideal, and surely the West Coast of Scotland is the epitome of that vision. If you wish to find romance by rail, if you want to go on one of the *Great Railway Journeys* and can't be bothered to save up for a ticket to India or South Africa; or if you want simply to relive some of the journeys of Michael Palin, then you must go down to your local station and buy a ticket for Kyle.

Trainspotting in Edinburgh Waverley

The thing about Great Journeys is that there comes a point where you are at your furthest from home, and there's nothing to do but turn around and go back again. When Michael Palin got to Kyle of Lochalsh, he caught a ferry heading down the West Coast of Scotland to Mallaig, where he got on yet another train, for Glasgow and so at last London. I would have caught that ferry if I could, but there aren't any ferries from Kyle to anywhere any more. If I was a real man, or if I'd been in the company of a film crew, I'd have hired a fisherman to take me on the two-hour trip to Mallaig. I'd have worn an oiled sweater, and would have helped my new friend raise some lobster pots on the way.

No film crew, and probably not a real man, so that's why I was sitting on a train through the Scottish Highlands, retracing my steps towards Inverness. The journey was even more spectacular in reverse, as overnight snow cushioned the mountains. At Inverness, rather than wait all day for another sleeper to take me back to Euston that night (after all, you can have too much of a good thing), I planned to stay on the train for Edinburgh and then spend a night there, recuperating after my Great Journey and doing a little Trainspotting.

I'd just arrived back in Inverness from Kyle, and there were twenty minutes before the train continued on to Edinburgh, so I nipped out, leaving my books and maps on the table, to get a sandwich, and try to suck down a couple of quick biftas. I drank two cups of Ritazza and felt slightly sick, before hurrying back to reclaim my place.

When I got back to the train, it was to discover that somebody had been through the carriage reserving places with those annoying little tickets which they stick in the back of the seats. Apparently I'd lost my spot, so I moved my stuff with bad grace away from the table where I had been so comfortable, and into a pair of so called 'airline seats'. They are so called because they are so close together that if you do not get up for a wander every so often, you will get deep-vein thrombosis.

The train was suddenly packed; on the trip over from Strathcarron there had been maybe five people, but from Inverness on, there were people in every seat, and even sitting outside the loos. My immediate travelling companions were smashers. Sitting next to me was Diane, late twenties, small, dark and pretty. She seemed to me like a nice lass. In the seat behind us were her two friends Sheff and Joe, the kind of guys who make you wonder why on earth we ever bothered getting down from the trees. They spent much of the journey leaning over to shout things at Diane. Diane spent most of the journey twisted round in her seat, talking to the two apes. I sat there, trying to read.

As we pulled out of Inverness, Joe started to pull cans of beer from a carrier bag, which he distributed amongst the party. I was already desperate for a fag, as the realization dawned that I was going to have to spend five hours in their company. There was no refreshment trolley on this train. Being forced to listen to their less than scintillating conversation was going to make reading difficult.

I was trying to concentrate on Christian Wolmar's book, *Broken Rails*. He compares nationalization with privatization, and shows how the mistakes of the first were either ignored or compounded by the second. It's a complicated tale, so stay with me; and imagine trying to follow it with two half-wits yabbering in your ear, and a pretty Scottish girl wriggling about in the seat next to you.

The First World War showed the government how vital the railway was to the national interest. The American Civil War of the 1860s had been the first truly modern war, recorded by photographers and utilizing trains to move troops quickly to the front. All wars after that would involve greater and greater degrees of slaughter, as the train enabled governments to feed more and more of their citizens into the muzzles of enemy guns. The First World War marked the realization of modernity's love affair with the machine, but it was the beginning of the end of the railway age.

Before the war there were some 150 train companies: some, like the Tal-y-Llyn, very small; others, like the Great Western, huge corporations with control over hundreds of miles of line. This was the legacy of Victorian laissez-faire economic policy, when two or sometimes three competing railways would build lines to the same place. The war had shown that this was inefficient. Most of the companies had failed to return a profit for years, and those that had filed only modest dividends to their shareholders. Nationalization was considered, but in the end, it was decided to amalgamate all the railways into just four large concerns; the Great Western, the London Midland and Scottish, the London North-eastern, and the Southern. In railway lore, this is known as 'the Grouping', and it happened in 1923.

The period between the Grouping and the Second World War is thought of as the Golden Age of Steam, largely because that's when lots of railway enthusiasts were born, and trainspotters are nothing if not terminal nostalgists. The *Flying Scot*, the *Golden Arrow*, the record-breaking run by *Mallard*; this was their time. *Brief Encounter*, *The Thirty-Nine Steps*, *Murder on the Orient Express*; the spy on the night mail, the *femmes fatales*, the bearded Chinaman, all had their being during the Grouping. So did the 1926 General Strike, when the great triumvirate of union power, coalminers, dockers and railwaymen almost managed to stop the country altogether.

The people who had shares in the pre-Grouping companies were given shares in the new companies, but even in this (perceived) halcyon age, dividends were negligible. The Second World War saw the railway at the forefront of national policy again; the Labour victory in the election of 1945 committed the government to nationalizing transport, and in 1948 the railways, along with road haulage and the canals, were finally brought under state control. But the government, in an honourable attempt to do right by the shareholders, gave them bonds at very generous rates of interest. This hamstrung British Rail right from the outset, as money that should have been used for improving the railway went into paying off the shareholders. Now Railtrack shareholders must be paid back. When Mr Byers put the company into administration, in late 2001, he was lucky that one group in particular of Railtrack shareholders did not kick off; the railway signalmen, Railtrack employees all.

Wolmar makes the point that, just as at privatization in 1995, the concern at the moment of nationalization was not primarily with transport needs, but with the demands of management and administration. The Modernization Plan of 1955, which aimed to pump millions of pounds into the railways, was hastily thought out, as each of BR's regional managers came up with a pet project, each loonier than the last.

Wolmar says that 'once in a generation the purse strings of the Treasury have been loosened and the industry offered serious investment funding', and we might add that the industry goes on to blow it all on sweeties. The railway cannot be run for profit. According to Wolmar, 'the golden rule is whether it is more rolling stock, extra train paths, better signalling to increase throughput, faster trains, longer trains, or whatever, the investment required will never earn a commercial rate of return'.

So you can never run a railway at a profit. Why should you need to? The roads certainly aren't run for profit; they cost a fortune, much more than drivers pay in road tax, but we are car junkies, and scared to count the true cost of our habit.

'Och, sorry, mate.' Wriggling Diane, twisting in her seat the better to hear Joe and Sheff's wit and wisdom, knocked my book from my hand. I couldn't bring myself to say the conventional ' 'S all right'. It bloody wasn't all right.

God, I hated Joe and Sheff. Diane was going to Edinburgh for a job interview in an hotel, and she was taking her friends along for the ride. Joe was lanky and enfeebled by drink, with the drawling voice of a useless English hippy. He kept telling stories about his one trip to Glastonbury, and how drunk he got. As much as anything, I'm disgusted by a man who goes to all the bother of going to Glastonbury simply to get drunk. Surely the point of Glastonbury is to alter your consciousness by less straightforwardly everyday means. Sheff was dressed in a tracksuit, the uniform of the professional car thief, and had the most annoying voice of anyone I'd ever sat next to. At first I thought he might be a chef, and that was why he was called Sheff. No. He was called Sheff because he was from Sheffield.

I've spent many a pleasant night in Sheffield, and I have nothing but good memories of my times there. The Super Tram is a knockout, even though it goes to the wrong place, and in the cafés they dip your bacon sandwich in cooking fat, which still leaves me open-mouthed with admiration. It's not a pretty place, but it really does have heart, in a way that Liverpool thinks it does, but I've always found strangely absent. The Sheffield accent is not great though. People moan about Brummies, but I like a Brummie voice. It is Sheffield, I've always felt, that has the most grating voice in England. And Sheff had been living in Scotland for years, so his already annoying voice was filtered through a kind of weird Scottish vocoder. Add to that the fact that he too talked with that vapid hippy drawl, and the whole was one of the most unpleasant sounds ever to issue from a human mouth.

Diane wanted to go to a comedy club when she got to Edinburgh, but Joe and Sheff just wanted to 'get wellied'. And as the journey wore on, it became obvious that Sheff was Diane's boyfriend. Oh, Diane! You are pretty, and young, and bright! Sheff must be at least fifteen years older than you; he is ugly and very stupid, and cares for nothing except getting out of his wee skull. I'm reminded of a Robert Graves poem, 'A Slice of Wedding Cake'.

Why have scores of lovely, gifted girls
Married impossible men?
Simple self-sacrifice may be ruled out,
And missionary endeavour, nine times out of ten.

Repeat 'impossible men': not merely rustic,
Foul-tempered or depraved
(Dramatic foils chosen to show the world
How well women behave, and have always behaved).

Impossible men: idle, illiterate,
Self-pitying, dirty, sly,
For whose appearance even in City parks
Excuses must be made to passers by.

> *Has God's supply of tolerable husbands*
> *Fallen, in fact, so low?*
> *Or do I always over-value woman*
> *At the expense of man?*
> *Do I?*
> *It might be so.*

Hmmm. Perhaps I had fallen into Graves's trap; perhaps I was over-valuing Diane. After all, look at the company she chose to keep. At least, or so I hope, she wasn't actually married to Sheff. I never take a Walkman with me on trains. Usually I like to read, and to listen to the train. Sitting with Joe, Sheff and Diane, I wished I had one, that I could turn up loud.

The *Railway Traveller's Handy Book* is packed with excellent advice, not least of which is how to deal with unpleasant travelling companions: 'Railway travellers are occasionally thrown into company with persons who know not how to behave themselves, or rather those who consider it the height of manliness and propriety to insult inoffensive and quietly disposed passengers.'

The author gives several examples of how to deal with unpleasant travelling companions, chief of which is to 'quit their company at the first opportunity'. But this really wasn't possible, as the train was packed, so I did the next best thing, and tried to sleep. I dreamed about Joe and Sheff; their whining voices, their beery breath, their unfunny stories about getting drunk. I dreamed of rescuing Diane, of whisking her away to a better place.

My mobile shrieked. It was my girlfriend.

'Uhhh?' I said, coming to consciousness.

'Hello, darling. Where are you?'

'Er . . . I'm on the train with Diane.'

'Who?'

'Er . . . I've just woken up. I'm not sure where I am.'

'Who's Diane?'

'Hello?'

'Hello! Who's Diane?'

'Er . . . I can't talk. I'll call you from Edinburgh.'

'Hello?'

'Hang on . . . I think we're just going into a tunnel . . .'

But she had gone. I was awake. I had been asleep for maybe twenty minutes; that was the nearest I got to a break from Diane and those imbeciles. Reading was all but impossible; I looked out of the window.

This is the old Highland Railway, built in the flush of enthusiasm which saw railways trace lines over the map of Britain, from nowhere much to the back of beyond. Everywhere got a railway, whether it needed one or not. As most of the potential passengers had been cleared from the Highlands, the railway had to rely on tourism and war to make anything approaching a profit. Tourism at the end of the nineteenth century often meant deer-stalking, although, like many companies, the Highland built its own spa hotels in an attempt to attract holiday traffic, most notably at Srathpfeffer on a branch from the line to Kyle.

War is always popular, and never out of fashion. And, as I have argued, it was vital to the development of the railway. During the First World War, Kyle was an important navy base. Mines for the Northern Barrage (which attempted to close off the Nord See to the Boche) were taken there by rail, and trans-shipped to war vessels. The British fleet was based in Scapa Flow off Orkney. Some 13,000 trainloads of coal were carried from South Wales to Northern Scotland over the course of the war. That's roughly ten trains a day. And every night, the Naval Specials left Euston for Thurso, travelling the 717 miles in under twenty-two hours. I'm moaning about being stuck with Joe and Sheff, but I must have had it easy compared to the sailors – twenty-two hours in poorly lit, badly heated carriages, jolting along for hour after hour, trying to sleep, and arriving in the biting chill of Thurso to wait for ships to carry them across to Scapa. Still, at least they could smoke.

The evidence of the railway's role in wartime has largely disappeared, but tourism is still plain to see, most obviously at Aviemore, the UK's leading ski resort. The mountains were covered in snow, and I hung from the window to see if there were any skiers using the train. One or two people got off, but not the crowds I had been expecting. It's a lovely station, though, with a turn-table for the steam engines of the preserved Strathspey Railway. Further on, at Blair Atholl, there was one of the ridiculous Scottish Gothic castles built in the nineteenth century for shooting parties. Both shooting and skiing are elitist pastimes – rise up, smash the system, etc. etc.

The short Scottish day was coming to an end. By Perth it was dark, like my mood. Diane, Joe and Sheff showed no signs of flagging in their unending conversation about beer, Buckie, whisky, etc. What particularly annoyed me was the way Joe and Sheff kept going to the bog for a smoke. I go in there for a smoke sometimes, I admit that. I'd smoked a spliff with Mr Venus on our run from Towyn to Porthmadog, for example, but on this occasion I couldn't bring myself to stoop to Joe and Sheff's level, not on a three-carriage two-loo train that was stuffed with travellers.

The train lavatory is too precious a resource to be treated with selfishness. It is to be prized by you, and passed on to your fellow passengers in a decent state. Because if you do a floater, you're going to be sitting next to the person who finds it for the next three hours. If you make a mess, everyone will have to look at it. Or sit in it. If you 'let one off', it's gonna be coming right back atcha down the corridor. If you 'knock one off', everyone will know from your guilty look as you walk back to your seat. If you smoke, everyone hates you. These are amongst the world's most public loos.

When I started this project, I asked my girlfriend if there was one thing she'd like to know about railways.

'Yes,' she said, 'there is. Why can't you flush the loo in a station?'

Darling, I can't tell you for sure. I can only hypothesize, based on a teenage experience in Switzerland. I would like to be able to tell you, but the literature is strangely silent. The historians seem uninterested. Or is something more sinister going on? Are the TOCs hiding something?

I turned to a working railway rule book, dating originally from 1972, which had been carefully updated by its owner each year until 1979. This is the book which has the answers to all questions railway. How to deal with an Insane Person, what to say to the passengers when the train breaks down, how to remove stray animals from the line, the lot. Surely the answer would lie within its plastic covers. I looked in the index. There was only one mention of the lavatory system, on page 123. This entry was headed *Prevention of Damage to Carriage Lavatory Water Tanks During Frosty Weather*. I turned to page 123, and found the entry. I read it. As you might expect, it deals with the steps to be followed to stop the pipes from bursting in the winter. Mostly, it is routine procedural stuff, but regular travellers (ha ha! Or irregular ones, too!) might like to know that Rule 3 insisted that when frosts are severe, the water tank should be emptied, and water cans provided in each of the lavatories. Can you imagine? Eeieuuu!

Anyhow, this was the sole entry about the loo in the working manual. Nothing about how they worked. Nothing about what to do if they were blocked. And, frighteningly, the whole entry had been crossed out in red ink and replaced with Special Notice, D.7668: *Prevention of Damage to Carriage Lavatory Water Tanks During Frosty Weather*, which I quote here in full.

Delete heading and instruction.

Delete heading and instruction. Nothing I have been able to discern from official sources has taken me one step closer to discovering the consequences of a stationary flush.

But I have a hypothesis, based on experience.

Steve Neil, the baddest boy in our class, was one of those bright lads who hate school so much that they go back up there at weekends and burn the mother down. Steve and I went on a school trip together in our first year at Tideway. It was a fortnight's camping in Switzerland. One day, me and Steve caught a train from the village we were staying in to Interlaken, the nearby town. The first stop was protracted for some reason. Steve went into the bog. Still the train didn't move. Steve opened the cubicle door with a triumphant swagger, and called me through to see what he had done. I looked down the bog pan. Where I expected to see water, I saw instead the edge of a sleeper and some gravel. The bottom of the loo was open to the air. Steve had 'laid an egg', which sat perkily steaming on the gravel, directly underneath us. We laughed a lot.

European friends ask me why the English find going to the lavatory so funny. I fail to understand how anybody could think that going to the lavatory wasn't funny.

As the train started to move, a flap of some kind came up. It was kept in place by the train's motion. (Ha ha ha.) When the train stopped, the flap fell open, and the track was revealed once more. At each subsequent halt, Steve and I made sure we left a little something behind us. This, then, is my hypothesis; that for some reason, there is a tube, or a pipe, which only connects to the waste tank when the train is moving. Why this pipe cannot be permanently connected is beyond imagination. The British system is clearly different from the Swiss solution of the early 1970s, but there must be a family resemblance. A recent conversation on the subject with a guard on a First Great Western left me puzzled. He told me that all the crap gets sucked out on to the line anyway.

'Only the sleepers and Eurostar have septic tanks. Every other train just dumps it on the track. Being a line cleaner is the worst job on the railway.'

But this still does not explain the *special* consequences of a stationary flush. He might have been winding me up.

So are there really 'chocolate logs' dotted all over the British Railway system, deposited by well-meaning passengers who never use the lavatory when the train is standing in the station? And why, when there are books about every other conceivable railway subject, is there nothing on the history of the steam-hauled shitter? Answers, please.

If Diane and Joe and Sheff had been nice, they wouldn't have smoked in the loos, and then I could have nipped in there for one. But because they were horrible, they did, so I couldn't. I was uptight. Of all my journeys, this was the one I had enjoyed the least for a long time; nothing to see but night from the window, unpleasant travelling companions who made concentrating on my book all but impossible, and no chance of a smoke. The highlight should have been the Forth Rail Bridge.

It is well known that the bridge is being constantly repainted; that is, as soon as the gang of painters get to one end, they go back to the other and start painting again. It takes a year, end to end. And always the same colour! Lawrence Llewellyn-Bowen would have something to say. At some point in their career, *Blue Peter* presenters will find themselves in a harness, dangling over the Firth of Forth, paintbrush in hand, slopping on red anti-corrosive paint. The bridge is fantastically over-engineered. It was the first major bridge to be constructed entirely of steel, whose extra strength, you might think, would have afforded the designers some latitude.

But it was also the first major railway bridge to be built after the Tay Bridge disaster. When it was completed on 1875, the Tay Railway Bridge was the longest in the world. Its engineer, Sir Thomas Bouch, was given the job of bridging the even wider Firth of Forth, and work began on the original Forth Bridge to a design very similar to that over the Tay. On 28 December 1879, the mail train from Edinburgh to Dundee crossed the Tay Bridge in a howling gale; the pressure of the wind and the pressure of the train combined were too much for the bridge, and the girders and the train crashed down together into the waters of the river. There were some seventy-five passengers on board, all of whom lost their lives. The only survivor was the locomotive, which was salvaged from the bed of the river and continued in service until 1919. The only beneficiary was the poet William McGonagall, celebrated as the worst poet ever to grace English literature. His masterful 'Tay Bridge Disaster' is still his most famous work. Sadly, it is very long, so I can only give a taste of this best-known of railway poems:

> *Beautiful railway bridge of the Silv'ry Tay!*
> *Alas! I am very sorry to say*
> *That ninety lives have been taken away*
> *On the last Sabbath day of 1879,*
> *Which will be remembered for a very long time . . .*

and so on.

Thomas Bouch was the most obvious person to blame for the disaster, and work on the Forth Bridge was abandoned. New ideas were sought, and Benjamin Baker and John Fowler submitted the plans for the cantilevered design which remains in spectacular use. Rigidity and safety were the two major elements in its construction, hence the over-engineering. It will take more than a few gales and express trains to bring it crashing down into the Forth. It was opened in 1890, when it must have been awe-inspiring. It still is. The over-caution of the Victorian designers has given us one of the world's great engineering achievements. Shame I couldn't see it. Bloody Michael Palin had a helicopter to film it for him when he crossed it – I'll have to go back by daylight.

We clattered over the bridge, which was floodlit, whether for the benefit of sightseers or for the safety of the painters, I am unable to say. I watched the girders flick past against the background of the dark river. The excitement of Joe and Sheff was mounting the nearer they got to Edinburgh. Where would they go first? What would be their first drink when they got there? I guess it's always the case that the further north you go in the world, the more concerned people are with getting pished. Perhaps this is why the Brazilians are much better at football than Scottish folk.

In Brazil it is hot and sunny. Sunlight twinkles on the aquamarine sea. The days are perfect; the boys drink a little wine, smoke a little spliff, play futbol, eat some fruit and fish, drink a little more wine, play some more futbol, and, as the sun goes down, they make love to the Girl from Ipanema under the immeasurable canopy of the stars. In Scotland, it is dreicht. Freezing rain falls from leaden skies. Life is cruel. You get up, do a few tinnies, gobble down a couple of wobbly eggs, kick a fitba around a lake of frozen mud for two hours, go to the pub and get wellied, eat white pudden and chips on the way home, and then shag Big Shona from Paisley in a bus stop. All British teams have to do to be able to take on the Brazilians is to change the British climate and its resultant culture in its entirety.

Which would mean killing Joe and Sheff, wouldn't it? Wouldn't it? It would, wouldn't it? Yes, that's it . . . kill them. Yes, that's right . . . kill them, yes, and push their bodies from the train. Or hide their remains in left luggage! Yes! YES! It was perfect . . . HA HA HA! HAHAHAHAAAAAAAAAAAHHH . . .

Engine No. 6024. "King Henry IV," on the 10.30 a.m. Paddington to Plymouth in Sonning Cutting, near Reading.

The Down Fishguard Boat Express.

CROSSING
NO GATES

In the years between 1827 and 1929, only seven murders were committed on British railways. Before the advent of the communication cord, it was commonplace for travellers to be locked into their compartments; ideal circumstances for those with murderous intent, one might imagine. The few cases that there were were sensationalized, and the railway was seen as a dangerous place to be.

Thomas Briggs was a successful banker. In 1864 he was found by a train driver beside the track outside Hackney Wick station with severe head injuries. Briggs was taken to a pub by the train driver. Imagine the scene:

' 'Ere, Maisie! Look wot I've fahnd!'

'Coo, 'e's in a right two and eight. What'll yer 'ave?'

'Il 'ave a pint of mild and bitter, and I think the gennelman could do with a sixpennorth of brandy?'

Deciding, for some reason, that the pub was not an ideal place for a man with severe head injuries, the driver took Briggs home, where he died shortly after.

In the meantime, two gentlemen had got on to the train at Hackney. What gentlemen were doing in Hackney, history does not tell us. Perhaps they thought they'd buy up property early, and sit tight until Hackney became genteel, with delis and chi-chi little galleries and Thai pubs selling Belgian beer. If this was the case, they are still waiting. On this particularly eventful trip on the North London Line, the gentlemen found their compartment spattered with blood. Now, of course, no one would be the least bit surprised to find a blood-smeared carriage on the North London Line, but at the time, it must have seemed somewhat unusual. They also found a large stick covered in blood, and an unusual hat. Again, history is silent as to what was unusual about the hat. The assumption was that Briggs had been battered by the hat's owner, and his body had then been dumped from the train.

During the investigation, a Mr Matthews claimed that he had bought this hat for his friend Franz Muller. Furthermore, Muller had just given Matthews' daughter a jewellery box as a gift, bearing the name of a Piccadilly jeweller, De'Ath's. The jeweller had read about the case; he remembered a hatless man who had brought in a gold fob watch, which he exchanged for several other items, including the box Muller had given to Matthews' daughter. The gold fob watch, on examination, proved to belong to Briggs.

Muller tried to escape, but he was arrested in New York and brought back to stand trial. He produced alibis from his girlfriend and her landlady; and it was pointed out that Matthews had once owned a hat identical to the one that he had given Muller; furthermore, Matthews' hat had been mysteriously lost. Was Matthews really the killer? Muller was found guilty of the crime and was hanged in November 1864. As a consequence of the case, the London and South Western Railway put little portholes between the compartments in all their carriages, so that dastardly deeds could no longer be carried out in private. These small windows were known as 'Muller Lights'. When someone in the marketing department of a major German dairy processing company read about the history of the case, he at once decided that 'Muller Light' would be the ideal name for a forthcoming line of low-fat yoghurt.

This case did not seem like a useful precedent. Perhaps I would do better to kill Joe and Sheff and then hide their bodies in left luggage. It had worked a treat for somebody in Brighton, in 1934. On 17 June inst. William Vinnicombe, a left-luggage office attendant, noticed a really rather disgusting smell coming from a trunk that had been deposited in the cloakroom ten days earlier. He called for the Railway Police, who opened the trunk and found the headless, limbless torso of a young woman in an advanced state of decomposition. The left-luggage office was searched for clues, and the body of a baby was found in a basket. A few days later, another cloakroom attendant, this time at King's Cross, detected another noxious stink. This time, a case was found containing two legs and two feet. Post-mortem examination of the torso showed that it had belonged to a pregnant young woman, aged perhaps in her mid-twenties. The head was never found, though there were reports that it had been seen in a pool at Black Rock, where Brighton Marina is now. No one ever accounted for the dead baby.

A second body was found in a trunk at the home of a waiter known as Tony Mancini. There was no evidence to link him with the torso at

Brighton station, but he was arrested for the murder of Violet Kaye, the second trunk body. Mancini claimed that he had found Kaye's body and had hidden it because of his long police record. Incredibly, he was acquitted at his trial. Forty years later, he admitted to a national newspaper that he had killed Kaye – owing to the rules of double jeopardy, the Director of Public Prosecutions declared that Mancini could not be tried again. He never admitted the first case; the headless woman in the trunk was never identified, and no one was ever brought to trial. It remains one of the best-known unsolved murder cases, although, over the years, suspicion has come to focus on Edward Massiah, a Hove doctor with a sideline as an abortionist. It could be that Massiah hid the body of the young woman after an attempted termination had gone wrong. In 1938, after the death of another young woman, Massiah left Britain and went to live in Trinidad.

God knows, I was ready to kill Joe and Sheff. But could I cope with the publicity? And if I went down, would I be spending more time with people like Joe and Sheff rather than less? I was supposed to be heading for Edinburgh Waverley, but I couldn't face another moment in their company. I could kill them, or get off the train. So I got off one stop early, at the much less spectacular Haymarket. My legs, my arms, my neck, my stomach, all ached to move again. I yearned to bring my nicotine levels up to normal, to stop those bastards talking about shit for five solid hours in my ears. I stood on the platform and sucked down a fag. Only when the soothing smoke had delivered a little poison to my system was I ready to face the street.

Ever since that morning, the snow had followed me south and east, and now it started to fall from close above my head, as though sprinkled by a stagehand sitting just above the sodium lights. I hailed a taxi, which took me to my hotel, a dog-eared three-star tourist place, just off the top end of Princes Street, almost empty at that season, waiting with faded tartan carpets for Festival and Americans and paydirt.

I unpacked, and then walked down Princes Street towards Waverley station. There were a couple of drunks, clearly employed by the Scottish Arts Council to play the part to perfection, dancing in the snow to the skirl of a busking piper. Outside the station were several *Big Issue* sellers, standing in the snow, and no one buying. I had a curry and walked back to the inhospitable hotel. I wanted an early night, because in the morning I was going trainspotting.

Trainspotting, by Irvine Welsh, was published in 1993. It sold millions. Lots of railway enthusiasts, feeling at last that a book had been written especially for them were severely disappointed. The film of the book was a box-office smash – and it contained no trainspotting whatever. The lads on Platform Five at Crewe were not happy. If you use Trainspotting as your search term on Google, you will get lots about the book, and the film, and nothing about the activity. You might imagine that the world of Edinburgh junkies and the world of railway enthusiasm are poles apart. Cheese: what spotters have in their sandwiches; chalk: what junkies have in their veins. But I was not so sure, and I wanted to chase up some connections.

Trainspotting is written phonetically, an always risky attempt to help the reader hear characters' voices. It puts some people off the book, but it works if you stick with it. At the book's centre is the character of Mark 'Rent Boy' Renton, a clever working-class junkie. He is sur-rounded by a company of assorted druggie types: Spud, more of an acid head than a junkie, Sick Boy, a needle-sharp and opportunistic ladies' man, and Frank Begbie, the psychopathic non-using 'mate' of all the junkies. I thought the book went some way to catching the atmosphere of the user's world. No book could get it entirely. We need a new Joseph Wright of Derby to paint portraits of user life, lit only by the TV screen and the flare of disposable lighters. I thought that it wasn't funny enough, and that not enough people died, but I thought it brilliantly done. I particularly liked the bit when Renton and Begbie steam the InterCity train.

I've never seen the film. I should have, I know, but I never have. It looked to me like entertainment which could only glamorize the cult of junkie as lifestyle choice, which didn't seem to me to need glamorizing at all.

A *Trainspotting* moment. In 1986 I was living in a junkies' house in Brighton. It was all I could find at the rent I could afford. I was the only non-junkie in the house. My landlord and landlady lived in two rooms at the top of the house with their two children. The only clear spaces on the floor were the filthy mattresses, one for the kids, one for the parents. The rest of the two rooms was covered in paper, tin cans, needles, bottles. The kids were usually naked. The bog was right at the bottom of the house, and they couldn't be hacked to get down there, so their room was always full of kids' plastic potties, brimful with piss and shit.

I was working as a boardmarker in a bookie's shop. One day, I came home from work to find my landlady in the hall.

'Howay, man, I hope you don't mind, but I had a miscarriage in yer bed.'

'God . . . I'm so sorry . . .'

'It was the only room in the house I could have the doctor in.' She leaned closer and patted my arm. 'But don't worry,' she said. 'I've changed yer sheets.'

I didn't want some film trying to take me back to that place, those people, that time.

My old songwriting partner, and one of my closest friends, Gary 'the Dutchman' Dutch, was a junkie. I watched him put junk before his talent for years. He was scared of how good he was.

He used to come up from the south to Lancaster to write with me. He liked Lancaster because no one he knew there was using. He would bring a little bit up with him for the first night, but then he'd stay clean for the week or so that he was up north. He told me that when he went home to wherever it was that he was dossing at any one moment, all he had was a five-pound-bag-a-week habit. But every time he left, I would notice that a couple of my CDs were missing. He started using more and more. He stored his keyboard at his parents' house, where he couldn't get it until he needed it. So that he wouldn't sell it. He was effectively homeless. He hung out in Seaford. Lots of his mates had moved there from Peacehaven. Any money he could get together, he spent on gear. For food, he went skipping. Skipping is where you wait until a supermarket has closed, and then go through their skip, looking for food that is just past its sell-by.

'We got some fucking great stuff, though,' Gary told me. 'Whole fucking Black Forest Gâteaux, pies, the lot.'

All around him, his mates were dying. Bruce was knocked down by a train. Potty Pete got septicaemia. Melanie, Duggs and Big Al all took some good gear that was going round, and if there's one thing junkies can't tolerate, it's good heroin. Killed 'em. Month after month, Gary was going to funerals. He went to five in one year. We'd almost lost touch; on his last trip to Lancaster, he'd stolen some things from me, things I finally couldn't forgive him for.

I hadn't seen or spoken to him for over a year, when he phoned me up out of the blue.

'It's too much, man. I'm coming to live in Lancaster.'

One of his closest mates, Eddie, had been murdered over a junk deal. A week later, Gary found out that another of his pals had actually been the one to kill Eddie. Dutchie freaked, and came to the only place where he'd ever managed to stay clean. He still lives there now, and he's still clean.

He came down to stay with me in the summer. His kid sister Julie had just died, a fortnight before. She was three years younger than Dutch, beautiful, talented and funny. She loved Gary. Gary was her hero. She was a junkie too. She'd had a series of strokes. She'd been through de-tox a couple of times, but it hadn't taken. Gary always smoked, chasing the dragon over strips of silver foil, but Julie jacked up. Her veins couldn't take it any more. She got blood poisoning, which led to the strokes. She fell into a coma, and died after a couple of weeks in Birmingham Infirmary. Gary was gutted. He used to stay with her in London, and they certainly did heroin together. I'd never asked him, though it crossed my mind: did Julie start doing gear with you, Gary? And was that your last junk funeral?

I asked him about *Trainspotting*. I could see that he didn't like being asked, though he did his best to answer. He'd seen the film, and hated it. He said it made being a user look like a branch of showbiz.

I don't want to watch a fucking film about junkies. I like films about trains. Films and trains have always gone together. The Lumière brothers' first films showed trains coming into stations. When the first narrative features were shot, they were about train robberies. Trains were what film was about.

I didn't want to see the film, but I did want to see if I could find anything of *Trainspotting* culture while I was in Edinburgh.

In the morning, after breakfast, I walked from my hotel back towards Waverley station. It was still snowing. It lay six inches deep on the pavement. I caught a bus to the Foot of the Walk, and tried to find the derelict Leith Central station. In the book, Renton and Begbie go in there for a piss, and get approached by an old dosser who asks them if they have come trainspotting. Renton realizes that this old tramp is Begbie's father. This is why the thing is called *Trainspotting*, for those of you who have only seen the film. I asked for Leith Central, and I was told that the old station had been knocked down to be replaced by a shopping mall and a swimming centre, just like it says in the book. I walked through the shopping centre; it smelled of hot fat. Outside, nothing much was happening in the snow. An old woman smoking a fag and wearing wellies came out from her tenement with a bag of rubbish which she left on the pavement. The pubs were opening; old men filed out of the betting shops and into the bar, shaking snow from their thin jackets. I caught another bus, this time out to Newhaven.

Gary and me played a gig in Edinburgh a couple of years ago, and what we really wanted to do before we played was to get on one of the buses that were going to Newhaven. We didn't have time before our show. Now I had the chance. It was still snowing hard, harder than before. The bus dropped me off by the little fishing harbour. Edinburgh's Newhaven is much less defined and much less grim, at first sight, than my home town. It is a small part of Leith, which is a small part of Edinburgh. Out on the end of the little breakwater was a fisherman covered in snow. I walked out and joined him.

'Good fishing weather,' I said.

He smiled at me. 'Yeah, it's facking great, innit?'

'You're not from round here.'

'Nah, mate, I'm from Elephant and Castle. I cam up for the fishing.'

'Is it any good?'

'Nah, mate, it's facking bollocks. But it's a fack sight better than Elephant and Castle. Me sister lives here. I'm finkin abaht movin up.'

He reeled in his baits and examined his hook. 'Oi, you're not from rahnd 'ere neiver.'

'No. I'm from Newhaven in Sussex. I just wanted to see this Newhaven, too.'

'Newhaven–Dieppe? Oh yeah? Oi – you an' me? We must be facking mad.'

He was facking well right, 'n'all. It was facking cold. The snow dropped and dropped. Only occasional buses swished by on the dock road. I said goodbye to the cockernee and walked back down the fishing quay. I saw a café, the Harbour Café, just like at home. It was hot and full of steam. Old men and women sat eating bacon, egg and fried slice, and reading the *Daily Star*. Slightly plump women in their early forties wearing too much makeup and nylon tabards were leaning over the tables wiping up. It was my kinda place.

I talked to an old couple at the next table and asked them how Newhaven had changed.

'Uts fool o 'em yuppies now,' said the woman. 'Snot like it wose.'

'What about drugs?'

'Ach . . . it's runein this toon. Runein it,' said the old lady, shaking her head. The man made a face and changed the subject.

'Weir yu frum then, son?' he said.

'I'm from the other Newhaven. In Sussex.'

'No, thiz nivver another Newhaven, is ther?' said the woman.

'Yeah. It's a ferry port. Ferries to France go from there.'

'Wull, ah nivver knew that! Did you, Daddy?'

'No, ah dudn't. Wossut liek?'

The nylon-clad waitress brought me my bacon, egg and fried slice. 'It's much like this,' I said.

I phoned for a taxi on my mobile. He struggled to get to me through the snow.

'Where to, sir?'

'Er . . . I know it sounds stupid, but could you take me to some of the estates they used for filming *Trainspotting*?'

The driver laughed. 'People always ask me that. It was filmed in

Glasgow, pal. It's too disgusting here. No one would believe it. I could take you to Niddrie, though. That's shite.'

'No, it's all right, guy. Just take us back to Waverley.'

He dropped me off at the top of the steps, and I slithered up the hill in the snow towards the bus station. An *Issue* seller stood under the lee of a building. I stopped, and made to buy a copy.

'Cheers, mate. Fust woan ah've sold aw fucken moanin.'

I gave him a tenner.

'Aw, I can't change that, mate.'

'If you leave me here, I'll sell the paper. You go and get some change.'

'Straight up? Yers trust us?'

'Course. Here you go.' I gave him the tenner and he gave me the magazines. The snow was stopping; more pedestrians were skating past.

'*Issue!*' I shouted. '*Big Issue!*'

It's so easy, this drugs thing. All you have to do is to make heroin available on prescription. That used to be the case in this country. You could register as an addict; you could stand in line with Mister Jimi at the Chelsea Drugstore. William Burroughs used to claim that Britain had the only sane heroin policy in the civilized world, and if William Burroughs didn't know, then who did? When the scheme was abandoned by Thatcher the Gear Snatcher, there were less than a thousand registered addicts in the UK. There was no significant heroin problem in the 1970s. Now every shithole is buried in the stuff, white powder falls from the sky.

You wouldn't have millions of heroin addicts. Junkies are not really heroin addicts because they don't take enough to become truly addicted. The shit they take is 95 per cent Ajax. That's why good heroin kills them; they're not used to it, and they overdose easy. As your addicted population stabilized, they would be able to get jobs and homes. Heroin, taken properly, is not that harmful; less harmful physically than alcohol, certainly. You would take heroin off the streets, and bring your crime rate down significantly at a stroke. Legalization would also offer economic benefits for places that grow it, places where nothing much else can grow; places like Afghanistan.

'*Issue*! *Big Issue*!'

Heroin isn't really the problem. It's actually less addictive than nicotine. Junkies are addicted to the junkie life. Renton undermines his own whining junkie rhetoric. He tells the reader that he feels like his bones are being crushed when he's hanging out, that it's shit to say that cold turkey is a bit like flu. Then he talks about scoring bad gear, gear that is barely heroin at all. What's to be addicted to? Cold turkey really is a bit like flu. Heroin's not the problem. Junk gives you something to live for, something to get out of bed for. You have to get your bit of money together, go and make the connection. It's something to do; it fills a void. It's the void that's the problem.

After twenty minutes or so of me standing in the snow, being carefully ignored by passers-by, the *Issue* seller came back with my change. I gave him the papers.

'I didn't sell any, I'm afraid.'

'That's all right, pal. Thanks fer trusting us.'

'Thanks for trusting me.'

His name was Kevin. He used to work in the casual building trade, but when he started getting epileptic fits, he couldn't get work on the sites any more. It was the junk that had started him having fits. Now he was on a methadone programme. He slept in a shop doorway at night, unless he could sell enough papers to get into a hostel.

That's some void.

I went back to my hotel, packed my things, and headed again for Waverley station. Like Paddington, it's built in a valley. The North British Hotel that overlooks it is much more impressive from the outside, but Waverley is a fine station from inside, built from a warm stone, and passenger-friendly. It's the only station named after a novel, incidentally. When the GNER train came it was comfortable and clean. It was five minutes late leaving, for entirely honourable reasons; it was waiting for a connection. Connections are good. The staff went out of their way to keep the passengers informed. As we pulled out of Edinburgh and trucked through the south Edinburgh estates, the buffet steward made an announcement.

'We do have full catering facilities on board this train, but there will be a slight delay before the commencement of these services.'

I love it when people talk like that.

The train ran south. From the window, I could see that the snow was getting thinner on the ground, and by the time we crossed into England by the Royal Tweed Bridge, it had gone.

I was thinking about the void. Some people feel it more than others. If you are unlucky, or stupid, or blind, you fill it with junk like the Dutchman did, or drink, like Joe and Sheff. If we are lucky, we can fill it with love and work. Or God. Or hobbies. That's what railway enthusiasts are doing. That's what trainspotting is. It fills a gap. Some railway enthusiasts use their hobby to blank out the real world, to stop it howling around their heads. To numb themselves. To escape into a world of romantic fantasy. It becomes narcotic.

I think the void grows from a lack of engagement with the world. We are divorced from nature, from ourselves, from our past, so recently lost. We are unconnected. Junkies and train travellers alike, we all need to make our connections.

The train pulled into Newcastle. This is where railways are from; this is the home of the Newcastle Road. The rails on a Newcastle road were always about four feet, eight and a half inches apart. George Stephenson was born next to one of these old roads, the Wylam Wagonway. When he started building railways of his own, it was natural that he should build them with the rails four feet, eight and a half inches apart. He didn't really give the question much attention. He saw the importance of having one uniform gauge, so that the network could be linked together, but there was no question in his mind that this uniform gauge should be the Newcastle gauge. Other gauges had advantages over what we now call the standard gauge. Brunel's seven-foot-wide gauge, if it had been adopted, would have meant that modern trains could have run faster, and safer. If more narrow-gauge railways like the Tal-y-Llyn had been built in rural areas, the lower maintenance and running costs make it much more likely that they would have survived for a lot longer . . But it was the gauge of the Newcastle Road that was adopted as the national, and eventually international norm.

The Newcastle roads were built in the seventeenth and eighteenth century to accommodate a wide range of wagons which were already in use. It was natural that the rails should be placed so far apart as to accommodate the average axle width of an seventeenth-century farm cart. The average width was about four feet, eight and a half inches. The wheels on carts were this far apart, so that they could fit in the ruts of the ordinary late medieval and early modern roads. These roads had not been improved since they were built by the Romans. The wagons were running in very old grooves, grooves that had been cut by the Romans' chariots. The average size of Roman military horses' arses, meant that the average distance between the chariot wheels was about four feet, eight and a half inches.

The train you are sitting on is following in the tracks of the Romans' chariots. We are intimately, and at all times, connected with our past, with life, with love, if we could just see it. If we could make the connections.

Funky Kingstown

My first experience of Irish trains was several years ago when I travelled with my trainspotting ex through Scotland, Ireland and Wales. We didn't have much money, so we did the whole thing by public transport. We established that if you are patient, and don't mind standing around in bus stops and train stations for hour after hour, then you can pretty much get anywhere, however inaccessible it might seem at first glance. Over the course of ten days, we got a good long way.

We caught a train from Euston to Glasgow, and from Glasgow to Ardrossan. We caught a ferry from Ardrossan to Brodick on the Isle of Arran, and a bus around Arran to Lochranza, where we caught another ferry for Cloanaig on the eastern coast of the Mull of Kintyre (try not to sing the song). We caught a bus from Cloanaig to Tarbert, from Tarbert to Campbeltown, and at Campbeltown we caught a ferry for Ballycastle in Northern Ireland. We spent the night in Ballycastle, and in the morning we caught a bus to Portrush, where we stayed for a few days with some old college pals of my trainspotter ex. This is the part of Northern Ireland where they paint the kerbstones red, white and blue. We saw a bungalow with a For Sale sign and an LVF flag in the garden, just so no left-footers accidentally bought the place. And I thought it was supposed to be fresh coffee that helped sell a house. Not around there; there it's the appropriate flag for the appropriate paramilitary organization.

Then we caught the train from Portrush down to Belfast. That train was in no hurry to get to Belfast; it captured something of the languid progress of a Parliamentary stopping train meandering across England before Beeching got stuck in. Like so much of Northern Ireland, it was run-down and unloved. The North, if you've never been there, is a very lovely place, but its tourist facilities recall Soviet-era Russia.

I'm always a tourist in Ireland. I have no discernible Irish roots, shocking though it is to admit. Uniquely among contemporary writers, I have no Irish blood or childhood links to Ireland. I could never be President of the United States. I just love it there. I like to see the sights, eat in fine restaurants, stay in top-class hotels and drink stout. In the North, the sights and the stout abound, but the hotels are Stalinist and much of the food Trotskyite at best. Like Russia, Ireland chose not to go with the standard gauge that was adopted by the rest of the world; the trains run on tracks that are five feet, three inches apart. They are big trains, therefore, and comfortable, but it takes three hours from Portrush to Belfast, when it would take you maybe an hour to drive. This was fine by my trainspotter ex, however, as it gave us an opportunity to discuss our relationship, that mysterious third entity in the lives of couples who are not getting on . .

The first-time visitor to Belfast cannot help but be a bit spooked. You get over it, but you feel a little nervy at first. And this was the summer of 1998, and I had a date with the television, and the small matter of England vs Argentina. It didn't feel great that, if you supported England, you sided with Ian Paisley, Mad Dog Adair, and 300 years or more of injustice. (Pub quiz question: when did Universal Suffrage arrive in the UK? Answer: 1972, with the removal of the property qualification for voters in Northern Ireland.) Martin McGuiness and the rest of the IRA Army Council, of course, were cheering on the Argies.

From the functional modern station, we caught the bus up the Ormeau Road and over the railway bridge, scene of many a good-natured sectarian riot. My Celtic-supporting Scottish Nationalist pro-Republican trainspotter ex loved to point out shops where massacres had occurred. She told me that her friends, with whom we were going to be watching the match and staying the night, were members of Sinn Fein, and hysterically pro-Argentinian.

She was winding me up. Our hosts could not have been milder. She was a doctor, he was a computer games designer, and they usually voted Alliance. As for the Big Match – they sided with Collina, the referee, and thought there was something to be said for both sides. It seemed appropriate, though, to watch Beckham's petulant little kick in Northern Ireland, petulance capital of Europe. In both cases you think,

'Grow up. Get a life.' Perhaps Northern Ireland will go on to marry Posh, and run its legs off to show that it has matured, one day.

The following morning, we caught the train from Belfast to Dublin. The ticket clerk was one of the rudest men I have ever encountered. My trainspotter ex told me that everyone in Northern Ireland is rude at first meeting, in case they are inadvertently nice to a member of the other community. This bloke obviously would rather have been anywhere else on earth than in the ticket office at Belfast Central. We took the train, in the livery of Iarnrod Eireann (Irish Iron Road; isn't that good?), down the line between Belfast and Dublin which was persistently bombed during the Troubles. Keeping the line open was an act of political faith.

As we crossed the border into the Republic, my heart lifted. I hadn't even realized until then how gloomy I had been feeling. There is an invisible line, one side of which is racked by hate and war, the other side of which no one much gives a fuck, and they like going down the pub for a bit of a singsong. I've never met anyone in the Republic who has ever visited the North; they blank it from their minds.

I bought a fluffy cinnamon fleece in Dublin, the first I had ever owned, to celebrate passing my fortieth birthday and the consequent lack of interest in looking sharp. Then we caught another train, south from Dublin, for Rosslare. This has never featured as one of the *Great Railway Journeys*, but I don't know why as it's a cracker. You get sea, mountains, pastoral beauty, estuarine sunsets; you get to go through the fine town of Wexford, and you should do it tomorrow. We got on to the ferry at Rosslare for Fishguard, where Mr Venus would be waiting to meet us, and I watched Ireland slip away behind us. I liked the Irish railways, I decided. I would use them again.

The following summer, I decided to take my youngest daughter to Cork, so that she could kiss the Blarney Stone. I'd kissed it when I was a kid, and it seemed to work for me. I remembered that stunning train ride down from Dublin, and thought our Blarney trip would be an excellent opportunity to use the Irish railways again. I phoned the Irish Rail Information line, to find out about trains from Rosslare to Cork.

'Ach, sure, no, you don't want to do that!' said the perhaps over-helpful lady at the other end of the phone.

'Don't I?'

'No. That's a terrible long journey, and you'll have to change at Limerick Junction' (the nearest thing Ireland has to Crewe).

'Oh. What should I do?'

'Take the bus. Far quicker and easier. Much cheaper, too.' This is a useful definition of good service; when someone tries to talk you out of the thing you want to buy and they are supposed to be selling, because they think there is something better. So she talked me out of the train (instead we caught the overnight ferry from Swansea direct to Cork) but she only increased my enchantment with Irish railways.

Later still, in the autumn of 2001, I was on a driving tour of north-west Ireland with my new girlfriend. We landed at Larne, and drove north along the Antrim coast road, to Portrush again, and then on to Derry. From there we crossed the border, still with the same sense of elation that I had felt three years previously, and made for the first town in the Republic, Letterkenny. In England, Wales and Scotland, pitching up at a little country town chosen just by looking at the map can be a risky business. In Ireland, you can't go wrong.

We knew nothing of Letterkenny until we arrived; the excellent shops were all brightly lit and open late, and the newly painted streets were full of happy, well-dressed people going cheerfully from pub to pub. We found a great hotel and had a choice of three first-class restaurants to eat in. And Letterkenny was no exception; as we drove down through Donegal, Sligo and into Mayo, every little country town we came to was similarly thriving. Until we came to Mulrany.

Mulrany is not really a town, I guess, but more of a straggling township between hills and the tidal inlets of Clew Bay. It is in the far north-west corner of County Mayo, set on the small strip of land which joins the Corraun Peninsula to the mainland of Ireland. We had decided on Mulrany because we wanted to cross the next day on to Achill Island and stay a few days there. Mulrany seemed the obvious stopping-off place after the long drive from Letterkenny. But there were no lively shops, and only one pub, a miserable, fading place where we took a miserable, fading room for the night. There was only one restaurant, although that was still superb; we had tangy Clew Bay mussels and lemon sole straight from the boat, served with the kind of mashed potatoes clouds are made from.

In the morning, we went for a walk around what there was of Mulrany. High above the village on the side of the hill was a huge derelict building, a stranded hulk of a place, washed up on the highest tide and left to fall to pieces. We walked up through the grounds, thick with rhododendron, fuchsia and fungus, and stood in front of the building. It had fake Dutch gables; the doors and most of the windows were boarded up. There was a faded sign; the Mulrany Grand.

This was a derelict hotel, a large one, with a hundred rooms or more. It looked to have been abandoned for twenty years at least. We looked through the windows; there was slime running down the walls, as tiles had started to slide from the roof, exposing rafters. We looked down the path we had climbed up, and noticed a causeway running from the steps at the end of the hotel grounds, carrying a path over salt marsh and tidal creeks to the beach, perhaps a mile away. Even from here, we could hear the crash of Atlantic breakers. This had clearly been a major resort. Now sheep wandered about in the courtyard of the old hotel, and kept the lawn in front of the building neat. Everywhere else, it was a semi-tropical jungle, like Heligan before it got found. We followed the remains of a path through the tangled gardens, climbing up the hill at the back of the hotel. We passed a cracked and empty swimming pool and the ghost of a croquet lawn. We followed the path until we came to a gate, leaning on its hinges; pushing it open, we were astounded to find ourselves standing on a railway platform.

Fuchsia bushes exploded over the platforms and were colonizing the trackbed; the rails had long gone. The station buildings, a ticket office-cum-waiting room together with a staff house, still stood, and looked to be in better order than the hotel. At the end of the opposite platform stood an imposing water tower, a solid brick base supporting a large cast-iron tank; this too was masked by fuchsia. The weathered signs saying 'Mulrany' were half obscured by rhododendron bushes.

It was like finding the head of Ozymandias hidden by flowers. This had been one of Ireland's grandest resorts; countless summers had been spent here, children laughing as they ran along the causeway to the sea, sedate Edwardian couples alighting from the train, to be met by porters waiting to collect the piles of heavy hide luggage. A whole culture had grown and disappeared with the coming and going of the railway. The line closed in the 1950s, by which time the hotel was already in decline. After several gallant but ultimately doomed attempts to keep the place going, the Mulrany Grand finally closed in the early 1980s. Irish people still pass through Mulrany in their cars, on the way to their holiday cottages on Achill, but few of them stop any more.

If Ireland is a contender for the most romantic place on earth, as surely it must be, and if abandonment, decay and loss are central to the romantic worldview, then the shell of the Mulrany Grand and its attendant railway station must count as one of the most romantic places imaginable. The trackbed looked to be in good order; the terminal buildings are still standing, as we found later in the day, ten miles further on, overlooking the sound which separates Achill from the Irish mainland. A few days later, heading towards Knock, we passed under the viaduct which dominates the small town of Newport, and that looked to be in good nick too. This would be a great railway to revive, running from the Iarnrod Eireann terminus at Westport to Achill. Rebuilding the line would only need a romantic imagination. And, I suppose, a lot of money.

I still wanted to go back to Ireland to travel some more on the trains. But I wanted to find a line which was unromantic. I think Irish people get fed up with romance. They sometimes find it dispiriting that Irish civilization has been appropriated for repackaging as Oirish, currently the planet's default culture. I had a line in mind, one which would bring into focus the grimmer side of railways and dispel the pungent romanticism of the abandoned line to Mulrany. I was put on to it by a guy who works at RTE, whom I'd met at a wedding.

'Railways, is it? Did you know that the world's oldest commuter railway is in Ireland?'

'No.'

'Well, it is. The line from Kingstown to Dublin is the oldest in the world.'

I looked it up; he was right. Kingstown is now called Dun Laoghaire; the line is about six miles long. I had visions of strap-hanging Dubliners commuting after work down to Bray, agents of Europe's tiger economy, mobiles bleeping, no one talking; a proper suburban line for a modern Ireland. What could be less romantic? Only one thing; I invited my esteemed snapper, Mr Perry Venus, to join me on the trip.

Mr Venus is a funny man. His permanently abstracted scowl, his fatalistic air, his deep-rooted cynicism all serve to make him one of the funniest men I know. But I don't know that you would call him romantic. He's sexy, I think. He has a highly developed sense of the finer things in life. He has an artist's eye. But romantic? His wife may find him so, though I doubt it. You do not find Perry Venus misty-eyed beside silent pools saying, 'Hist! Canst thou not hear the sigh of the water nymphs?' Anyway, all my trips to Ireland had been with lasses. It would be Mr Venus's birthday. What could be less romantic than going to Dublin with your mate for a piss-up on his birthday? And then to take a six-mile train ride in a grubby DART carriage? It was perfect. We arranged to meet in Holyhead; he would drive up from mid-Wales, and I would catch the train up from Euston.

Journeys to Ireland are political journeys. After the Act of Union between Great Britain and Ireland in 1801, the Irish Parliament in Dublin was abolished, and Irish MPs sat at Westminster for the first time. MPs could look forward to long miserable journeys from their constituencies to sit in the House. You can't expect MPs to suffer for long; it was clear that communications needed to be improved. And then of course Paddy, a likeable enough fellow, but excitable in his cups, doesn't really work unless he gets an occasional clip round the ear from the British Army. He can get a bit uppity, can Paddy, if you don't show him who's boss. So it became expedient to be able to move large numbers of troops up to the Irish ports, quickly and efficiently. The history of transport is inseparable from, a) the comfort and convenience of politicians, and b) their need to cling to power through the deployment of military strength.

Holyhead was recommended by a commission as the ideal port for the new Irish packets, and boats started to cross between the newly constructed harbour on the tip of Holy Island, off Anglesey, and Howth, just outside Dublin. Passengers landing at Holyhead found themselves dropped on Holy Island. No roads worth the name ran through Holy Island or Anglesey. There was a difficult ferry crossing to face, over the treacherous waters of the Menai Straits, between Anglesey and the mainland. The Royal Mail coaches could not operate west of Shrewsbury, and between Shrewsbury and London the old Roman road of Watling Street was in the control of seventeen separate Turnpike Trusts, all of whom kept their stretches of road in varying states of repair. In 1815, Parliament voted for a new road from London to Holyhead. The man who was chosen for the job was the pre-eminent engineer of his day, Thomas Telford.

Telford had built roads for the government before. A vast scheme of improved communications was promoted for the Scottish Highlands. Politicians were worried by depopulation in the Highlands, although the cause was hardly difficult to find; as Telford said when he went to survey the territory, 'Men are being eaten by sheep.' The improvers felt that Highlanders needed to make more use of the sea, which hitherto had played only a small part in their culture. Those Highlanders who were not forced to emigrate were stranded on dour Highland beaches, given nets, and told to get on with it. Now, liberal hearts were bleeding. Fishing harbours were proposed, together with a system of roads which would link the Highlands with the rest of Britain.

Certainly, the roads were negligible, apart from the system of military roads built by General Wade after Culloden. Indeed, so bad were the roads that the only way into the county of Sutherland was a track along a beach that was covered over at high tide. Telford was appointed engineer for this ambitious new scheme; in eighteen years, he supervised the construction of 920 miles of new road, building dozens of state-of-the-art bridges to span the fast-flowing Highland rivers. Most of these bridges are still in use. Oh, and he built the Caledonian Canal through the Great Glen while he was at it, just for good measure. He was a shoo-in for the Holyhead job.

Telford's solution proposed improvements on the existing road between London and Shrewsbury, and then an entirely new road through North Wales. He built roads after the Roman model. His methods of construction involved laying a massive foundation of paving-stones, held together with carefully graded smaller stones. MacAdam, his great rival in road-building (and whose name survives as Tarmac), built cheaper and quicker, but the Holyhead road would be the best in Britain.

And it crossed the Menai Straits on the most spectacular bridge of its age. The suspended span of the Menai Bridge is 579 feet long, with an air draught of 100 feet; this to allow full-masted Admiralty ships to pass underneath unhindered. By 1826, the Menai Bridge and its smaller but hardly less spectacular sister at Conway were opened, and the road from London to Holyhead, and thus Ireland, was complete.

Thirty years later, there would be grass growing up the middle of the roadway, as it was superseded by a superior technology. The steam-hauled train had stretched out to meet the Irish packets.

By the late 1830s politicians could see the time advantages that the railway had brought. The road was OK, but they wanted to be able to catch the train to Holyhead. George Stephenson had surveyed the line as early as 1838. He recommended the coastal route. In the twelve years since the road had been completed and the railway surveyed, civil engineering had advanced beyond recognition. He also recommended that the railway cross the Menai Straits on Telford's suspension bridge, but the far greater loads imposed by the railway made this impossible. He therefore proposed a site about a mile away, where the Britannia Rock sat in the middle of the Straits. A central pier could be built on the rock, which could then be joined to both shores. How this could be achieved, no one was entirely sure. Robert Stephenson was appointed engineer; the line was started in 1845, and by 1848 was complete between Chester and Bangor, and between Llanfairpwllgwyngyllgo-gerychwyrndrobwllllantysiliogogogoch and Holyhead. All that was necessary was that Robert Stephenson build a bridge between the two ends of the line. His solution was the Britannia Bridge, one of the Great Railway Bridges of the World.

This time, I wasn't going to make the mistake I had made at the Forth Rail Bridge. This time, I was crossing by day. I saw the journey as a kind of hymn to Stephenson, starting in his great terminus at Euston, slicing through the Chilterns and the Northamptonshire uplands on the London and Birmingham, leaping the Menai Straits by way of the Britannia, before rolling in to Holyhead for the boat to Dublin.

The morning I set off from Euston for my rendezvous with Perry in Holyhead, the train was fairly empty; a suit with a laptop, some Home Office files and a book on prison reform worked at an adjacent table; behind me were two elderly ladies heading for the North Wales Country Music Festival in Colwyn Bay; a woman in a wheelchair travelling with her daughter was in the corner, talking in that comic book 'Yore avin a larf, int yer?' *EastEnders* voice that I can never quite believe really exists outside of Walford.

The line follows the canal for much of the first part of the journey, as train lines often do, since the canal engineers had already done a lot of work finding a level route. North of Watford, ladies and gentlemen, *mesdames et messieurs*, if you look to your left, you can see the Ovaltine factory; and if you look immediately to your right, there on top of the hill is the Ovaltine Farm. This farm appeared on all Ovaltine tins for many years, and at first glance it looks like a typical prosperous southern counties farm, half-timbered and with extensive barns and outbuildings. On closer inspection, you can see that it is a façade, a Hollywood farm, and not a real building at all. The implication, that Ovaltine uses lovely fresh products from this very farm, was perfectly legal back when the farm was built in the 1920s, but modern advertising legislation probably frowns on such pretence, so for many years, the farm has been falling into disrepair. On this trip, I noticed that it was covered in scaffolding; the time had come for a long overdue makeover. The farm is part of this line, and part of Ovaltine's proud heritage, and I was glad that they'd decided to do something about it.

At Milton Keynes, a few more passengers got on the train. North of Rugby, I saw that the canal was choked with weed, the worst I had ever seen. An uneventful trip.

As we approached Nuneaton, the train slowed to a crawl. I looked out of the window to see what the problem was. It looked like weird art vandals had been at work. There were several very pink joints of meat wrapped in cloth and scattered along the line. What a waste, I thought. Some kind of protest, perhaps. As we came through the station, I saw ambulance crews and police standing forlornly at the platform's end, waiting for the train to pass. There was a woman holding a microphone, interviewing one of the policemen. I felt sick. Human meat, presumably a suicide. That's what we all look like, when we've been chopped up, at least, when we've been chopped up by a train; just like any other joint of meat. There was nothing remotely human about the remains that I had seen smeared along the lineside. I didn't get the impression that anybody else had noticed; the suit kept working on his files, the Country fans kept talking about line dancing, the cockernees kept up their gor-blimey-guv'nor chatter. It was very strange; almost as though I had dreamed it. There is a restaurant on platform five at Nuneaton station, an imaginative and to-be-welcomed use of old railway buildings; I shan't be eating there myself. I still feel sick, passing through Nuneaton.

At Stafford, the spotters were out in great numbers to see a diesel-hauled train. There were at least fifty of them, mostly with cameras, thronging round the, so far as I could see, entirely uninteresting engine. I know that I am missing something essential, but it doesn't matter how far I travel, or how many spotters I meet, or how much I read and research, the engines don't do it for me. I'm fascinated by the Permanent Way, the people who built the railway, the details like advertising and ticketing, and even the operation of the railway; but I cannot for the life of me get the slightest bit enthusiastic about the engines. Especially workaday old diesels. I don't like motorbikes either, and the rhetoric often seems the same about railway engines and bikes; throbbing, powerful beasts, a great surge of power, etc. No wonder women suspect that there might be something phallic going on.

No, what I like is the way the lines merge and move apart, like they do at Crewe, the buildings, the lineside furniture, the abandoned and wrecked carriages that close in and move along the train as you come in to Crewe. The Home Office suit got off, and a great many fifty-something Country music fans got on. After Crewe, the line for Holyhead leaves the West Coast main line, and I started to look forward to a trip on a stretch of line which was new to me. We passed the Railway Age; it looked empty.

Ten minutes out of Crewe, the train broke down. As is all too often the case, the train crew made no announcement to let the passengers know what was going on. We just sat there for half an hour. The Country fans sitting behind me took this opportunity to sort out their tickets for the festival. They only had one ticket for the line-dancing event in Ben's Bar, but they had three for the George Strait Tribute Night in the Dance Ranch; they agreed to sort it when they got to the holiday camp at Colwyn Bay. I went into what train managers touchingly call 'the vestibules' (that is, the bit at the end of each corridor where the loos are) and hung out of the window for a fag. A guy was walking up the line in an orange reflective jacket.

'What's happening?' I asked.

'They've got a blown compressor. The fitter's on.'

I wished I hadn't asked, really. Men like this always assume that men like me know what compressors are, but I haven't got a clue. But it was good to know that the fitter had arrived; presumably the thing would be fixed fairly quickly now, and could get back to compressing stuff.

I went back to my seat, to find buffet staff distributing free cups of coffee in paper cups with 'Compliments of Virgin Trains' printed on them, presumably kept on hand for just such an occurrence. This is a marker of how often breakdowns happen, and is singularly unimpressive. Another perpetual annoyance are the taped announcements at stations, 'The train to (insert station) . . . is running . . . approximately . . . (insert time) late. I . . . apologize for . . . any inconvenience caused.' I'm not sure that pre-taped apologies count as apologies at all. They are contingency plans, which is another thing altogether. And who is the 'I' of this universal apology? Is a tape machine taking responsibility and hoping to do better in future? If the train companies had any real remorse, or any genuine feel for PR, for that matter, they would at least get a member of staff to make a real live apology. They might even get staff to go down to the platform to see if anybody needed help. But no – let the computer do it.

The *Railway Traveller's Handy Book* has this to say of railway passengers in general:

A person in a railway carriage may be likened to a prisoner of state, who is permitted to indulge in any relaxation and amusement to while away the time, but is denied that essential ingredient to human happiness, personal liberty. He is, in fact, confined to a certain space for so many hours, and cannot well remove from his allotted durance without annoying his fellow passengers. The materials for railway amusement and relaxation embrace conversation, reading, card-playing, smoking, musing, and sleeping.

Conversation I didn't fancy; there were only the Country music ladies and the cockernees; all seemed perfectly nice, but all were engrossed in their own travelling companions. I didn't have any cards, I wasn't sleepy, I couldn't smoke, and I'd been reading since London. I thought I might try musing for a bit.

So I sat there musing, and I mused that soon Mr Venus would be arriving in Holyhead, and that I wouldn't; and I knew that the boat to Dun Laoghaire that we were booked on to would be going without us. And I knew what Mr Venus didn't, that I had forgotten my mobile. So there wasn't any way to tell him that I was going to be at least an hour late, and that he would have to negotiate us on to another sailing. Then I remembered that InterCity trains have a phone by the buffet, so I tried to phone him. It didn't take money, so I bought a card from the buffet for a fiver, but I was buggered if I could get it going. Whether I was putting it in upside down, or the buffet had conned me, I still don't know. The most likely explanation was old-fashioned stupidity, but there. I kept getting up and down from my seat, anxiously trying to get the thing going, and failing every time. And I am so pathetically hetero and English that I couldn't bring myself to ask the buffet staff what to do. My girlfriend, when she reads this, will hold her head in her hands and despair. Time passed; it was getting urgent. Perry would be arriving on Anglesey at about this time; it was only an hour away from our sailing, and I was still stuck ten minutes out of Crewe. I looked at the phone again, and realized from the instructions that the thing took credit cards. It felt like a minor miracle. A few weeks earlier, in order to pass an idle moment, I had filled in an on-line application for a credit card, and for some reason that I am still unable to fathom, the bank decided that I was a suitable person to have such a wondrous thing. I'm really not, and they've regretted it since, but there I was, at forty-three, for the first time in my life a credit-card holder. I put it in the phone, and it worked. God bless capitalism! God bless the bank's obviously completely inept credit-checking department! I got through to Perry on his mobile, just as he was pulling into the car park at Holyhead, and explained the situation. Just, in fact, as he was passing through a police checkpoint; I could actually hear them telling him off for talking on a mobe while driving.

'I'll call you back,' he said.

'Er . . .' The line went dead. I waited ten minutes, and phoned him back.

'What happened, man?' he said. 'I called your mobile, but all I got was the answer machine.'

'Sorry. Forgot it. Anyway, have you had any luck changing the tickets?'

'Not yet. I'll try you again in a few minutes.'

'No, I've forgotten my . . .' He'd gone.

And then, at last, the train started to move. We came into Chester's old-fashioned station, and then out past Britain's oldest and smallest horse-racing course, the mile round Roodee. Mr Venus and I used to work for the same firm of turf accountants in Brighton, and our heads are stuffed full of this kind of racing trivia. Shortly after the race-course is the bridge over the River Dee. This was Stephenson's second attempt to cross the river and it replaces one which failed in 1847. The original bridge had three 100-foot spans, each constructed using cast-iron girders. In just the same way that the Tay Bridge failed thirty years later, the bridge collapsed with a train crossing over. Five people were killed; Stephenson had been lucky that so few died. It was the last long-span bridge built from cast iron. Cast iron is brittle, a fact that Stephenson should perhaps have taken into account before he built the bridge; but engineering only advances through failure. The Tacoma Narrows Bridge in the US is a well-known case in point; engineers pushed the envelope of what could be done with a suspension bridge, and the result is the well-known film of the bridge swaying, buckling, and finally failing in the wind. The Millennium Footbridge over the Thames is another recent example of new technology being found wanting. Sometimes, there is no way for engineers to discover these kinds of truths other than to build the things and see what happens.

I phoned Perry and told him that we were on the move again. He told me the devastating news that our rearranged ferry crossing will take us, not into Dun Laoghaire (which was the whole point of the trip), but into Dublin Port, from where we'll have to catch a bus into the city centre. Bum. Still, this was a splendid train ride, hugging the North Wales coast, the muddy brown waters of the Dee estuary on one side and the high foothills of Snowdonia on the other. The line crosses the Holywell Embankment, one of those feats of Victorian engineering which are not so much to look at now, but were a right bugger to build.

By Prestatyn, the line had left the Dee estuary and followed the sea coast proper; a bungaloid coast, a be-caravanned coast. Out to sea, small gravel boats were dredging. We passed through Abergele. Abergele was the scene of an appalling railway disaster, in 1867. Two wagons, loaded with casks of paraffin, did not have their brakes properly applied during a shunting operation. They started to roll down the shallow incline towards Abergele station, and though the brakesman tried to catch them so that he could screw the brakes on correctly, they were moving too fast. They rolled away around the curve, and before the brakesman could do anything, they collided with the Irish Mail. The coals from the engine ignited the paraffin, which totally destroyed the front portion of the train. Thirty-four people were killed; as the Board of Trade inspector said of the victims, 'They can only be described as charred pieces of flesh and bone.'

We came into Colwyn Bay, and from all along the length of the train, big blowsy lasses with big bouffant hair-dos climbed down on to the platform. These were the crowd for the North Wales Country Music Festival, and may God bless them and all who sail in them. I like big lasses, me. I like a bit of Country too, and so does Mr Venus; I almost wished that we were going to the Festival, instead of on a six-mile suburban train ride. But then I thought of the railway thrills ahead; the tubular bridges, Conway and the Britannia Bridge across the Menai Straits. And then I was very much looking forward to passing through Llanfairpwllgwyngyllgogerychwyrndrobwllllantysiliogogogoch (the longest railway platform sign in Britain. The town is usually abbreviated to Llanfair PG; it was, incidentally, the site of the world's first meeting of the Women's Institute). So I thought, to hell with Country, and big lasses, at least for today. Sing ho! for the line to Holyhead, and Stephenson's amazing bridges, the apex, the apogee of the career of arguably the greatest of railway engineers! Huzzah!

Robert Stephenson had been left with the puzzle of how to take a railway across the Menai Straits. At the place his father had chosen, the bridge would be almost 1,400 feet long. The same Admiralty restrictions that had applied to Telford still constrained Stephenson, twenty-five years later; the air draught between the high-water mark in the Menai Straits and the bottom of the bridge could not be less than 100 feet. And Stephenson was embroiled in the inquiry looking into the failure of his bridge over the Dee. He knew that a suspension bridge wouldn't be strong enough, and that, after the failure of long-span cast-iron bridges, he was going to have to use wrought iron – stronger by far than cast, but difficult to work with. Other than that, he was unsure. Nothing of the kind had been attempted before.

Then came one of those serendipitous failures by means of which engineering advances. A warship, the *Prince of Wales*, built from wrought iron, became jammed during her launch at Blackwall. She was unsupported for 110 feet of her length, without showing any sign of strain. Stephenson decided that wrought-iron tubes would be able to support the railway. What he proposed was to build what were essentially gigantic box girders, and to run the railway inside them.

Three towers were built, the Anglesey, the Caernarvonshire and, in the middle of the Straits, the Britannia, 200 feet above high water. The giant tubes were welded and riveted together on the shore, and were then to be floated out into the Menai Straits and lifted over 100 feet into position. Each of the main tubes (there were four altogether) were 430 feet long, and weighed 1,500 tons. Nothing on this scale had been hitherto attempted. Although Telford had used the float and lift method for the chains of the suspension bridge, each of his chains weighed a mere twenty-three tons. On 19 June 1849, Brunel stood by his friend's Stephenson's side as the first of the tubes was floated out on four pontoons into the tidal cauldron of the Menai Straits.

The idea was that the tube would be floated into place beneath the towers, and then left low over the water for a few weeks while preparations for the lifting went ahead. A huge crowd gathered on both sides of the Straits. The wind blew, the tide raced. The first tube was to be guided into place between the Anglesey and Britannia piers, but as the tube swung into position, the capstan controlling the cable which was bringing the tube in towards the Anglesey bank broke catastrophically. The cable ran free, and it looked as though the pontoons carrying the tube would be swept downstream. Incredibly, the foreman in charge of the capstan grabbed the rope on the end of the cable and called to the spectators to help him. Hundreds of them rushed to help, and in the mother of all tug-of-war contests, they managed to pull the tube into position. All that remained was to lift the 1,500 tons of iron into place, and then repeat the operation three times. The Britannia Bridge opened fully in October 1850. There are only three other bridges built to this design on the planet, and they were all engineered by Stephenson; the slightly smaller Conway Bridge on the way to Anglesey was a dress rehearsal for the Britannia. Then there is one in Egypt, and one across the St Lawrence Seaway in Canada. And I was going through half of them! I was thrilled skinny.

The train broke down again just outside Llandudno Junction station. Clearly, whatever the compressor was compressing remained steadfastly amorphous. It was only twenty minutes this time before another engine was attached to the front of our train, and we were pulled ignominiously into the station, where three coaches were waiting in the car park to take us on to Holyhead. You have to hand it to Virgin Trains, they run one hell of a coach service. But there would be no Stephenson bridges for me.

There was a faint smell of sick on the coach. Sitting behind me were a couple of young women, one clearly a foreign student, a Canadian Chinese girl from the look and sound of her. Her English companion said, 'Well, you can't come to the UK and not experience the shambles of the train system.' Oh, how I agreed. How I wanted to get Richard

Branson's smirking beardy face and rub it in the sick stains on the carpet. We followed the A5/A55 through Bangor ('The City of Learning') and over the new bridge on to Anglesey. I didn't even get to see Telford's bridge. The girl sitting beside me was clearly depressed too. First, because no one ever likes sitting next to me on buses, and second, because she was going home to Holyhead.

'It's a nothing place,' she told me. 'I grew up here, and I've come back to visit me gran, cos she's not very well, but there's nothing here. No one ever goes into the town, they just get on to the boats.' Very much like Newhaven, I thought.

Venus was waiting to snap me as I climbed down from the coach in Holyhead. We shook hands, and made our way into the ferry terminal. I might have missed the Stephenson bridges, we might be going to the wrong port, but by God we were going for a lads' night out in Dublin, and we were going to enjoy it. Still huzzah!

We boarded the ship, a fast, modern and very large Super-Cat, called the *Jonathan Swift*. These new ships are like motorway service stations, but with a better view. They share a colour scheme; migraine turquoise, gum-disease pink. There is a huge car park. The catering facilities are very similar; a Burger King, a KFC, a shitty sandwich bar, a self-service restaurant which sells puddingy lasagne and grey sausages. There's a couple of bars, and I admit that you don't get those in service stations, but if you did, they'd be as horrible as these bars. There are shops that sell nasty things to give as presents to people that you'd forgotten to buy presents for. There are not terribly amusing amusement arcades, with the less cultured type of lorry driver playing fruit machines. There are airline-style seats. But, if you walk past all this, there is also a small rear-deck where you can stand and watch Holyhead fall away. And you can smoke there too. As the ship slipped her moorings, there were maybe fifty of us up on this rear-deck, smokers one and all.

Venus snapped some of the harbourside furniture; buoys beached on the breakwater, the rusting hulk of a tug. He snapped some of the passengers, especially some thirty-something lasses off for a good time in Dublin. They liked this very much; they played with their hair, and one of them gave Venus a most encouraging look from under her lashes.

'Forget it,' I said. 'You're married.'

'What?' he said, smiling.

'You big fat tart, you know what.'

'It is my birthday,' he said.

'Not till tomorrow.'

We stood on deck until the *Jonathan Swift* came out from the lee of Holy Island, happy to feel the rise and fall of the deck under our feet. We're nautical men, me and Mr Venus, Pisceans both. Salty dogs. It's in the blood. Well, not nautical, exactly. More what you'd call boaty. We've done a lot of trips together on canal boats, anyway. As we came into the Irish Sea proper, though, we were once again reminded of the difference between the salty stuff and the languid waters of the Shropshire Union Canal.

'Shit, those are big waves,' said Perry, as the boat started to dip and yaw in the massive swell. He turned a little pale.

'Shit, yes,' I said. 'Shall we go down?'

'God, yes.'

The sea was so big that we could barely make our way to the airline seats beside the picture windows. We gripped railings, and lurched from table to table, incidentally becoming intimate with several families who had had the good sense to be already sitting down before we hit the swell.

At last we managed to get sitting, and we held on to the edges of our seats for dear life. You could see the huge waves rolling towards the ship, striking us abreast, yawing and rocking the floating Hilton Park.

'I don't really like the sea,' said Perry, and I must admit, at that moment, neither did I.

'Do you remember that trip off Aberaeron?' he asked.

'Yes.'

We had taken our wives and my two children for an hour-long ride on a trip boat which ran off Aberaeron beach. It was a little boat, and very rough that day; Perry and I clung to the side of the boat and closed our eyes. When the boat landed, we were first off, and we stood on the beach shaking with fear, glad just to be alive. Our wives, and my two daughters, aged at that time three and twelve, decided it had been such fun that they would go again. We thought they were being most unwise, and rather than stand on the beach and watch our loved ones tossed on spumy waves, we slunk off to the pub for a reviver. I had forgotten this rather shameful episode until I found myself once again in rough seas with Mr Venus. In our defence, neither of us can swim.

Halfway through the trip, I thought I might try and have a fag. This meant retracing my steps, lurching into the same families, gripping the railings with both hands, and hauling myself on to the little observation/smoking deck.

Perry was grey-green, the colour of the sea. 'Don't leave me,' he whimpered.

'I need a fag,' I said. 'I can't stand it any more.'

'I'm coming with you.'

Our fellow passengers watched with a great deal of amusement as we lurched and staggered through the boat, climbed the stairs, and stepped out into a banshee gale. We held on to the bulwarks with one hand while we tried to light our fags with the other. Not easy in those conditions, but we managed it. There were two other smokers out there. The wind smoked most of our fags for us. I was happier out there, feeling that it would be handier for the lifeboats, but Perry was freezing, so we got back to our seats.

A stewardess, mysteriously unaffected by the Richter Scale Eight movement of the ship, came strolling casually by and gave us all sick bags. I didn't need mine; I wasn't sick, just scared. Perry didn't use his either, though he came very close. As we came in to the mouth of the Liffey and Dublin Port, and the sea became calmer, we wept with relief. We gathered our bags together and hurried down the gangway. Now we knew why they were called packet boats.

I've caught boats from Dublin Port before, and I have nothing against the place. It is modern, convenient and well organized. The only problem is, there's no trains, and I was looking for trains. To get into the centre of town, you can hail a taxi, or you can board a crowded bus with lots of other tourists. We got on the bus, standing room only, and rattled past warehouses and factories to the bus station by Connolly station. This cheered me up as I knew there would be trains in the morning.

It was snowing now, and Perry and I had no idea where we might stay. I knew a couple of cheap hotels up by the Joyce Museum, but in fact we tried the first hotel we came to, which was called Wynn's. Perry was still feeling sick, and although Wynn's looked expensive (and was), he'd had enough. We booked ourselves a twin room and smoked a reefer, as it is well known that spliff stops you feeling nauseous. At dinner-time, with Perry feeling a little revived, we walked across the river to Temple Bar to see if we could find ourselves something to eat. I fancied something half decent, so we went to a little restaurant that I had visited with my girlfriend only six months before, after our visit to Mulrany. Everyone else in there was in couples; Perry and I had a splendid little dinner *à deux*. Our heads almost touched in the dim candle-lit interior as we whispered to each other about what we were going to do in the morning. I don't know about Perry, but this dinner was the gayest thing that I've ever done.

Now we should have gone out on the pish in Temple Bar, but we were both feeling full and tired, so we went back to Wynn's Hotel, watched a little TV, and fell asleep. Lightweights, these days, both of us.

I had now retraced the journey of a nineteenth-century MP heading back from London to Ireland, except that I had been on a lot more replacement bus services and had ended up in entirely the wrong place. After breakfast, we headed for Connolly station, so that we could at least ride the Dublin to Kingstown line. Our boat was scheduled to leave Dun Laoghaire that afternoon, and I was not going to be fobbed off. So far as was possible, I was determined that this time there would be no fuck-ups.

Connolly station was not the terminus of the Dublin and Kingstown Railway, but it was the nearest to the hotel, and we didn't need to be anal. After the disappointments of the day before, at least we were back on a train again, after all. The line I wanted to travel is now a constituent part of the DART, the Dublin Area Rapid Transport system, which carries 80,000 passengers a day, at least half of them over the line of the Dublin and Kingstown. We stood on the platform, waiting for the first train south. The DART trains are green and boxy; wider than those on the island of Great Britain.

We got in the train; this was a Saturday, and there were not many passengers heading south. There were a couple of girls, a gaggle of youths, and a filthy old tramp with his boots off and his stockinged feet up on the seat in front of him, drinking vodka and orange from an old squash bottle. We knew it was vodka and orange, because every few minutes he would get out a bottle of vodka and add it to the orange squash. He was smoking a dog-end. There was a sign above his head saying, 'Seats are not for feet. No Smoking'. He was talking to himself in a voice full of hate: 'Click-clock, Click-clock. Clocking click. Clicking clock.'

His voice sounded like Father Jack's, and as the journey went on, Venus and I became convinced that he really was Father Jack on a jaunt from Craggy Island up to Dublin for the day.

We crossed the Liffey and came to Pearse Street station, built on the site of the original station buildings. We were now on the line I had come to see, Ireland's oldest, and the world's first real commuter line. The bigger ships were unable to get into Dublin Port, despite the extraordinary two-mile-long pier which extends from the mouth of the Liffey into the Irish Sea. Kingstown was also a burgeoning holiday resort for well-to-do Dubliners, though one of the many objectors to the line thought it preposterous that people would want to travel as far as six miles for a swim and a breath of fresh air.

The contractor chosen to build the line was William Dargan, whose name had been put forward by Telford; Dargan had been a contractor on the Chester to Holyhead road, and Telford thought highly of his work. The line was to be built largely along the shoreline, and, in a revolutionary break with all previous railway practice, stations were to be built in key residential areas. The promoters of the line, like all early railway promoters, were not really expecting great volumes of passenger traffic, apart from the MPs and a few well-heeled travellers who currently used the stage-coaches, so it was particularly far-sighted to put in these intermediate stations. Early railways were designed for long-distance traffic and were built with few stations, all of which were spaced far apart. The Dublin and Kingstown Railway was the first to build lots of stations close together.

As soon as the line opened in 1834, it was swamped with passengers. Suburban communities sprang into life alongside the line; the novelist Charles Lever wrote of the line that

The 8.30 a.m. is filled with attorneys; the ways of Providence are inscrutable; it arrives safely in Dublin. With the 9.00 train come fresh jovial looking fellows with bushy whiskers and geraniums in buttonholes. They are traders. 9.30 is the housekeepers' train. 10.00 the barristers – fierce faces look out at the weather . . . 11 o'clock, the men of wit and pleasure.

In its first year, a million passengers were carried on the line. Now it has been subsumed into the line of the DART, but all along its length, you can see the communities which owe their existence to this revolutionary length of rail.

The tramp was a classic of his ilk. As we came out of Pearse Street station and passed over the Grand Canal Dock, he was beginning to take the Father Jack thing very seriously indeed.

'Click-clock, clicking clock. YA FECKER! Ya blirt ya, ya FECKING CONT! Ya bastard clicking clocking BLIRT! YA FECKERS! Ya bastard click clock click clock stuff ya, YA FECKING BASTARDS!'

And so on.

It is not nice to laugh at people who are less fortunate than yourself. Perry and I were well-brought-up lads. Now we are *Independent*-reading liberals. We are not the kind of folk who laugh at tramps. Perry and I had done very well. We did not giggle at the virtuoso display of swearing skills. We looked at the Lansdowne Road rugby stadium, hard by the track. We looked for the evidence of Dargan's original line; the Italianate bridge and bathing place built by the promoters of the railway to appease Baron Cloncurry, who did not want the thing running through his land unless his right to bathe in peace was guaranteed. We gazed at the fantastic views over Dublin Bay that the commuters who have been using this line for almost 170 years have been lucky enough to enjoy on their way to work every morning. But swearing is funny. Old people who disapprove of it don't know what they're missing. And this guy was the Mozart, the Shakespeare of swearing. And the absolute highlight of the old milestone inspector's peroration was when he actually shouted, 'ARSE!', exactly like Father Jack. Perhaps this was the very tramp that the writers of *Father Ted* had based Jack on. Venus and I could stand it no longer; from trying to hold in our laughter in a restrained, middle-aged educated men kind of way, now we were cacking our pants. We wept. We shrieked. All the other passengers, much too polite to take any notice of the old man, turned around and looked at us in disapproval. We were relieved when the train pulled into Dun Laoghaire (previously Kingstown) some twenty minutes after leaving Connolly. We stood on the platform, taking deep breaths, regaining our composure.

'What now?' said Perry.

'That's it,' I said.

'What, that? We came all this way to go twenty minutes on a half-empty suburban train? For my birthday?'

'Yeah.'

'Are you sick in the head?'

'No. It's a commuter train. The first commuter train. Commuter journeys are generally short journeys.'

'Right.'

We walked from the station across a car park to the smart new ferry terminal building at Dun Laoghaire. Our sailing had been cancelled due to rough weather. This was good, because it supported our view that our crossing of the previous day had indeed been a bit like rounding Cape Horn in a ship's gig. But it was bad, because there wasn't another sailing for five hours; even then, it would sail only if the wind abated.

'What shall we do?' said Perry.

There didn't seem to be much to pass the time for five hours in the ferry terminal, unless we followed the example of a couple of severely hungover lasses, who slept prettily on seating in the departure lounge.

'I know. We'll go visit the Martello Tower.' Venus is the only person I know who got right to the end of *Ulysses*. Well, that's not quite true. I've got a copy, yes, and I got to the end, yes, to Molly Bloom's soliloquy. And I got to the bottom of the first page, Buck Mulligan in the Martello Tower, kidneys smelling of urine, etc. It was the bit in between that I skipped. Perry's done the whole thing. Several times. So a visit to the Martello Tower was his idea of fun. After all, it was his birthday. I'm just like that, I guess; the kind of guy who's willing to go the extra mile for a friend. We walked back to Dun Laoghaire station, and asked what stop we should get off at for the Martello Tower.

'Sandycove. It's the next stop. It's only an extra mile. You'd be quicker walking.'

'No thanks. We'll take the train.'

We waited for the train. Four lads were playing football on the platform, and, unsurprisingly, given current British and Irish form, they consistently lost control of the ball, which dropped from the platform on to the tracks. One of their number would check to see if there was a train coming, then hop down on to the rails to rescue the ball. We watched this inept display until our train came, and then we went another stop, and walked down towards the Martello Tower. Perry was thrilled, he really was. And I could dig going to Joyce's Martello Tower. It might give me much needed ammunition if I ever had to pretend to have read the thing.

It was a long walk, much more than an extra mile, even after taking the one-stop ride from Dun Laoghaire. The snow of the previous day had not waited around, and we walked in brilliant late-winter sunshine. A stiff Force 5 wind rasped off the sea. It was very cold, and my bag was full of heavy railway books. We walked along the promenade at Sandycove and up a short climb to the little headland where the Martello Tower stands. It was closed.

Poor old Perry. It was his birthday, and here we were standing outside the Martello Tower from *Ulysses*, and there was no way we were getting in. I didn't know what to say to the lad. The only thing that would cheer him up would be some fat lasses covered in goose grease for him to take intimate photographs of . . . but where were we going to find anything like that on a freezing cold winter's morning on the shores of Dublin Bay?

Well, the Lord moves in mysterious ways. Just around the corner from the Martello Tower is the Gentlemen's Forty Foot Bathing Place.

We saw the sign and were intrigued. We followed steps down to the sea, past some Art Deco changing huts. There was a boulder, presumably forty feet high. And there, diving from the boulder into an icy sea, were several big old girls covered in goose grease. They went in colleen-coloured, swam a few strokes to the bottom of the steps, and emerged a glorious salmon-pink. It was Perry heaven. Despite the freezing cold, these plucky Irish girls were happily diving into the waves for him to photograph. There were men, too, elderly guys in Speedos, also covered in goose grease. They were less easy on the eye, but Perry snapped them too. He suggested that for the next twenty-five years or so, we visit places which have a tradition of Christmas sea-bathing, one a year, and then write a book about them. Genius. Anyway, the moral of this story is that somewhere close to a railway there is a little bit of heaven just waiting for you. All you need to know is which station to get off at.

Back at Dun Laoghaire, we found out that the next boat had not been cancelled; the wind had dropped sufficiently for the sailing to go ahead. We were glad, as our cash had run out and we were tired after our uneventful morning. The HSS *Explorer* was another floating service station. I stood on the deck and watched Ireland slip away behind us. Perhaps no sea voyage is more poignant than this, the leaving of Ireland. Millions of emigrants had stood on ships and watched these shores disappear over the horizon. Now only Perry and I were up on the deck to see it go; everyone else was hiding away below deck, queuing up for Burger Kings. I wished more people were up here with us, taking real time out, watching the sea, watching the land recede. Why are Burger Kings better than this? You can get them anywhere, but this was something to behold. We went downstairs for a beer after the last trace of land had faded from sight, and met an old Irish guy at the bar.

'Ah, sure, they were rubbish, the auld boats. I remember the Irish Mail, terrible old hulk. It took bloody ages to load the thing, and all by hand. And nothing to do on the boat except sit. Then you'd get to Holyhead, and there'd be a filthy dirty auld steam train to take you to Crewe. Took bloody hours, it did. It's much better now. You can get a drink, and a bite to eat, and when you get to the other side, there's those marvellous new trains. Do you know, there's even a thing where you can plug in the headphones of your Walkman and listen to the radio?'

My romanticism wilted, but did not wither away entirely. I would still rather stand on the deck and feel the wind in my face than sit cooped up in front of a fillum or a fruit machine. But then, I'm a tourist.

Back in Holyhead, there was one more thing I wanted to do. I was driving back to mid-Wales with Perry to stay at his place, but he agreed that I could catch the train as far as Bangor, so that I could do the Britannia Bridge. I got on to one of the modern Sprinter trains, and noticed that the guy on the boat was right; there was a socket for headphones. That was a railway pastime unknown to the author of *The Railway Traveller's Handy Book*. I didn't have any headphones, so I sat and looked out of the window. It was late afternoon and the light was fading fast. It was dark by the time we reached the Menai Straits; I caught a glimpse of Telford's floodlit road bridge as we entered the Britannia's tube, but of the Britannia, other than a momentary darkness, I saw nothing. Of course, you never really do, from the train. You're inside a tube. At least I could say that I had been over it.

Perry was waiting for me at Bangor station; he took some photos of the London Midland and Scottish Railway company crest that still adorns the waiting room.

'Thanks for that, mate,' I said.

'No problem. Mon called.'

'Did she?'

'Yeah. She said you'd forgotten your mobile.'

' 'S'right. I gave her your number instead. How is she?'

'Fine. She asked me where you were.'

'What did you tell her?'

'I told her you were on the train.'

Lancaster the Pretty Way

I knew that I had to be there in Lancaster for Madeleine's surprise fortieth birthday party. That was one I didn't want to miss. Madeleine is married to my good friend Saleel Nurbhai. Madeleine and Saleel (their friends call them either M and S or S and M, depending on mood) kept me alive for almost two years while I lived in a caravan and wrote a book, and I owe them a lot. Saleel phoned to invite me to the do and I promised him that I would be there. I lived in Lancaster for thirteen years, longer than I've lived anywhere, and I miss my friends there, so I've been back a fair bit since I moved away. Now I was going again. Another trip on the London and Birmingham? Yet another jaunt up the Grand Junction to Warrington Bank Quay, Wigan North Western, Preston, Lancaster?

I looked at my maps. I still had a lot of colouring in to do. There were whole tangled skeins of railways I had yet to unknot. In a lifetime of travelling about on trains, surely I should be able to run the marker pen over more lines than this? If I died tomorrow, would this be my legacy? Would my children, while sorting out my things, look at my railway map and say, 'Blimey, he never did the whole of the Settle–Carlisle Line. He never got beyond Barrow-in-Furness, the stupid old fool, and he fancied himself as a bit of a line basher. I'm afraid Father's was a wasted life.'

So this time I thought I might go the pretty way, like you do sometimes. Instead of going from Euston to Lancaster direct, I wanted to go from King's Cross to Leeds, get a quick look at the Middleton, then on from Leeds over the Settle–Carlisle Line, from Carlisle down to Barrow on the Cumbrian Coast Line, with a swift detour up the miniature-gauge Ravenglass and Eskdale, and from Barrow around Morecambe Bay; and so to Lancaster. Lancaster to Euston would be a perfectly acceptable return trip. I reasoned that I might be a bit too hungover after the party to bugger about on another colouring-in exercise.

But you try going to King's Cross and telling them you want to go the pretty way when you're buying your ticket.

'That's not just pretty,' said the trying-to-be-helpful young lady on the ticket desk, looking at a map, 'that's perverse.'

'Yes, I know, but that's what I want to do.'

'You could get a train from Euston direct to Carlisle.'

'I'm not going to Carlisle, I'm going to Lancaster, and I want to go via Leeds, Carlisle and Barrow-in-Furness. Then I want to come back to London.'

'Well, I don't think I can sell you a ticket. It's not a valid route. I'll have to sell you a ticket to Leeds, and then you can buy the other tickets as you go.'

This reminds me of my favourite joke. There's a guy who runs a Chinese restaurant in Bognor Regis, who thinks that he hasn't been home to see his old mum for a few years. So he goes down to Bognor station and asks for a single to Beijing.

'I can't sell you that here,' says the booking-office clerk. 'I can sell you a ticket to London, perhaps they can sort you out there.'

In London, the guy asks for a single to Beijing, but the ticket clerk can only sell him a ticket to Paris. In Paris they sell him a ticket for Berlin, in Berlin a ticket for Moscow, and in Moscow they finally manage to sell him a ticket to Beijing, via the trans-Manchurian. He stays with his family for a few months before he thinks he'd better get back to his business. So he goes down to Beijing station and asks for a single to Bognor Regis.

'Certainly, sir,' says the ticket clerk. 'Don't forget to change at Barnham.'

Admittedly, this is only really funny if you live in Bognor.

I had a weapon in my armoury which the guy from Bognor clearly didn't know about, and which the ticket seller was clearly not expecting.

'Have you checked the *National Routing Guide*?'

She blanched under her fake tan. 'N . . . no.' She was scared, and rightly so. The *National Routing Guide* is a work of such fearsome complexity that it makes Hegel's *Phenomenology of the Spirit* read like Dr Seuss. You should mention it if you ever want to scare booking-office staff.

'Well, could you?'

'I . . . I've never had to use it before. Hang on.' She disappeared into the back office and emerged with an ancient BR hand, obviously kept on for just such an emergency.

'What route is it you're after?' the old boy croaked.

I told him, and, shaking his head, he took the young ticket seller over to the locked cabinet where the *National Routing Guide* was kept. Now came a period of quiet contemplation. The queue behind me was growing both longer and more annoyed. I watched the two ticket sellers, one young and bright, the other infinitely old and wise, as they pored over the *Routing Guide*, trying to make sense of the index, desperately flicking over the pages, he running bony fingers down incomprehensible columns, she reading over his shoulder and trying to follow his reasoning. Twenty minutes passed before they looked up with a smile of triumph, and she came back to me. Ye Olde Booking Office Clerke shuffled into the back office.

'That *is* a valid route,' said the young ticket seller, triumphant from her gargantuan struggle. 'I *can* sell you a ticket!'

'I don't suppose you can sell me a ticket which includes the Ravenglass and Eskdale Railway, can you?'

Her face fell. 'I'm sorry?'

'I wondered if you could sell me a special ticket which includes the Ravenglass and Eskdale? It's a miniature railway, in Cumbria.' I smiled around at the fuming queue.

She sighed, and went into the back office, presumably to reawaken the ancient sage.

She was much quicker this time. 'No,' she said.

'Never mind, I'll get a ticket on the day. Do you accept euros?'

'Er . . . hang on. I'll ask.' Her teeth were gritted.

'No, don't bother. I just wondered.'

So I managed to buy a ticket which was valid for the most arcane route possible. You just have to ask.

Madeleine's surprise birthday party was due to start at 7.30 on Saturday evening, and I intended to take two days to get there; I left my house in North London at nine on the Friday morning. The train from Euston normally takes three hours; it was, I suppose, as though I had volunteered to take one of those horrific post-Hatfield journeys that meandered about the countryside and took nineteen hours to get wherever you were going. I have always enjoyed departure and the journey much more than arrival; in particular I like journeying slowly through England, that most foreign of places, home.

Something was clearly wrong the moment I turned up at King's Cross. In King's Cross, I always feel lost. There's a queueing system that I can't get hold of. The queues snake around the concourse and block the view of the too small and confused departure board. And the working girls always hassle me; I think I must look like a punter.

On this Friday morning the queues were as long as I'd seen them, doubling back on themselves, filling the station. I fought my way to the departures board, where I learned that the overhead wires had been blown down in the night, and no one could say when the next train would run. There is, and has been for years, a lot of fuss about the electrification of the West Coast main line. It cost hundreds of millions to electrify the line in the 1960s, and now it is being upgraded again – current projections estimate that the upgrade will cost £13 billion. Nothing like so much money was spent on the East Coast main line.

In fact, the electrification of the East Coast main line was carried out by a sparky called Frank, and was achieved using little more than old fuse wire supported on coat hangers. The whole thing cost £27, which was a lot of money in those days. Unfortunately, Frank had never taken on a project of this scale before (up until then, his biggest job had been rewiring a scout hut in Dunstable), and no one had told him that wind occasionally blows on the east side of Britain. The slightest puff of wind, therefore, brings down the catenary. Regular passengers on the East Coast line are beset with this no-wires-in-the-wind problem. And on the Friday of my departure for Madeleine's surprise party, once again the wind had brought them whipping down. There were no trains to Leeds, and little prospect of any; I had to be in Leeds by 12.30 to make sure of my quick trip to the Middleton Railway, before making my connection on to the Settle–Carlisle line.

But I'm a wily old railway bird, so I pushed through the bemused crowds on the concourse, checked with the information desk that my ticket would be valid on Midland Main Line, strolled through the underpass to St Pancras, and hopped on to a train for Sheffield, from which station, I naively trusted, connections to Leeds would be regular, fast and reliable.

Midland Main Line is my boss TOC because it still has smoking carriages. This fine institution has largely gone from the railway now. Why? Because they cost more money to clean than non-smoking carriages. The TOCs insist it's because there is no demand; tell this to the brave souls who stage a smoking protest in the buffet car on the London to Brighton train every night. The demand is there, and I fail to see the problem. After all, as it says in *The Railway Traveller's Handy Book*: 'some lines have smoking carriages provided where the enjoyment may be indulged in *without giving offence to others*; he, therefore, who is inconsolable on the journey in the absence of his beloved weed, should take care to acquaint himself with the fact whether there are smoking carriages or not.'

In the National Railway Museum, I saw carriages with signs on compartment windows saying, *Smoking – Players Please!* Nowadays, at Baker Street station on the Underground there are signs saying, *No Smoking – with Nicorettes!* It's called progress, I suppose.

As for those bastards who come and sit in the tiny handful of smoking carriages that are left and go, 'Pooh, it's so smoky in here,' or 'Hack hack hack, what a filthy habit,' and wave their porcelain hands in front of their darling sensitive noses, I say this: stay away. We are not 'giving offence to others'. We are locked in a freezing box miles from the buffet. We are not here for fun. It says *Smoking* quite clearly on the window. Go and sit elsewhere. All the other carriages are non-smoking. And yes, of course it's smoky in here. We like it that way; we spend a lot of money making it smoky. It's a smoking carriage. If smokers can put up with not smoking in non-smoking carriages, then surely non-smokers can return the courtesy, and only come in to a smoking carriage if they want a tab. Otherwise, fuck off.

Anyway, the ride from London up to Derby would drive anyone to fags, not to mention drink. It is not pretty. Is 'toilet' too strong a word for Luton? The train hurried through the Bedfordshire brickfields, and into Northamptonshire, where it stopped at Kettering, swings capital of the world. Not swing, you note (that's probably St Louis, Chicago or New Orleans), but swings, for Kettering is home to Wickstead Park, where a vast percentage of the world's playground equipment is manufactured. Many a bottle of White Lightning cider has been drunk on Wickstead Park swings.

The trainspotters were out in force in Leicester; thirty or forty of them. I spotted the train they had come to spot, and for once I was impressed. A massive Deltic diesel engine was sitting in Leicester station with its accompanying trainload of enthusiasts.

Those things are big; I thought of the prototype that I'd seen dominating the Turn-table Hall at the NRM. They only made twenty-two, but I still didn't write down the number of this one. I do like them, though; throbbing, powerful beasts, these babies deliver a great surge of power, etc.

North of Leicester, you stand to see one in the line of power stations which runs all down the Trent valley, and that's on a good day. We crossed the river by Long Eaton and headed north for Derby, where the ride picks up. But if you are looking for romance and charm, then it is thin on the ground. Derby is a fascinating railwayscape, with strange engines, experimental wagons and laboratory coaches filed on the tracks, but it is not pretty. I couldn't make judgement as to whether my friend on the Tal-y-Llyn was right not to want to move here, though. I still think it would have to be very grim to be worse than privatization.

Three women passengers got on at Derby and came and sat at the table next to mine. They were big lasses and Herculean smokers, wheezing and coughing and arguing. They argued about fags, about £4 that one party owed another, about the forthcoming excitement of the next day's lottery draw. They did not strike me as especially bright, although I could not help but admire the way they each added a vodka miniature to their cans of Guinness. They would have made a much more convincing fist of the gonzo trip to the Tal-y-Llyn than Perry and I could ever hope to, I suspected. Certainly, they were not impressed by the few sights that are worth looking at from the train window; star of the show, the twisted spire of Chesterfield church. I looked at my watch and wondered if I was going to make the Middleton railway, in Hunslet, which I guessed would be a fifteen-minute cab ride from Leeds station.

When the train arrived in Sheffield, I discovered that the whole station was in the process of major refurbishment, and information was thin on the ground. There did not seem to be any departure boards, nothing about which train was going from which platform. By the time I found a uniformed person, it was just in time for her to point to the departing train for Leeds. I asked her the time of the next train to Leeds; it would not go for an hour. My train from Leeds to Carlisle via Settle departed at 14.49; my train from Sheffield to Leeds would get me there two minutes before it was due to go. If I missed it, if the train from Sheffield didn't run dead on time, then there wouldn't be another train for two hours, and that would be too late, as there seemed little point in travelling over Britain's most scenic and romantic railway in the dark, especially since I'd already done both the Forth Rail and Britannia Bridges by night, and had found the experiences anti-climactic.

In the good old days, if you had two minutes to make your connection, you wouldn't have worried. You would know that the station-master would hold the connecting train until your train got in. But since privatization, this is a common courtesy which has gone out of the window. The TOCs get fined every time one of their trains is late. So they never hold up connections under any circumstances. I've often arrived at Lancaster from London on the last train which connects with the train to Barrow. It's a tidy step from London to Lancaster, even by the direct route, and with the best will in the world, the train can be ten minutes late. So passengers for Barrow are buggered. You see them fuming at station staff who've watched the last train happily set off, dead on time, two minutes before the train from London gets in. Then, after a lot of shouting, the staff arrange taxis for the sixty-mile road journey to Barrow.

This, of course, is insane, the product of a disordered mind. Let's say it again; the trains have never really run at a huge profit. They are part of a transport infrastructure. They exist to move people and goods from point A to point B, not to make money. Money spent on the roads is an investment, but money spent on the railways is a subsidy. Politicians are scared of motorists, but not of train travellers. The TOCs exist to make money; many of them are owned by large multi-nationals. Politicians are scared of large multinationals, but not of their own citizens. So the TOCs can do what they like as long as they keep their profits up, profits which come from public investment, sorry, subsidy. That's why, if your train is late, your connection has gone.

I didn't feel that I could risk it, so I went to stand in the taxi queue outside Sheffield station. I got chatting to the guy behind me. He was a returning back-packer. He'd just got in from a year in India and Nepal. He told me that the worst part of the journey from Kathmandu to Sheffield was the train from Heathrow home. I believed him. He said that he had kept a scrupulous diary of his trip, and was thinking of turning it into a book. I told him I was a travel writer.

'Where have you been?' he asked.

'Well, I'm there now. Sheffield. And later, Leeds and Carlisle.' I could see that he wasn't impressed. When I got to the front of the taxi queue, the driver told me that it would be fifty nicker to go to Leeds. So I decided to take the train anyway, but I knew it would be a close-run thing.

I can't say that I enjoyed the run from Sheffield to Leeds. It was a Virgin Cross Country train; this one was from Penzance to Newcastle. The nearer you get to a city, the more plastic bags you see hanging in bushes and trees, and in the South and West Yorkshire conurbation, you are never really out of the city as such, so the plastic bags hang like over-ripe fruit from the shrivelled shrubs by the lineside pretty much everywhere. I looked at my watch as we pulled in to Wakefield. We were still on time.

My mobile gibbered. It was my girlfriend.

'Hello?'

'Hello, darling. Where are you?'

'I'm on the train.'

'I'd like to welcome passengers aboard the 14.19 from Wakefield Westgate to Newcastle, calling at Leeds . . .'

'Hello? Who's that?'

'York, Darlington and Durham, arriving in Newcastle at . . .'

'It's our train manager. His name's David.'

'17.23. We'd also like to take this opportunity to remind passengers . . .'

'He's very loud.'

'. . . that smoking is not permitted anywhere on the train, this includes the lavatories and . . .'

'Yes, he is loud. He says this at every stop.'

'. . . vestibules. First class is in coaches A and B, and the quiet carriage is coach . . .'

'What is a train manager, anyway?'

'. . . C. Buffet facilities are available on this train for teas . . .'

'The guard. Guards became train managers at around the same time we stopped being second-class passengers and became standard-class customers.'

'. . . coffees, snacks and light refreshments. We thank you for travelling with . . .'

'I can't really hear you, darling. He's too loud.'

'. . . Virgin Cross Country today, and we hope . . .'

'I'll call you from Carlisle . . . hello?'

'. . . that you have a pleasant journey.'

She had gone; I got back to looking at my watch.

I made that connection, after all that fuss. The train was due to leave at 14.49; at 14.48, my train pulled into Leeds, and I broke the rule of a lifetime and ran for a train (what passes for running with me, anyway). Normally, my main exercise is going over to the pub for some fags; not only did the tightness of the connection force me to break into a trot, it stopped me from having a fag, since I was back in the land of the no-smoking carriage.

And I'd missed my planned visit to the Middleton Railway, which is not so much a restored line as the last of the independent coalmine railways from which the rest of the system evolved. This was the first line to get Parliamentary assent, in 1743. Steam engines started running on this line in 1812. The railway is still running today, just as much of a maverick as it has been for almost 250 years; it's the only volunteer railway line which survives by carrying commercial goods traffic, and I had wanted to see it very much. A line basher needs to be optimistic, but high winds and bad information had failed me, and I had run out of time. All I could do was jump on the train for Carlisle.

The train was full. The line follows the course of the Leeds and Liverpool Canal as it leaves Leeds; Kirkstall Abbey is the sure sign that you have left the ugly old city. Shouldn't be too harsh; the day was grey and wet, and I suppose everything looks better in the summer sun. Besides, one way and another, I lived in Lancashire for thirteen years. I went to Lancaster University, I support Lancashire at cricket and I have the Lancastrian aversion to all things Yorkshire. And I'm not *really* Lancastrian, so I have the zealous fervour of a convert, too. I always look forward to crossing the border. On this part of the trip, surrounded by Yorkshireness, I was, for the first time on a train, suddenly gripped by fear. What if the driver does a SPAD? What is a SPAD anyway? What if some nutter has left breeze-blocks on the line? What if a car driver, exhausted from knocking one off on the internet all night, falls asleep and drives his vehicle off a bridge and into the path of our train? The statistics insist that rail is the safest way to travel, but the horror stories get to you sometimes. And the accidents, though very rare, do happen. I was really worried, before deciding that it was just the normal foreboding that I feel whenever I'm in Yorkshire.

But almost as soon as the train left Leeds, the journey picked up. The sprawl of cities and industrial towns which had lasted almost unbroken since Sheffield gave way to the first glimpse of real Yorkshire country-side: high hills, fast-running streams and bright green fields. The small mill towns which straddle the gap between the railway and the canal are lively and attractive. Shipley, just outside Leeds, still has heavy industry, but the mills are on a human scale, and I feel that I would much rather work there than in Sheffield's cavernous steel plants. But then, I'd rather ponce about on trains with a notebook than go back to work in any factory. The writer's life does have drawbacks, but they are almost entirely financial. Even nice-looking factories I always found hellholes to work in, and no amount of money would get me back. But if I had to, say if a bloke had a gun held to my head, I would go for one of these small mill towns; the model village Saltaire, the canal town Bingley, or Keighley, where the preserved Worth Valley Railway meets the main line.

If ever you are in Keighley, incidentally, you can get great pies from the butchers, the like of which I've never come across anywhere else. They are steak and kidney pies, but they have cold crust pastry (like you get on pork pies), and they are truly fantastic. It's not so bad really, is Yorkshire.

At Gargrave, we made an unscheduled stop. The guard announced that it was 'a special stop for a gentleman who missed his connection'. So I felt extra guilty about my fulminating about the connection at Leeds. Something of the spirit of the old country railway, which existed to serve communities and passengers rather than shareholders and fat-arsed investment bankers, still survives. The gentleman was a cyclist, and he carried his bike over the footbridge, whether to wait for a train to take him back to where he should have got off, or whether to cycle off lycra-clad into the Dales, I could not tell.

The mill towns had all dropped away, and we were out in real countryside now. Most of the passengers had got off the train; from being almost full when we left Leeds, there were now only a few dozen passengers left. Tarred black plate layers' huts appeared from time to time along the lineside. The train pulled into Hellifield station, a personal favourite of mine. This must have been an important station once, with a large engine shed and four platforms, but it is out in the middle of nowhere, and if you did not know the long-gone importance of this line, it would be difficult to see why Hellifield needed such a grand station. Intricate wrought-iron columns support a glass canopy. Country stations with an extant Victorian glass canopy in original condition are as rare as hens' teeth, so British Rail wanted to knock it down. Railtrack, to their credit, I suppose, saved it; not from any high ideals about the preservation of the railway's heritage, but because they saw an opportunity to make a few bob out of it. They leased the waiting rooms to a restaurant; and better that than to see Hellifield fall into ruin.

At Settle Junction, the Settle–Carlisle line left the line from Leeds to Carnforth, and we were on the craziest and certainly most romantic mainline railway in Britain. In the 1860s, the Midland Railway, the mighty Midland, had felt left out. The other big train companies had main lines to Scotland. Why couldn't they? It wasn't fair. And all the coastal routes were taken. They thought they'd spotted a gap through the hills. It should be possible, their engineers argued, to build a railway to link the Ribble and Eden valleys. Then they could connect with their lines from Leeds to Lancaster, and from Leeds to Sheffield, Derby, Leicester and London. They would be able to run trains from St Pancras through to St Enoch in Glasgow. They were the biggest company, and the best. Their directors felt they deserved their new main line, the third to be built connecting London and Scotland. They started construction in 1870.

Six years later, when work had finished, the seventy-two miles of line had cost £3.5 million, making it by far the most expensive mainline railway built in Britain, mile for mile. Expensive in lives, too. It has been estimated that during the line's construction something like 300 men were killed. That's about one a week. No one knows exactly how many died, as the navvies were seen as largely disposable, so no accurate count was taken. At least 100 lie buried in the churchyard of St Leonard's, at Chapel-le-dale. There is a plaque in the churchyard, 'To the memory of those who through accident lost their lives in constructing the railway works between Settle and Denthead, 1869–1876'.

The line crosses the moors, the deadly moors, through immense tunnels and on breathtaking viaducts. It was never a huge success. When the Midland got their main line, they still couldn't compete with the London and North-Western in terms of journey times between London and Glasgow. The company tried to sell the route by virtue of the Midland's high degrees of comfort, with limited success. In the British Rail Development Plan of 1967, it was decided that the line had no future. In 1970, British Rail closed all the stations on the line except Appleby and Settle. In 1981, British Rail announced their intention to close the line, citing the cost of maintaining the Ribblehead Viaduct. A vocal and intelligent protest group campaigned to save it. National publicity brought increased passenger numbers to the Settle–Carlisle, and in 1989 the government agreed that the line should be 'developed and maintained'.

The line serves two useful functions. It brings much-needed public transport to remote rural areas, which otherwise would have to rely on buses. And it offers an alternative to the West Coast main line, when that overworked railway has to be closed for maintainence or resignalling. Good reasons for saving the line. For me, though, it is the men who dropped dead on Blea Moor for whom we need to keep this line running. If the line had been closed, the little meaning that the navvies' deaths may have had would have been thrown away for nothing.

Settle station was like a Gothic cottage. John Ruskin's support for the Gothic style did not extend to railway stations, despite the fact that St Pancras is probably both the best and best-loved Victorian Gothic building in Britain.

Another of the strange and evil tendencies of the present day is to the decoration of the railroad station. Now, if there be any place in the world in which people are deprived of that portion of temper and discretion which is necessary to the contemplation of beauty, it is there. It is the very temple of discomfort, and the only charity the builder can extend to us is to show us, plainly as may be, how soonest to escape from it.

Ruskin didn't approve of railways; in the same passage from *The Seven Lamps of Architecture* he says, 'No one would travel in that manner who could help it.' How much more he would have hated the car, the motorway, the screaming bright interior of a service station at four in the morning.

Oh, but this was good weather to be high in the hills, and wrapped up warm in a railway carriage. The line climbs over 1,000 feet on the twenty-mile 'Long Drag' from Settle to Ais Gill. The very high winds that blew down the wires on the East Coast line had grown wilder as the day lengthened. A day like this – black clouds flying in from the west, sleet beating against the train, snow on Pen-y-Ghent and Ingleborough, high wild winds – was the kind of day the navvies worked in to build this line. They would have had better days in this mountain country, forcing their way through heather to find whin-berries, watching butterflies on the limestone pavement, the sky high blue, but nothing could compensate for conditions like this.

The train was rocking in the wind, and the clouds were looking blacker by the second. New storms were coming over. I watched rabbits chasing one another in the fields. My ears popped, we had climbed so high. This may be Yorkshire, but I love this part of the Dales so much that I've always thought of it as a kind of honorary Lancashire. The train rocked its way into Ribblehead station. Nothing here has been modernized; the whole line has retained its original signage; all that has changed is that there are more passengers now.

In front of us was the Ribblehead Viaduct, one of the seven wonders of the railway; high, long and curving over the head-waters of this most Lancastrian of rivers. Then I remembered that we were in Yorkshire, and the dread came over me again. That viaduct was very long, and the winds were very high. It is highly inaccessible; if you look around you at the empty hills and stark moorland, it is difficult to imagine people here at all; but if you turn around and look over your shoulder, you see this great thing, bridging the hills, reminding me of nothing so much as Hadrian's Wall on its lonely march over the Northumbrian Fells.

The best was yet to come, after the long Blea Moor Tunnel. Rocking in the wind, the train flies over Dentdale on a shorter but higher viaduct. God's country, the South Surrey Hills, the Welsh Border, North Devon, Dentdale. However you approach this bowl in the landscape, you can't help but be overawed. A concatenation of stone-walled fields, tumbledown barns and streams, always seen at first from above, and always sunlit; even today, the sun breaks through the cloud for a moment to light up the valley.

The train pulled into Dent station, and I looked for my friends Kath and Duane's house, a little way down the long road from the station, the highest mainline station in Britain. It is isolated on the side of a mountain, and the village is hidden in the valley. This was the furthest I'd ever been on this line.

A few summers ago, I came out here with Chas, my evil sidekick and piano-player. We came out to a party at Kath and Duane's. Chas's van was *hors de combat* (no great surprise there), so we caught the train across from Lancaster, changed at Hellifield, and boogied up to Dent, carrying Chas's electronic organ between us. As much as anything, this signified our desperation for a gig. But still. We like playing at hippy parties, too. I'm fairly sure that Kath and Duane won't be offended if I describe them as hippies. After all, hippies is what they are. But what about 'old hippies'? Would that be testing the boundaries of friendship too far? How about 'first-wave' hippies? Might that suit the case? When I first met Duane, slender as a bird, shrivelled as a speed freak's bollocks, his hair as white as Hoffman's bicycle, I said to him, by way of small talk, 'What do you do?'

He closed his eyes, sucked at a large chillum packed with his excellent home-grown, pulled more air into his raddled lungs, held his breath, exhaled a jet of THC-deficient smoke, opened his eyes, and said, 'Breath work.'

He twinkled at me, a broad smile on his sunbrowned face. Which shut me up.

He's also an ex-MP, I happen to know. That's military police to you, sunshine. Also, that he was not christened Duane; he changed his name because in his long-distant youth, he was a huge fan of Duane Eddy. He is high in the top ten coolest guys I know.

And Kath I owe my life to. One miserable Glastonbury, a bitter cold and wet one, with thigh-deep mud, and mine and Chas's show in the Theatre Field both a critical and commercial failure, it was only the kind ministrations of Kath which got me through. She was running a crew on the Kids' Field; she had warm tepees, and an ever-boiling kettle, and amazing people to talk to, and dinner every night at seven. AND ALL I DID WAS MOAN! I don't even think I washed up. I owe her one, and this probably isn't it.

So we wanted to play at Kath and Duane's solstice party; the train ride out there was a bonus. Duane met us at the station to help us down to the house with Chas's electronic organ. Duane drives a sports car so ridiculously small that I can just about get my knee into the passenger seat. It's cool, though, a Sixties model, like its driver (and Chas, if truth be told).

'How are we going to get the keyboard in there?' asked Chas.

'You're not. You put your bags in here, and balance the keyboard on top of the car. Then I drive slowly down to the house with you two hanging on to it.' Duane twinkled up at us from his bucket seat. So that's what we did. We trotted alongside Duane's car the couple of hundred yards to the house, trying to keep the electronic organ balanced on the top of the car, while Duane tried to keep his speed below five miles an hour. Not easy; Duane maintains that brakes are a luxury on a car, and that the clutch amply fulfils all his modest braking requirements. But there we are; I'm here to tell the tale, and the keyboard was fine. Chas and I were a little out of breath but suffered no permanent damage.

We set up in the garden. Kath and Duane don't live in their house. It's handy for the loo and the bath, but mostly they live in one of two large yurts in their garden, pretty much all year round. It occurs to me that a book about trains might not be a huge hit with the hippy community; and, more to the point, people who read about trains might not know much about hippies. So I should say that a yurt is the Mongolian equivalent of a bell tent, with a felt outer covering stretched over a flexible trellis of thin wooden slats. If you thought that hippies lived in tepees, you are only partly right; these days they live in buses, old ambulances, even houses, some of them. But over the last ten years or so, the yurt has become increasingly popular, even trendy. It is the hippy's equivalent of a loft space in Hoxton. And Kath and Duane have two; one for living in, and one for parties and sweat lodges.

Chas and I set up our gear, had some food and a couple of pale ales and a few goes on Duane's chillum. When night fell (and this was the solstice, remember, and we were in the north; where it doesn't get dark until almost eleven), we played a set for the assembled company, maybe fifty strong, made up of beautiful people gathered from the Dales, North Lancashire and Cumbria. We played every number we knew, trying to keep 'em dancing till dawn, or as close to it as we could manage. Which was about half-two.

Duane wasn't dancing. He and his assistants had lit a huge fire earlier in the day to heat the large stones which they would use in the lodge. Duane was tending his stones. When we finally ran out of numbers to play, the sweatmeister started to pull the red-hot stones from the centre of the fire and carry them on a shovel into the sweat lodge. Kath and Duane's sweat yurt is so big they call it the Albert Hall of yurts. They can easily get thirty people sitting round the side for the sweating. A large hole had been dug in the centre of the yurt, and the hot stones were pushed in.

I backed out at this point. I don't like sweat lodges, for two very good reasons. They are: I don't like looking at hippy men's penises, and I don't like foxy hippy chicks looking at mine. Chas and Duane are always trying to persuade me that people take no notice of such things in a sweat lodge. Well, I would, so I'm not going. Instead, I sat around the fire with a half-dozen or so fellow refuseniks to talk and drink and smoke. It was that rarest of beasts, a clear solstice night. The stars shone down on us as we laughed and put the world to rights. From inside the sweat lodge, we could hear hissing as Duane poured water on to the stones. We could hear chanting, too; Duane likes a directed sweat, and insists that everyone in one of his lodges makes it into a ceremony. Suddenly, he emerged from the sweat yurt, naked as Pan, and led the thirty or so participants down to the beck that runs through the garden. They jumped into the stream, steam rising from their bodies. And then back into the yurt for some more sweating. And then back down to the beck for some more cooling off. A sweat lodge, in short, is a sauna leavened with hippy spirituality and ceremonial verve.

Ever the innocent bystander, I not only ducked out of the sweat lodge, I'm afraid I nodded off before sunrise. I crawled into one of the living yurts that had been erected in the garden and slept like a middle-aged bloke who was pissed and stoned, who was wearing a dinner suit and who was lying under a couple of blankets on the cold ground, i.e.

fitfully. But I slept, and was eventually woken, not by revellers coming in for a pre-breakfast nap, but by the undoubted sound of a steam engine.

I found my specs and crawled out into the sun. A large black steam engine, smoke rising almost vertically from its stack, with a long train of carefully preserved BR stock, was sitting in Dent station, just a few hundred yards away up the hill. It was an excursion. I could make out figures leaning from the windows, though I was too far away to see their greaseproof paper packages of sandwiches. They must have been able to see, down in the valley, a house with a garden full of yurts, the remains of a still-smouldering bonfire, a couple of hippy mums making tea while a gaggle of naked kids rorted around, and a large, very hungover bald bloke in a rumpled dinner suit, peering sleepily up at them, trying, under very difficult circumstances, to make out what sort of an engine it was.

If I'd have known there was going to be steam on the Settle–Carlisle that day, I would have taken my binoculars. That would have freaked my hippy hosts out; few if any active hippies understand the pleasure of watching the trains go by. Some of the kids looked up from the stream to watch the train pull out of the station, and as children so often react against their parents, I feel sure that at least one of them resolved to be an engine driver one day, rather than a crystal healer or even a breath worker, whatever that is. Or, I suppose, a faded cabaret artiste. Sweat lodges; steam trains – boys like playing with hot things. The Golden Age of Steam lives on in Kath and Duane's yurt.

The line is ideally suited to these steam excursions; it's a proper main line, so you can go quite fast, but it doesn't carry much traffic any more, so you don't get in anyone's way. The line is spectacular from start to finish; its future lies in tourism. After Dent, forestry crept up to the line. Townspeople don't like the big conifer plantations, but I don't know that they are worse than turning your land over to sheep. More people work in the forest than worked on the great Highland sheep-walks. At Garsdale, a branch line used to run down to Hawes (perhaps the most unfortunate name of any town in England), on through Wensleydale and down to Northallerton, where it joined what we now call the East Coast main line. And at Kirkby Stephen, another branch headed east towards Darlington, passing through almost nowhere. It was always optimistic to build lines in country areas, and they are all insanely over-engineered; every tiny village with a station and a siding and four or five staff. But I would have thought this was an argument for keeping these lines open, or at least mothballing them. They were very well made, on the whole, and they might be useful again one day. Why bother ripping up the lines?

27 July 1927, and these branch lines acquired a special significance as a total eclipse of the sun ran in a diagonal band across the north of England. Both the LNER in the east and the LMS in the west ran special excursions for people to see the sun go out. The LNER posters for the event say 'last chance until 1999'. By the time of the 1999 eclipse, the branch lines had closed, the victims of Dr Beeching's hatred for slow trains which wind through the countryside. If he'd had his way, many more lines would have closed, and I suppose we should count ourselves lucky. Kirkby Stephen station has survived almost intact, with gas lamps bearing the name of the station, as well as the original signage. The station, like almost all the stations on the line, is high above the town. If you want to walk up from the town to the station, you face a 300-foot climb. But after Kirkby Stephen, the line begins a slow descent down into the valleys. There were hundreds of rabbits flocking alongside the railway. We pulled into Appleby, home of the Horse Fair.

Appleby is as good an example as you'll find of a small Cumbrian hill town, sleepy and roses-round-the-door pretty. But during Horse Fair week it is wild, as Romanies from all over the country congregate for their annual beano. For weeks before, you see bowtop caravans coming through the lanes of Lancashire as the travellers make their way north. The justly famous scenes where the horse traders wash their animals in the river are worth the long train ride, or the drive over the moors; visitors should not forget that they are outsiders, *gadjos*, and that this is a Romani occasion. Despite many attempts, and unlike the railway, it has never been appropriated by the heritage industry or tamed by the benighted inhabitants of Appleby.

As the line dropped, it became more pastoral and less rugged, but it had one major surprise in store. The line crossed the Eden Gorge, a real romantic landscape, with rivers and towering rocks and the impression of a distant castle, a maiden singing lonely for her lover in a locked tower room. Soon after, romance melted away. The passengers' mobiles peeped back into life. Approaching Carlisle, the plastic bags started to appear in the hedgerows, and the odd burnt-out car had been abandoned by the lineside.

I don't care what you say, Carlisle is a funny place. I met a *Big Issue* seller by the station who was trying to raise money to get to Cardiff. 'It's too weird here,' he said.

I always get lost in the old city. I can't get my bearings. I tried walking to the B&B I had booked over the internet, but I couldn't find it; I hailed a taxi and he drove me all of 200 yards, the shortest and therefore most embarrassing taxi ride I've ever taken. Then I wandered about looking for something to eat, with little success, settling for one of those second-rate curry houses that are to be found everywhere in England, full of people trying to make the best of things. Then I got lost again, trying to get back to my B&B. I stopped one guy and asked if there was an off-licence about; he looked frightened and shook his head. 'There's nothing like that around here, mate.' This, five minutes' walk from the city centre.

The B&B was one of those places where they always seem startled to have visitors. They put me at the top of the house, and there were dozens of dead flies on the window-sill. Which didn't matter too much, as the view from the window was the backyard of the house, and the wall of a garage. I drew the curtains, to shut out the view and the dead flies. In the hall, there was a display stand of leaflets about the attractions of the Lake District, but with the best will in the world, they are all fifty miles or more away.

Nobody comes to Carlisle on holiday, do they? Cumbria is two distinct counties, no longer Cumberland and Westmoreland, but north-west and south-east. To south and east you have Windermere, Kendal and Appleby; to the north and west, Carlisle, Workington and Sellafield. Penrith sits on the cusp of the two halves, and is thus, I would wish to argue, the most typical Cumbrian town, both touristy and industrial, with the hills dying away on one side and the northern plain opening up on the other. I took a train up there once from Lancaster with my trainspotting ex, on a *Withnail and I* day trip. We were looking for the Penrith Tea Rooms ('Bring us fine wine and cake . . .'), but when we got there, we discovered that the tea-room scene was filmed in Stony Stratford, which, although the residents try to deny it till they are blue in the face, is the posh end of Milton Keynes. Disappointing, no?

Everything was made better by Carlisle station. It's my very favourite. It's not the long, low, neo-classical front that does it for me, but the combination of its tobacco-dark interiors, and some hot choo-choo action. Engines stand, powerful beasts, etc., throbbing on the central tracks, waiting for a train to be called. Branch lines curl in, from the west coast, from Leeds, from Newcastle. And the great main-line trains come through, the Deer-stalker Express, Auden's Night Mail, 'bringing the cheque and the postal order'. If ever you want to spend one day of your life as a trainspotter, spend that day at Carlisle.

And the buffet is to die for. Dark mahogany woodwork sucks up the light. Antediluvian boilers bubble on top of the polished counter. To make it perfect you need a bored-looking lass in a floral apron and a headscarf smoking a fag and half-heartedly drying a tea cup.

'Wot can I get yer, ducks?' she would drawl, in that film cockney accent brought to perfection by Dick Van Dyke in *Mary Poppins*.

'I'll have the same as whatever you're 'avin, Doris.'

'Oooh, who's the cheeky one!'

'Cam on, Doris, what'll yer 'ave?'

'Don't mind if I do. I'll 'ave a gin 'n' water. It's early for me, mind.'

'Two gin 'n' waters it is, then, Doris.'

You do get a bored lass, but she's wearing a Café Ritazza uniform, her name is Jade, and she's not allowed to smoke at work. At 9.30 in the morning, I was waiting for the train down the West Coast, and I didn't feel much like gin and water, even if it was on offer. Rain beat against the window of this most perfectly preserved of station buffets.

Jade chatted to her mate while I read in my paper about the 'not-for-profit' company that is due to take over from Railtrack.

What's a company for, then, if not for profit? Do we have 'not-for-profit' roads? Yes, we do. Roads are not expected to run at a profit. We need to abandon the idea of profit and loss when we are talking about infrastructure. It should be accounted for differently. And mass transit should slow down. Freedom of movement is a basic human right, one which is denied everybody except white folks, who can go where they like. Speed is a luxury, one which is freely available to those who can pay for it. There needs to be a redistribution, a remaking of the equation. More freedom to move wherever you like, at much slower speeds. The train was announced, and I walked across to the platform.

Fucking Ritazza coffee got me wound up again.

Out of Carlisle, the countryside was flat and featureless. The light hinted at the presence of the sea, still miles away to the west. We passed through Wigton, home of Lord Bragg. If ever a man needed a wig less; it would make more sense if he was from Harefield. Or Barnet. Then through Aspatria, which appears in lots of weather forecasts, for reasons I don't know. If there is a weather station there, I didn't see it. Sometimes Aspatria makes the rugby scores on Sports Report. Didn't see a rugby ground either. Still, I'd always wondered where it was.

The sea came up to meet the line at Maryport which, like so many of the West Cumbrian coastal towns, seemed to me entirely grim. An Irish wolfhound, big enough to blot out the dim sun, chased the train alongside the line. I felt that he wanted to get out of there. The line ran by the sea, which was grey and brown and gritty and muddy. If it is possible for sea to look neglected, this sea looked neglected. Unloved. It is poisonous, of course, the most radioactive sea on earth. It looked it.

The train approached Workington. I remember when Workington were in the Football League, back in the days when the four teams who finished bottom of the Fourth Division had to apply for re-election. Workington were blackballed; probably because none of the other clubs wanted to travel so far to such a place. I saw the local supermarkets, Aldi and Netto, and what must still be the largest employer, the Corus rolling plant, clinging somehow to life. Like all steel towns,

Workington has seen better days, but when those days were, God alone knows.

A dad got on with two sons, taking them out for a day trip on the trains. The guard came round to inspect the tickets, and the dad said that he didn't know how far he was going; he just wanted to take the boys on some trains.

'What about the Ravenglass and Eskdale?' said the guard. Dad had clearly never heard of it, although it can't be much more than thirty miles south of Workington, and is a gift for those difficult access weekends, I would have thought. The guard explained about the La'l Ratty, as the line is known, and the dad agreed that it might be worth a try. He bought tickets for Ravenglass. I showed the guard my ticket. He frowned.

'This isn't valid for this route,' he said.

'It most certainly is. They checked for me in the ticket office at King's Cross. In the *National Routing Guide*.'

'What did you say?' said the guard, turning pale.

'I said, *National Routing Guide*. You could check for yourself.'

'No . . . I mean . . . I haven't got one. Not here. They'll have one at the office. I could phone them, and ask.'

'Make sure you mention the *National Routing Guide*,' I said with a smile.

He wandered off, never to be seen again.

All along the line, old concrete railway sleepers were piled by the sea wall, holding back the dying waves. There were wind farms all along this coast, which always strike me as modern and full of hope. The people who moan about them want a clip round the ear. Would they rather have Sellafield?

Oh, they say, but they're so noisy! Well, they're not. They swish. I like the swish of the great blades. Sellafield is almost silent; it hums with quiet menace. As my mum says, it's the quiet ones you have to watch.

Still the line clung to the shore. The sand was black. Prefab huts and houses lined the beach, some of them looking rather luxurious, others semi-derelict. St Bees Head loomed in the distance, and the sun was coming out as we pulled into the seventeenth-century town of White-haven, the nearest thing this coast has to an attractive settlement. Then we were under the shadow of St Bees Head, where there is a grand-looking public school, with boys playing on the grass in front of the building. Along the beach there were more of the strange holiday homes, and on the landward side, caravan parks sprawled along the coast. Would you come here for your holiday, or send your son here to be educated? We turned a corner, and there was the thing which had made its shadow felt ever since we joined the coast – Sellafield.

One of the kids asked his access dad what it was.

'It's a way of making electric.' And so it is, I suppose.

It looks like Barad-Dur or Gormenghast, monstrous tower rising upon monstrous tower. I have never seen it in sunlight; gloom collects in the heights of its minarets, steam hisses from unknown sources. It is vast, covering acre after acre of poisoned ground. It's a way of making electric. Well, part of it is, anyway. Much of it is a factory for reprocessing plutonium and other nuclear waste. And much of the waste arrives by train in huge flasks. I lived beside the North London Line for a couple of years, and I saw these flasks come by our house, past parks and gardens, schools and hospitals. This is the end of the journey for this disgusting filth. BNFL (still owned by Her Majesty's Govern-ment) assure us that these flasks are safer than an ice-cream cone, that you could lick them and feel no ill. They tell us that the sea is just fine and dandy for swimming, that the fish which come out of it are gorgeous and yummy. They should have their faces rubbed in it, like a kitten which shits on the carpet.

Ah, but, the problem is, they have lots of great big guns, and we don't. So they rub our faces in it instead. They tell us we need more nuclear plants, in order to stop global warming.

'Couldn't we try using less electricity?' we bleat.

'No', say our masters, 'because, you see, we have these big guns, and they are pressed to your children's heads. Your job is to shut the fuck up, do what we tell you, and make us even richer and more powerful. We like money and power so much that we're quite prepared to destroy life on the planet. Stop moaning, and have a go on the lottery.'

Anyone who has read this far will be beginning to suspect that I don't like politicians.

Mind you, the trains were good down this coast. Wordsworth and Ruskin were highly vocal in the attempt to stop the lines coming into the Lakes, and I'm glad they failed. The horror of Sellafield receded, to be replaced by one of the most beautiful train rides in England. There is a lovely signal-box outside the station at Seascale, and I watched as the driver and signalman exchanged tokens, in the kind of scene beloved by railway photographers. Incredibly, there is a golf course between the Sellafield plant and the railway line. I like a game myself (though you shouldn't tell girls, as golf is second only to trainspotting as a turn-off), but I'm afraid that I fail to see the attractions of this particular course. Sellafield is far and away the biggest employer on the Cumbrian coast, though; the economy is entirely dependent on it, and I guess the workers have to do something to relax other than raise money for leukaemia charities. (There is a mysterious cluster of childhood cases of leukaemia around Seascale. The authorities are baffled as to what might cause it.) We passed another nuclear plant at Drigg and crossed the estuarine confluence of three rivers at Ravenglass, where I got off my train and walked through the car park to the terminus of the Ravenglass and Eskdale Railway.

The La'l Ratty is not a narrow-gauge railway, like the Tal-y-Llyn; it is a miniature-gauge, a bit like the ones that go round parks. The rails are fifteen inches apart. It used to be a narrow-gauge mineral line, with rails three feet apart, built to carry haematite iron ore down to the main line for the steel works at Workington and the shipyards at Barrow, but the ore ran out at the beginning of the twentieth century and the line was closed. But in 1915 a company bought up the old line and converted it to fifteen-inch gauge for the burgeoning tourist industry. Incredible that there should have been a tourist industry in 1915, but there was. The policy in the First World War was to try to allow life to continue as normally as possible; the idea of the total war economy grew out of this mistake.

The miniature engines were supplied by Henry Greenly, who had essentially come up with the idea of building trains to this scale. It's interesting stuff, is scale. When does a train become a model? Somewhere smaller than this? Greenly's engines are miniature reproductions of the great main-line engines of his day, and so therefore would seem to count as models. But they pull trains loaded with passengers into the Cumbrian mountains summer after summer, and so would therefore seem to qualify as real trains.

Because I was going to Madeleine's surprise birthday party, I was dressed in my natty new pin-stripe suit and my favourite bookie's overcoat; ideal for a day at the races, but, I suspected, a little dressy for a ride on a miniature train. Everyone else was wearing cagoules and fleeces, in couples or family groups; I was the only solo traveller and I felt a wee bit self-conscious. The train pulled in to the station. A driver and a fireman were crammed into the tiny open-topped engine cab, and they also had a huge Irish wolfhound-like dog with them. It didn't look too comfortable. I bent myself double and squeezed into one of the tiny carriages.

Oddly, many of the people who had come down on the train from Carlisle and got off at Ravenglass didn't get on to the train; they stood in the tiny station and watched silently as the engine pulled out. Perhaps they just liked to watch. Access dad didn't get on with his two sons, either. Perhaps it was too expensive, but it did seem a bit tight on the boys. As we pulled out of the station, I could still see the towers of Sellafield on the horizon, soon forgotten as the line started to climb up into the hills; past a watermill, through woods spotted with clumps of tiny wild daffodils. If Wordsworth had only welcomed the train, he could have wandered lonely as a trainspotter.

Sitting behind me were a family group – Mum, Dad, and two little girls. We passed some rolling stock, waiting perhaps to make up the next train. One of the little girls looked at the carriages and the crest emblazoned on the side.

'Daddy, Daddy, what does R and ER stand for?' Dad says nothing.

It was the same thing I'd seen on the Tal-y-Llyn, a thing you see all the time. The little girl asked the question five times; five times her mother and father ignored it. I've asked before, but it never ceases to amaze me. Why bother having kids if you don't talk to them? If you are so stupid that you don't know the answer to the questions (in this case, Ravenglass and Eskdale Railway, of course), it's OK to say, 'I don't know. We'll ask someone.' Or make it up. Anything, please. Just say anything. I longed to answer the little girl's question, but I chickened out, as usual.

The big hairy dog in the engine cab was leaning out, his ears back in the wind, looking longingly at the Herdwick sheep along the line, at the streams and waterfalls, at a pheasant who hopped off the line and out of the way of the train, at the high mountains which rose up in front of us. We came to a small row of railway cottages. The train stopped and the driver and his dog jumped out, leaving the guy I had thought was the fireman to take over. He was pretty cool; he was unshaven, wearing wraparound shades and smoking a cheroot. Clint Eastwood driving a tiny steam engine, if you can picture such a thing. Soon we reached the end of the line. The little girl whose questions had been so carefully ignored said, 'I'm bored now. I want to go to the gift shop.'

Of course she was bored, as no attention had been paid to her or her sister on the whole trip. A novelty rubber or a Thomas the Tank engine badge would have to substitute for her parents actually talking to her.

End of the line – out of the carriage and into the tea shop. I took my tea outside. This was real Lakeland scenery. Sellafield may be only seven or eight miles away, but it was possible to forget it, as high screes and mountains climbed away from the valley. On the horizon was Scafell Pike, the highest mountain in England. The air was cool and fresh. I heard a horn and looked up the hillside.

A cascade of hounds came pouring over the scarp, followed by a dozen or more hunters, all on foot in this high country. The horn called again, and the cries of the hunters were carried across the valley. It was a wonderful sight, which I had never seen before. These Cumbrian hunters have always insisted that hunting on foot should be exempted from any ban on fox-hunting, because theirs is a predominantly working-class pursuit, whilst hunting on horses is for nobs. This is a spurious argument, of course, as cock- and dog-fighting are also working-class, as is glassing someone for looking at your bird. Working-class does not equal good, as working-class people know. The hunt is going to go, and I guess that's a good thing, but I'm glad that once I saw the hounds tumbling over the fells like a doggy waterfall.

On the way back down I travelled in an open carriage, in an attempt to simulate Fanny Kemble's wild ride alongside George Stephenson in the *Rocket*, though we were actually going about half the speed. Sitting in an open carriage is a mistake, as every time the driver blows his whistle, you get showered by hot mist. I hoped my suit would stand the strain and still look half decent for the party later. The first primroses were coming up; the last snowdrops were fading. A gaggle of geese flew over the river estuary at Ravenglass, which is one of the places where Arthur is reputed to have sailed for Avalon. There was an hour until the next train to Barrow, so I went across to the Ratty Arms for a drink and a bite.

Sitting in the bar, I was drinking mild, one of my weaknesses, which is getting harder and harder to find. Without wanting to sound like a real-ale get, soon everything will be gone except lager. Seeing the hunters made me think how everything will soon be homogenized, sanitized, and all we will have is one culture, one language, one way of being, and that way of being will be corporate. If people cannot talk to their children, show them the infinite variety of life, teach them to live it as an adventure, then we might as well pack up and go home, wherever that might be. Those little girls on the train, ignored by their parents, are being taught that life is nothing but a series of shopping opportunities. It seemed to me, sitting there, supping ale, that it is the gap between the educated and the non-educated that is the real problem, a gap which is widening. I really shouldn't drink in the day. I just get maudlin.

Back across to the full-size line to wait for the train to Barrow. There was an elderly gentleman sitting in the shelter waiting too. He told me that he'd fallen asleep coming out of Barrow, that he'd meant to get off at Millom, several stops down the line, but hadn't woken up in time, so here he was, waiting for the next train home.

'It's always been rubbish, this line,' he said. 'But at least in the old days it were cheap.'

'Really?'

'Aye. It used to be half a crown return from Millom to Barrer on a Saturday, so you could get t' dance. Mind, y' had to run to catch train back. Y'd see everyone from Millom running t' Barrer station to mek last train.'

Difficult to picture the old geezer, hair slicked back with brilliantine, sprinting in a demob suit back to Barrow station. But there; difficult to picture me with spiky punk hair strolling through Newhaven to catch the train to Wales. It is an image my children find especially hilarious. But I like the idea of the entire youthful population of Millom haring towards the station from the dance.

The platform was almost non-existent at Ravenglass; there were wooden steps to help people clamber into the train when it came, and I helped the old gentleman up into the carriage. The guard stood watching.

The winter light sparkled on the carriages of the train running on the line between the foothills of the Cumbrian mountains and the sea. The light changed as rain closed in quickly from the west, chasing in across the sands. This is the most beautiful line in England. It would have been easy to forget Sellafield, had there not been more nuclear sites still to come.

Barrow ('in-Furness'; before 1974, this was an isolated outpost of Lancashire) was one of two towns promoted by the Dukes of Devonshire in the nineteenth century. The other was Eastbourne. An astute family: Barrow was once one of the busiest ports on earth, and the railway was constructed to carry iron and iron ore. Eastbourne was built in the sunniest place on the South Coast to take advantage of the growing holiday trade afforded by the growth of the railway. No two places could be less alike, but they were once part of the same investment portfolio. It's as if Disney and Ford were the same company, which, I guess, one day they might be. Eastbourne has lost much of its *raison d'être*, but Barrow still functions as an industrial town, if only just.

It is another nuclear town. They build nuclear submarines here. But where Sellafield looks like hell, Barrow looks astounding. You cross the docks and see submarines waiting for a refit; all along the river wall there are huge sheds where half-built ships lie like pilot whales run up on to the shore. Barrow is a spectacle at night when the sheds are lit up; also at five o clock in the afternoon. In the old days, everyone worked at Vickers yard; now there are far fewer employees, but it is still one of the few places left where you can see a workforce emerge at knocking-off time, running and on bikes. It is a living Lowry painting. An ugly, friendly place, whose sole purpose is to build warships. This whole coast is reliant on morally indefensible industries; but close them down, and you would destroy it.

There was no platform information at Barrow about which train to catch to Lancaster. There didn't seem to be any staff, either, until I spotted a gangly youth in a little hut by the station entrance. When I pressed him, he admitted that the train to Lancaster was on platform two. He also said that the train was only going as far as Arnside, several stops before Lancaster.

'And will there be a bus there to take us on?'

'I guess so,' he said.

I really wanted to kill him. Not just punch him; kill him, slowly and painfully. Madeleine's surprise party was due to begin in a friend's second-hand bookshop at half past seven, and I'd timed the journey so that I arrived in Lancaster at ten past, which gave me just enough time to get in place before she arrived, all unsuspecting. After spending two days on trains to get there, I would not be amused if I turned up late. I know it's not the fault of station staff when the line is closed for engineering, but I do mind when they are unhelpful and surly. The train pulled into the station and I got on, anxious about my timing. Sitting at the table next to me were two line bashers.

These guys had covered their table in maps, railway atlases and notepads. So had I: I smiled, and tried to talk to them, and asked them where they had been, but they were not having any. They told me, when pressed, that they had come up from Bristol, but more than that I could not get out of them. Even when the guard came round and tried to get me to pay extra; even when I mentioned the *National Routing Guide* and sent him scurrying for cover; even then there was no flicker of brotherhood between us. Perhaps they were worried that I had coloured in more of the map than they had.

The guard did tell everyone though, before he disappeared, that although the train was indeed terminating at Arnside, where there would be a slow bus waiting to take people on through Silverdale, Carnforth and Hest Bank before arriving in Lancaster, there would be a direct coach waiting for us in Grange-over-Sands, which would be going straight to Lancaster, so that anyone who needed to catch a train to London could make their connection. So I settled back to enjoy the ride. I was sorry to be missing the Kent Viaduct, which carries the line into Arnside over the Kent Estuary; sorrier still that I was missing Carnforth, most romantic of all railway stations on this line, since it was the location for the filming of *Brief Encounter*. But the Leven Viaduct was fine, and as I got off at Grange-over-Sands with most of the other passengers, I reflected that this was a cute little station, by Austin and Paley, who built Lancaster's Victorian Gothic cathedral. The line bashers stayed on, so that they could colour in the bit of line between Grange and Arnside.

So we waited for the bus outside Grange station. Strange that it wasn't already waiting. I looked at my watch; it was 6.15. It was going to be tight if I was to be hiding in the back-room of Tracey's bookshop in time for Madeleine's arrival. But the bus would be here any moment, I surmised. There were about twenty of us whom the guard had told to get off to wait for the direct bus replacement service, and some of them were at least as agitated as me.

'Where's the bloody bus, then?' said a woman in her fifties. 'Ah've got to mek connection; me daughter's waitin fer us in London.'

There were nods of assent from around the group.

'I'm writing a book about trains,' I announced, 'and there's always a cock-up of some kind, no matter where you're going. Just you try getting across the Britannia Bridge by daylight.'

'Nonsense,' said a portly gentleman in a pork-pie hat, who looked the very spit of Arthur Lowe. 'I take this line every week, and there are hardly ever any problems.'

'Really? You surprise me.'

'Well, statistics always have the answer.' He pulled out his diary from his inside pocket. 'My wife and I, together and separately, have severally travelled on seventy-one trains this year. Forty-two were on time, or within two minutes; twenty-eight were between two and ten minutes late, and only seventeen were more than ten minutes overdue.'

You can't argue with that. If Captain Mainwaring tells you that the trains are good, then you don't contradict him. He asked me about my book. I told him that I wanted to write about trains, and train travel, without really taking note of engines or engine numbers. I told him that I thought that kind of thing put people off. He was not pleased.

'I can't stand railway writers who don't have a clue what sort of motive unit they're on. I tell you the people I admire, and that's the stop-watch bashers.'

'Really?'

'Yes. I had an old chief who died when he was ninety-four, who was timing trains until he was ninety.' So there you have the secret of long life; or, at least, how to make life seem bloody long. Take a stop-watch with you on train journeys and watch your life tick away, second after painfully slow second.

'If trains are so bloody good, where's bloody bus?' said the agitated lady. There were, of course, no staff to help us, but there was a newsagent on the station who was still open. I went to ask him if he knew anything.

'Oh,' he said. 'The bus doesn't come on a Saturday. Leastways, it didn't last week.'

I reported back to my fellow passengers, and after a short conference, four of us decided to band together to get a taxi into Lancaster. It was twenty-eight quid, seven quid each. The agitated lady, two middle-aged gentlemen and I piled into the cab which had been waiting patiently on the station forecourt, presumably against just such an eventuality. The lady went into the front, and we guys sat in the back. We left the other sixteen or so passengers waiting for a bus which wasn't going to come, among them the Captain Mainwaring lookalike with the touching faith in statistics.

'Stupid old fool,' said one of my companions of the Arthur Lowe figure. And I had to agree. They might still be there; sixteen emaciated figures, standing outside Grange-over-Sands station. We didn't really talk much on the run from Grange down to Lancaster. My fellow passengers needed to connect with the train from Lancaster to Euston. I needed to be in the bookshop. We were all too anxious to gossip.

At 7.25, we pulled into the car park of Lancaster station, and my fellow escapees hurried off for their train. I toted my bag, and trotted off to the shop where the party was to be. All Madeleine's friends and family were waiting in the shop for her arrival; I was the last to turn up, with less than a minute to spare.

'Quick,' said Saleel, 'into the back-room.' We pushed our way into Tracey's tiny stock-room, and waited for our cue. When it came, we emerged, maybe thirty of us, and shouted, 'Surprise!' Madeleine was overwhelmed, clearly very touched. We queued up to give her a birthday kiss. When it was my turn, she said, 'Ian! Ian, you've come so far!'

'Yes, I've come a long way. I wasn't going to miss this, was I?'

'Did you drive?'

'No. No, I came on the train.'

Branch Lines to East Grinstead

My parents were divorced in 1968, the same year that steam trains finally ceased operations. Since you can allegedly prove anything with statistics, it is almost certainly possible to map the decline of the steam train against the rise of divorce, and to demonstrate that there is a link between the two.

The Golden Age of Steam evokes images of happy families, all setting off together on summer holidays to Paignton or Porthcawl. Paddington was alive with excited and happy children, rosy-cheeked, well-behaved characters from the pages of Enid Blyton. The station hissed with steam and was filled with that glorious smell. Mum and Dad were arm in arm, looking forward to spending time together, dancing in the ballroom, walking on the prom, watching the kids play in the sand.

But as steam gave way to electric and diesel, the kids became increasingly fractious, and wanted to go to Torremolinos or Disneyland. The family catch the Gatwick Express in silence. Mum and Dad are barely speaking at the best of times, which is not right now; they are looking forward to getting to wherever it is they are going so that Mum can tap off with a Spanish waiter, and Dad can get pissed and make a move on the attractive holiday rep.

Yes, the disappearance of the steam trains certainly has a lot to answer for.

By 1968 divorce was no longer the preserve of the fabulously wealthy, and had been democratized. But it was still very rare. In all my time at school, I knew nobody else whose parents were divorced; and at college in Lampeter in the late Seventies, I knew only one other person who was the child of divorced parents. Although now, I'm very glad that my parents got divorced, and love my stepfather with all my heart, at the time I was gutted, and cried night after night. I missed my father painfully, and photos taken of me at school show a child who was incredibly unhappy. I found it difficult to understand that my parents no longer loved each other; and some of their aggression towards each other was taken out on me, although I'm sure they never realized it. After their divorce, I never saw my parents together again, which I found puzzling. I wanted to know that they still cared for each other, that they could still, at least, be friends; they couldn't, for reasons I now understand much better. My journeys by train shuttling between them was their only chord of communication.

Well, kids, what goes around comes around. Although I don't think it inevitable that the children of divorced parents will get divorced themselves, I am divorced, and I'm an access parent too. I don't know if I have the emotional makeup to make a great access dad. My elder daughter lived with me, and I think I did all right. I was grumpy and bad-tempered, I hated her boyfriends, I stood at the bottom of the stairs shouting 'Turn that bloody noise down', I set seemingly arbitrary rules which, although I tried to explain their necessity, I enforced without recourse or appeal. I was a proper dad, and my daughter got the chance to see me in all my moods; we laughed, we cried, we starved and we ate together. We grew up together, and learned together how to make a family.

But my younger daughter has always lived with her mother. This worked OK until she was seven, because they lived just around the corner in Lancaster, and it was possible for my little one to spend time with me and her half-sister; real times, grumpy times, happy times, fun times, dull times. But when she was seven, her mother decided to move 250 miles down the road, and it was not possible for me to follow. So I became an access dad; from spending real telling-her-off and moaning times, at which I am great, now I had to be a treat, a laugh. I don't know that I am that much of a treat. I don't know that dads are supposed to be a treat. I think we're supposed to be complex figures; fun is only part of a portfolio of stuff that we're supposed to bring to the party. It is difficult, attempting to offer some kind of guidance for life, standing in queues at theme parks.

But there you go; a treat is what I am, and my job is to come up with amusing ideas for weekends like hundreds of thousands of other dads you see trooping around visitor attractions. Sometimes, I try to come up with highbrow days out. My daughter Minnie wanted to go to the London Dungeon; I said OK, as long as we went to the Tate Modern afterwards. She loved the London Dungeon; I was utterly mortified that I'd taken her there, and I would urge other access dads looking for a great day out to avoid it at all costs. I was speechless with anger, at the Dungeon, at myself for giving way, at Minnie for enjoying it. So I took her to the Tate Modern in silence. She liked the gift shop. But that was about it. I took her into the Rothko room.

'Whaddya think, our kid?' I said, able to speak again.

'They're brown squares, Daddy.'

God, children can be Philistine. I mean, yes, sure they're brown squares, but . . . I wished I had the vocabulary to come back at her with something enlightening, but I am an historian of science by training, not an art historian, and for the life of me I couldn't think of anything useful to say. After all, brown squares is what they are. That was not a great day out.

And theme parks bring out the very worst in me. I know the kids love them, and, as far as I can judge, so do most of the other adults, but I cannot see the attraction of standing in line for three-quarters of an hour just to be tipped upside down, soaked, and scared shitless. I take Minnie to these vile places as seldom as I can, and when I get there, I sulk. The last time I got nagged into it, we went to Chessington World of Adventures, and it was only the fact that Charlie, my elder daughter, came with us to ride with Min that stopped me from killing somebody. I would rather spend the day in the dentist's chair than go back to another theme park. No, for a really great access day out, you simply can't beat a nice trip on a preserved railway.

When she was a little 'un, one of Minnie's favourite days out was Steamtown in Carnforth. I really hoped to revisit Steamtown for this book, but sadly, it is currently closed. It is the most down and dirty preserved steam-train place there is. There's nothing much to it other than steam locomotives; huge Russian ones, impressive British ones in various states of decay and/or restoration, working ones, narrow-gauge ones, even several degrees of miniatures, from Li'l Ratty size down to the kind you hook your leg over and ride on top of. Minnie loved sitting on the little wagons which were towed behind a tiny engine with an enthusiastic gentleman driving. If you are really lucky (and this is true of any miniature train, and not just Steamtown), the wagons will become uncoupled, and the engine will head off without you, leaving the passengers astride the tiny seats shouting at the driver to come and pick them up. This happened so often on our visits to Steamtown that I began to suspect the thing of being a setup.

The highlight of any day out on a preserved line for the tinies is Thomas the Tank Engine. Carnforth did it; everywhere does it, they have to, to survive; they run Thomas specials, Thomas weekends, and Thomas Christmas events.

If you follow one of those brown heritage signs with a little chuffer-puffer on it, round about Christmas-time, you will come upon a preserved railway with a train pulled by a steam engine which has a badly drawn picture of Thomas the Tank Engine's face stuck on the front. One of the volunteers who help to run the line will be dressed as Santa Claus, and he will distribute rubbers shaped like Thomas to the excited little ones. The dads will be looking at the engines; the grandmas will be remembering when they had a crush on Ringo, forever immortalized as the voice of Thomas the Tank Engine.

It is a double-edged sword, your Thomas event. The preserved-railway movement has mixed feelings. It brings them income and gets passengers travelling on the line, which is good, but, you see, Thomas is not just any old engine with a bit of round cardboard stuck on the front, but an ex-London–Brighton and South Coast Railway 0-6-0 class E2 shunting engine. And that is bad, because it's not authentic, in a world where authenticity is king.

Certainly, the author of the books, the Reverend Wilbert Vere Awdry, would not have been pleased to see the brute facts of railway engineering and operation played with in this fast and loose way. Awdry was a buff, and the son of a buff, and he fought battles with the books' illustrators in order to preserve their factual integrity. He was a clergyman, 'not a very able clergyman', according to the Bishop of Dallas. Awdry's father was an itinerant clergyman, who filled in when parish priests were on holiday. Wilbert travelled by train with his father, who taught him the finer points of the genteel art of trainspotting.

Before the widespread availability of realistic model railways, railway enthusiasm was a gentlemanly pursuit. The *Railway Magazine* was full of articles by authors with names like 'A Dweller in a London Caravansary', or 'Brunel Redivivus'. It contained poetry, like this example from 'C.E.A.', published in 1898:

> *Hurry up! Hurry up!*
> *The train is going to start;*
> *How many packages have you got? –*
> *A rug and a bag – is that the lot?*
> *Where for? For Bath?*
> *A Second Class Smoker? Yes –*
> *Right at the other end of the train,*
> *And you'll have to be quick, I guess!*

('The Porter to the Unpunctual Passenger')

With the advent of models, the interest spread to new social classes, and to younger age groups. Modern trainspotting was launched in 1943, when a seventeen-year-old schoolboy, Ian Allen, published his first *abc* list of locomotive numbers. Awdry was one of the last of the gentleman enthusiasts, a railway clergyman, of whom there were many. The vicar in *The Titfield Thunderbolt* was an accurate picture of the breed; not terribly worried about the God stuff, but very fond of steam engines.

The same year that Ian Allen published his first book, Wilbert Awdry sat down at the bedside of his son, who was suffering from scarlet fever, and started to make up stories about steam engines. He started to write them down on scraps of paper, in order to be able to answer his son's uncanny ability to spot technical anomalies. He even drew an engine with a face, to go with the stories. When his son asked for the engine's name, Wilbert told him that it was called Edward, and Edward is the star of the first book, *The Three Railway Engines*, which was published in 1945; Thomas the Tank Engine didn't appear until the second book, published the following year. From the beginning, Awdry was in dispute with his illustrator, C. Reginald Dalby, because he felt that Dalby was too concerned with making the pictures nice to look at for children, and was not really worried about the engines' relationship to 'the prototype', as railway modellers call reality.

This concern with verisimilitude pervades the books, which are packed full of engineering and operational detail. Minnie gets fined every time she uses the word 'boring', but her judgement is right in this case. They *are* a bit boring. It was the TV show rather than the books, which launched today's Thomas craze. And the buffs don't like the TV series, because it strays from the narrow path of hard fact and railway authenticity.

Parents like the TV series, though. When their kids are ill, instead of having to go to all the trouble of making up stories to entertain them, they wrap the weans up in a blanket, and lay them on the sofa in front of a Thomas video. It is a shame that Awdry didn't much enjoy the TV series himself; it started in 1984, and he died in 1997, aged eighty-five. The point of the stories for railway enthusiasts is that they are about trains, and they mirror developments in the real railway world. Kids, poor misguided fools, think they are nice little stories about funny choo-choos.

The stories are set on the island of Sodor. This is a dry clerical joke. There is an Anglican Bishop of Sodor and Man. 'Sodor' was probably the name of the diocese which included all the Western Isles, from the Hebrides right down to the Isle of Man. It is possibly derived from the Norse Sudr-eyjar, or Southern Islands, as distinct from Nordr-eyjar, the Northern Islands, Orkney and Shetland. In 1334, Man was detached by the Church from the Scottish Islands, but the diocese was still called Sodor. Since people had become unsure where Sodor was, at some point in the seventeenth century the name was amended from 'Sodor' to 'Sodor and Man', so as not to confuse anybody, even though it really meant 'The Isle of Man'. So Sodor became an island somewhere in the

Irish Sea in Awdry's imagination, a place large enough to have its own reasonably extensive railway system, but small enough to remain independent of the decline of the steam train on the mainland.

Train fans love the stories, of course, and there are several websites which aim to identify the various engines used in the stories. Innocent enough, one might imagine. But there is a dark side to Thomas, as I discovered when undertaking the research for this book. In a highly damaging report entitled 'Occupational Stresses of Sentient Locomotives', the Cambridgeshire Society of Imaginary Psychology point out that Thomas and Co. are 'subject to stress caused by lack of control, the threat of unemployment and workaholism'. Their case is devastating, unanswerable, and highlights the exploitation of the sentient locomotive by the Fat Controller. They cite the example of Henry, who, 'not wanting to go out in the rain . . . was punished by being bricked up in a tunnel for a considerable period of time'.

There is no question that the Fat Controller, Sir Topham Hatt, cuts a sinister figure. In Will Self's wildly unpleasant and funny novel, *My Idea of Fun*, Satan calls himself 'The Fat Controller'. Perhaps we should be careful about letting our children read and watch these stories of expressploitation.

Still, old Minnie used to love her days out at Steamtown, and I used to love taking her. Carnforth perfectly illustrated my thesis that there are two different railways, the real railway of quotidian horror, and an imagined romantic railway. There is Steamtown itself, which is based on the site of an old graveyard for steam engines. Carnforth was the apex of the so-called 'Black Triangle', the last part of the country to use steam power. Those locomotives which had not already been sent to the notorious scrap yard at Barry (or stored in Box Tunnel for the government to use in time of national emergency) were stored here at Carnforth. Preservationists would come here to buy engines to do up for the burgeoning preserved-line movement.

And then you have the old station on the West Coast main line, a fine example of Victorian railway neo-classicism. Trains still stop here, but the station is unmanned, the buildings are unused and falling into disrepair. The great trains for Scotland come thundering through like something out of a *Boy's Own* comic; and express trains are romantic, even though you know that really, loads of people are sitting on their cases outside the bog. But mostly Carnforth is romantic because it provided the setting for the most romantic railway story ever told. It was here that *Brief Encounter* was filmed.

Directed by David Lean from a screenplay by Noël Coward, *Brief Encounter* is the greatest British weepie ever, bar none. It won the Best Film Award at the first Cannes Film Festival, and was nominated for three Academy awards in 1946; Lean was the first British director to be so nominated. It stars Trevor Howard as Alec and Celia Johnson as Laura, and deals with a short-lived and unconsummated love affair between a middle-aged doctor and a middle-aged housewife.

He lives in Churley, she in Latchworth; but they meet in the refreshment room of Milford Junction, once a week for seven weeks. It is full of fantastic period detail: the lending library at Boots where Laura goes every week to change her book; the Kardomah Café with 'a dreadful ladies' orchestra'; and the illicit thrill of forking out a bit extra to sit in the balcony at the cinema, all of which must be puzzling for younger, unhistorically inclined viewers, since surely Boots is a chemist, not a library, and a café is a place to drink latte and eat stale biscotti to the strains of a Muzak version of 'Why Does It Always Rain On Me?' And since when were cinemas anything other than inelegant boxes? My favourite detail is the moment when Laura sits on a park bench smoking a tab, and says to her dull husband Fred (the whole film is narrated by Laura, and takes the form of an internal narrative, a never-voiced confession to Fred of her doings): 'There was nobody about and I lit a cigarette. I know how you disapprove of women smoking in the street. I do too really, but I wanted to calm my nerves and I thought it might help.' Superb stuff.

But it is Milford Junction where all the really important action takes place. From the first meeting in the refreshment room, where Alec helps Laura remove a piece of grit from her eye, to the brilliantly anti-climactic moment of their last farewell, the station is all-important. The whole affair is symbolized by trains; the 5.40 to Churley goes in the opposite direction to the train for Latchworth, just as Alec and

Laura must pass one another and never quite meet. The film ends with Laura running out on to the platform, where she comes close to throwing herself under the express as it thunders through Milford, and then cuts to Laura's sitting room with kindly Fred in his armchair, uttering his heart-breaking line, 'Thank you for coming back to me.' However the period detail dates the film, it still makes me weep buckets, and I defy the stoniest heart not to shed a tear. You can still visit the sad dereliction of Carnforth station and imagine Alec and Laura sipping tea in the refreshment room.

That Carnforth station, once an important junction (not to Churley or Latchworth, both of which sound irredeemably southern, but to Barrow and Leeds) is in its current state is a national scandal. The express still rattles through on its way to Glasgow, but there is no refreshment room for new Lauras to wait in. Surely, some use should be found for such an important and romantic place. (I am very pleased to say that Carnforth station has now been fully restored. Now all it needs is a few more trains to stop there.) I cannot see that most of the things that are being built now – an out-of-town supermarket, furniture warehouses, motorway service stations – can ever hold such significance. Ugliness spreads like gangrene across the body of this country.

I remember how it hurt me when I was child that I never saw my parents together after the divorce. My ex-wife and I are pals, so we always make a point of doing something together with the kid every six months or so. Maybe I'm being naive; maybe it makes things worse. If Minnie sees us getting on, she might wonder why . . . well, why we couldn't get on. But I think that you have to try; that if this doesn't work, then you have to try something else. You have to show them that Mummy and Daddy still care for them, and that they care together. That Mummy and Daddy care so much, in fact, that Mummy and Daddy are going to force them to come on a trip on the Romney, Hythe and Dymchurch Railway, even when they are thirteen and would much rather Mummy and Daddy stop troubling them with the fall-out from the divorce, stop trying to assuage their liberal guilt; and above all, stop taking them on train trips and just let them get on with hanging about in shopping malls with their mates. But this is what we resolved to do.

I had got the inspiration from Billy and Betty, the children whose father took them on a spotters' holiday. They went on the Romney, Hythe and Dymchurch Railway, and according to the author, they were 'all as happy as kings'. When they got home from the trip, Betty whispered to her father at bed time, 'It's been a lovely, lovely day.' Surely Minnie couldn't help but enjoy herself.

Minnie and her mum, Lily, live in Brighton, so the first part of the trip involved me getting down to Brighton from London. At the time, I was working in a large second-hand bookshop in the Charing Cross Road, and on the weekend chosen for the fun day out, I had just been supervising a changeover in our stock, a gargantuan task which involved emptying some 30,000 volumes out of the shop into an artic, and then bringing in and reshelving a similar amount. This was hard, sweaty work; and second-hand books are not always as clean as they might be. The only washing facilities we had in the shop was one cold tap, and though I had tried to clean myself up a bit, I was filthy by the time I knocked off work and got to Victoria.

I hoped that I might get a seat to myself, but I was unlucky. The train was packed, and a group of maybe ten middle-aged and clearly reasonably prosperous men got on and sat down in the seats around me. They had been to see cricket at Lord's, and they were pissed. And they were still drinking, and they were shouting. Poor behaviour in public places is not the preserve of working-class football fans; it belongs to all men who have had one too many. I tried to read my book, but I was very conscious that until I got to Brighton and could get me a bath, I was more than a little stinky. The men were looking at me and passing comment; he's bald, he's reading, all right specs, and so on. As we came into East Croydon, the guy who was sitting next to me said, 'And I can't sit next to him any more. He fucking stinks.'

I lost my rag.

'Yes, I fucking stink. I have a physical job, and I've been working all day. I don't have a shower at work, and I haven't had a chance to go home, so I fucking stink.'

There is one major difference between drunk football fans and drunk cricket fans. If you said that to drunk football fans, they would more likely than not twat you one. The cricket fans were horrified at their friend's rudeness. He started trying to befriend me, apologizing, offering me drink, telling me his life story. All his mates were telling me that he was rude because he was rich. The man who told me that I stank was a merchant banker, and like all the group, he lived in Haywards Heath. I refused the drink, but reading was now hopeless; I had to talk to them and try to be nice, in order to help the banker cope with his embarrassment. I was reminded again of *The Railway Traveller's Handy Book*, with its tips for dealing with annoying fellow passengers:

There is the inquisitive passenger, who wishes to know more respecting yourself than you care to reveal to a stranger. When you recognize such an individual, take up a book or newspaper, and commence an attentive perusal of it . . . [this had already failed] *. . . or go off into a sound sleep, and respond to his interrogations with a loud snore.*

This guy was really trying to turn me into a friend, to demonstrate that he was not an asshole, and until I acknowledged how lovely he was really, there was no way he was going to let me sleep.

'Have a drink? What's your name? Do you like cricket? We've had a great day at Lord's. I'm so sorry I said you were smelly,' etc., etc. And all his mates were joining in, telling me about their day, trying to make me their pal. One of them even invited me to his house. All things considered, by the time they got off at Haywards Heath, still kow-towing, still trying to cover their embarrassment, I felt that I would almost rather have had a kicking from a bunch of Crystal Palace supporters.

And as for their embarrassment? After they got off, it was me who had to carry on to Brighton with a carriageload of people who were all too aware that I had a personal hygiene problem.

I walked down to Lily and Minnie's flat, had a bath, and passed into blissful unconsciousness on the sofa bed. In the morning we drove to Dungeness for our family day out. Lily was driving. Minnie sat in the back. We headed out eastwards, towards Hastings.

'Do we have to go on a train ride?' Minnie kept saying. 'Couldn't we go to a theme park?'

'No, darling,' I said. 'It will be fun. Just like when we used to go to Steamtown to see Thomas the Tank Engine. Do you remember?'

'No.'

'Yes you do,' said Lily. 'Don't you remember going to Steamtown with Frank?'

Frank was one of Lily's ex-boyfriends, with whom she had a disastrous affair after our divorce.

'No,' said Minnie.

'You went to Steamtown with Frank?' I said.

'Yes,' said Lily.

'But I used to take Min to Steamtown. Steamtown was always our day out, wasn't it, Min?'

'Was it?' said Minnie.

'Well, it is open to the public,' said Lily. 'Anyone can go there. I don't have to get your permission to take Minnie out. Or to take her out with Frank. We can go where we like.'

'Yes, but Steamtown was where I took her. It was our place. God, I hated Frank.'

'Don't start.'

'What the fuck you saw in Frank, I never could tell. He was a fat mummy's boy, he looked like Mick Hucknall, he was boring . . . and you took him to Steamtown with Minnie.'

'He had a huge knob.'

That shut me up. I sulked, and looked out of the window. Min looked out of the window. Lily drove.

'Anyway, we never went with Frank to this railway we're going to today,' Lily said brightly.

'I don't want to go on a railway,' said Minnie.

'Well, we're going anyway,' I said.

We drove through Hastings and down into Rye, where Lily's grandfather used to live. He had died a few months previously. Lily started crying as we passed through the town.

'I haven't been here since Granddad's funeral,' she said. This started Min crying, too.

'Don't cry, Min,' I said. 'Great-Granddad was ninety-three. Old people die.'

'Don't be so fucking insensitive,' said Lily.

'Don't argue,' said Min.

'Not far to the railway now,' I said.

'I don't want to go on a railway,' said Minnie.

'Well, we're nearly there,' said Lily.

We drove out from Rye, through Camber Sands ('Can't we go to the beach?' 'Shut up, Minnie, we're going on a railway'), and out into the flat country that stretches from Rye down to the tip of the Dungeness promontory. This is eerie country, with gravel the predominant soil type. The nuclear power station came into view; we drove through the straggling settlement of Dungeness, marram grass the only thing that grew in the gravel. Most of the houses were glorified beach huts; there were inshore fishing boats pulled up on the beach. It was a lonely and unearthly place. It struck me as odd that Britain's two best-known miniature railways, the Ravenglass and Eskdale and the Romney, Hythe and Dymchurch both operate in the shadow of nuclear power stations. The tiny terminus station of the RHD railway was between the old lighthouse and the power station. Apart from these, the only other thing to see was Derek Jarman's beach garden, built from stones and the flotsam that Jarman found on his walks along the beach.

'Look, Minnie. Look at the garden. It's very famous.'

'It's a pile of stones.'

There was a train waiting in the station to take us on the fourteen-mile trip to Hythe, steam-hauled. We bought our tickets and found ourselves an empty carriage. All three of us are tall; we had to bend almost double to get in, and we sat with our knees pressed uncomfortably together while we waited for the train to go.

The Romney, Hythe and Dymchurch Railway is one of the things that makes Britain great. It is kind of pointless and eccentric. It goes from Dungeness, which is a very odd place, to Hythe, which is a rather workaday one. It was the brain-child of two men, Count Elliot Zborowski and Captain J. E. P. Howey, both mad-keen railway enthusiasts. Zborowski had a miniature steam engine, built to run on fifteen-inch gauge, the same gauge as the La'l Ratty. He and Howey decided that it would be a good thing to have a miniature railway of their own, where they could run Zborowski's engine for the amusement of themselves and their friends, but which could, in addition, carry fare-paying holiday-makers. Zborowski was a famous racing driver (his car was called *Chitty Chitty Bang Bang*, the original for Ian Fleming's book and subsequent film), who had won many races at Brooklands; he was killed before he and Howey were able to decide where they were to build their railway.

Howey, undeterred by the death of his friend, continued to investigate possible sites. He eventually decided on the route across Romney Marsh, and he hired the greatest miniature train engineer to build it, the Brunel of miniatures, one Henry Greenly. Greenly had been involved in the miniature-railway movement from the start. He had advocated the three gauges which he felt were viable for building model railways that people could actually ride on; fifteen, ten and a quarter, and seven and a quarter inches. These are the so-called 'minimum gauges'; above this, you get narrow gauge; below this, you get model railways.

Greenly built locomotives to all these gauges, based on the mainline trains of the day. In 1904 he wrote the first useful book for train modellers, called *The Model Locomotive*. He had built lines in parks and pleasure gardens all across Europe, and was instrumental in the design of the locomotives for the Ravenglass and Eskdale. But the Romney, Hythe and Dymchurch was to be his greatest project, his London and Birmingham, his GWR.

There were those in this isolated corner of West Kent who didn't want the railway. They couldn't see the point of having a tiny little train rattling over the marsh. They wanted a standard-gauge railway; but by 1925, almost all railway construction had finished, and promoters knew that a standard-gauge line would never pay. Nobody was going to build a full-size line across this empty country, so they were going to have to settle for a miniature. Reading the details of the public inquiry which was convened to discuss the line, one recalls the objections to the construction of the Liverpool and Manchester line, a hundred years before, but in miniature. Like George Stephenson, Greenly managed to persuade the doubters that his line was feasible, and it was opened from Hythe to New Romney in 1927. It passed through the fabulously named 'Duke of York's Holiday Camp for Boys', and the Duke of York himself (later George VI) performed the opening ceremony by driving the first train. Howey was not content, and a year later, the extension across the shingle bank to Dungeness was completed.

Howey had asked Greenly to build him a line which would last for his lifetime, and Greenly did exactly that. After the captain died, the line passed into new ownership, which discovered that it was starting to fall apart. Now, much like its northern counterpart, the La'l Ratty, the Romney, Hythe and Dymchurch is owned by a private company, and supported by a Preservation Society, which helps to keep the thing running. I told Minnie all of this fascinating history as we rattled along at fifteen miles an hour, and I thought she was going to kill me.

But instead she stared from the window of the tiny carriage. We had sat as far forward as possible, so that I could see the engine as it went around the curves. Again I break my engine promise; it was *Samson*, one of the original engines designed and built by Greenly in the 1920s. Occasional glimpses of an engine do not, however, threaten my theory that steam-train travel is not really any different from any other kind of train travel; certainly Lily and Min were finding it anti-climactic in the extreme.

'It's not very pretty, is it?' said Lily.

'It's grandparentish,' said Min. And I could see what she meant. The line passed between rows of bungalows with gardens struggling to grow despite the fact that there was no soil as such, merely a lot of shingle. None of the gardens along this stretch of line seemed to have been influenced by Jarman's example. Jarman's garden (and I disagreed with Minnie; I thought it rather wonderful) worked with what there was; shingle, beachcombings, a handful of native shoreline plants. These retirees' bungalows were attempting to reproduce the classic English suburban garden, despite the slight handicap of salt, wind and no soil. As they say up north, there's nowt so queer as folk. The best garden apart from Jarman's was the one which had a fantastic model village with a three-and-a-half-inch-gauge garden railway running through it. Minnie quite liked this garden, too; at least, she cracked up at the sight of it. We arrived at New Romney, and decided to break our journey.

'All the local children use this line to get to school, Min,' I said. 'Wouldn't you like to go to school on a miniature railway?'

'S'pose.'

There is a toy museum at New Romney Station, which just managed to elicit a flicker of interest in Minnie's teenage brain. It has a great model train, which I liked very much. There was also a horrid vulgar family of six – Mum, Dad, Gran, and three kids – all screaming at one another in the loudest voices imaginable with no trace of self-consciousness whatever, the parents letting the kids wander about on the line with no regard for whether or not there were any trains coming. And they were the kind of people who give smoking tabs a bad name. The youngest child, aged perhaps two, had Coke in her baby bottle, and pierced ears. If she'd asked for a fag, they'd have given her one.

Me and Lily and Min walked up through New Romney to find a bit of lunch. It is a pretty village, cut in half by the A259, with nowhere safe to cross. The walk from the station up to the village was grand-parentish in the extreme, with more of the bungaloid growth that stretches almost unbroken from Portsmouth to Dover. We walked back to the station in time to find the horrid common family getting on to the train for Hythe. I made sure that we got into another carriage.

From New Romney to Hythe, the line leaves the back gardens of bungalows and enters the empty flatness of the marsh proper. It passes through Dymchurch, which calls itself 'The Children's Paradise'. Minnie brightened.

'Can we get off here, Daddy?' she asked.

'No.'

'Why?'

'Because we got off at New Romney, and there isn't time.'

'But New Romney was boring.'

'Sorry.'

I meant it. I still mean it. Sorry, Min. New Romney was a bit boring, and if I had thought about it more, we could have got off at Dymchurch, and you could have gone to the Children's Paradise, and I would have been happy too, because Dymchurch is home to one of my favourite fictional characters, the utterly amoral vicar, Dr Syn. If ever you find the Dr Syn books, written by Russell Thorndyke, Dame Sybil's brother, please don't buy them. They are hard to find (very hard, as it goes; a paperback reprint from the early Seventies will cost you about twenty-five quid) and I'm still trying to accumulate the lot. Leave them be, and with any luck, I'll come along behind you and grab them with a triumphant shout. Dr Syn is a retired pirate, who has come to Dymchurch in order to live the life of a blameless late-eighteenth-century clergyman. But at night he becomes the Scarecrow, leader of a ruthless band of smugglers, the Night Riders, who use the landscape of Romney Marsh to baffle the hapless Customs officers. There is a biannual 'Syn Day', where the good people of Dymchurch dress up as the Scarecrow and his men. These books need to be in print; one of the reasons we should have got off the train at Dymchurch was to see if there was a secondhand bookshop that might have a copy of at least one of them. Perhaps there is no such shop – I dread to think what Minnie would have said if she'd been forced to go on a train to visit a secondhand bookshop for her access weekend. We'll try again next year, darling.

The sheep along the line did not even look at the train as it passed; they were even more indifferent than the sheep by the Tal-y-Llyn, who I thought were about the coolest sheep there were. This is probably because the Romney Marsh sheep know that head for head they are the most valuable sheep in Britain; the French love sheep which have been raised on salt marshes and are quite happy to pay a premium price for them. These fat sheep were destined to be turned into *navarin* in three-star restaurants in France; no wonder they were a bit snooty.

An hour after setting out from Dungeness we arrived at Hythe, and to my utter delight, there was a superb selection of secondhand books in the gift shop. I bought Min a rubber shaped like Thomas the Tank Engine as a memento of our day out, and I bought myself several rare and difficult-to-get-hold-of volumes, including L. T. C. Rolt's *Lines of Character*, which I'd been after for years. Minnie did not seem as pleased as I was. I guess at thirteen, the delights of the novelty rubber are finally beginning to wear off. Lily did not seem pleased, either. She seemed to resent the money I was spending on secondhand railway books; and she argued that I should give her this money, so that she could blow it on luxuries, like food for our daughter.

'Man does not live by food alone, dear,' I said.

'All right, give me the money, and I'll buy books with it.'

'But you're not that interested in railway books, are you?' I said.

'No. I'd buy good books.'

'Stop arguing,' said Minnie.

'It's all right darling,' I said. 'Mummy's only joking.'

'I'm bloody not,' said Lily.

'Come on; it's nearly time to catch the train back to Dungeness,' I said, trying to cheer everybody up.

'Can we get off at the Children's Paradise, Daddy?'

'Sorry, Minnie. This is the last train.'

Minnie was sulking at me, because for two solid hours she had been sitting in a tiny cramped railway carriage with her bickering parents. Lily was sulking at me, because I had accidentally allowed her to see that I had spare money. I was happy as Larry, however, rattling past the ghosts of caravan parks long gone, trying to peer over the fences of beach bungalows. To cheer them up, when we got back to Dungeness. I bought them both tea in the station buffet. The loud vulgar family were at the next table, eating with their toothless mouths open, shouting at the children.

I thought, at least they found a way to stay together. At least they all love one another.

On the journey home, I nudged Lily as she tried to drive. Minnie was asleep in the back of the car.

'What?'

'I thought that went rather well. Don't you think?'

Lily stuck her tongue out at me and smiled.

'Wait till Min finds out where I'm taking her tomorrow,' I whispered.

Lily laughed.

'You are evil, Marchant,' she said.

'She still owes me after our trip to Chessington World of Adventures. After that, I get to choose where we go for the next five years.'

'Till she's eighteen?'

'And beyond.'

We got back to Brighton, and when I climbed into the sofa bed that night, I glowed with a sense that I had done a Good Thing. And that I had another Good Thing planned for the following day.

Minnie's friend Rebecca, also thirteen, was coming round, and I had promised them a surprise day out. Lily stayed at home, cleaning or something, but she lent me her car for the occasion.

'Where are we going, Daddy?'

'It's a surprise.'

'It's not another railway, is it?'

'Of course not, darling.'

'You promise?'

'I promise.'

Minnie and Rebecca climbed into the back of the car together, so that they could whisper thirteen-year-old things to each other, and I drove out of Brighton towards Lewes.

'Please tell us where we are going, Ian,' said Rebecca.

'That would be spoiling the surprise.'

'Is it a nice surprise?' said Rebecca.

'It certainly is!' At Lewes I turned north on the East Grinstead road.

'Is it far?' said Minnie, after a few miles.

'No. Look. We're here!'

I pulled into the car park of the Bluebell Railway.

'I don't fucking believe it,' said Minnie.

'Minnie!' I said. 'You know you're supposed to say "fecking".'

'It's a fecking railway,' said Minnie.

'Yes indeed.'

'You promised it wouldn't be a railway,' said Minnie.

'I know. I lied. Never trust a grown-up. Come on.' Minnie and Rebecca followed me with dragging feet through the car park and up to the station building at Sheffield Park, headquarters of Britain's best-known preserved railway, the Bluebell.

One of the pretensions of the preserved lines is that they capture the atmosphere of a real country railway. The staff all wear antique-style uniforms and have watch-chains and whistles. The station buildings are covered in metal advertising signs celebrating the great days of smoking. There is a fire in the wood-panelled waiting room, and Edmundson tickets waiting in racks to be dispensed by the enthusiastic volunteer staff. But like any heritage project, these pretensions are undermined by the sheer weight of visitors. The car parks are packed; new restaurants have been built to cope with the numbers of people who are willing to pay for a bit of nostalgia, albeit largely the nostalgia of their grandparents. If the line had had this many passengers when it was open, it would never have closed. And the railway enthusiasts are caught on the horns of this dilemma; they wish the line had stayed open, but then they wouldn't have been able to play trains; they are sorry that the line has closed, but they are glad that it has, because they like playing trains.

I bought tickets for me and the girls to the end of the line, currently in Kingscote, but which will soon be re-opened to its original destination in East Grinstead, England's strangest town. This old branch line ran from East Grinstead to Lewes. It was promoted by the Earl of Sheffield (who had the good sense to live in this idyllic corner of East Sussex, which is about as far away from Sheffield as it is possible to be), and it is difficult to see that it served much purpose other than bringing guests to the Earl's pile at Sheffield Park; guests including the Australian cricket team, who always came down to play a match against the Earl's XI when they were in the country. Cricket buffs will know that the Australian equivalent of our County Championship is the Sheffield Shield; the good Earl contributed the trophy.

There were six intermediary stations between East Grinstead and Lewes, and not one of them was anywhere near the communities they were supposed to be serving. And, as is so often the case with these country railways, they are over-engineered to the nth degree. Each of the stations had a substantial brick-built station house, with ticket offices and waiting rooms and living accommodation for the station-master.

There was a clause in the Act which approved the line that obliged the company to run 'four passenger trains each way daily on this line, with through connections at East Grinstead to London, and stops at Sheffield Bridges, Newick and West Hoathly'. These rural communities, puffed up with a sense of their own importance, wanted the finest possible station architecture and the grandest possible service, despite the fact that the line passes through sparsely populated country, even today.

The countryside is pretty because it was poor. The twentieth/twenty-first-century perception of the country as a land of milk and honey was not the case until at least after the First World War, when commuters began to spread their net wider. The quaint country cottages were scenes of appalling poverty. My mother was born into a Sussex rural community. When she was a child, they didn't have a loo of any kind, just a bucket in a neighbour's barn. She can still remember hiding in the barn and watching her grandmother pissing into the bucket while smoking a clay pipe. Apart from a tiny handful of landowners, and an only slightly larger group of tenant farmers, most people in pretty, chocolate-box rural southern England lived lives of poverty of which we can barely conceive. The money was in the North and the Midlands, though Northerners all get on their high horses and tell you that they allus had it tough; but compared to Sussex and Surrey up until the Second World War, this is simply not true. Most agricultural workers raised their families on a wage of ten shillings a week. It is no wonder that so many of the country lines limped along, barely able to pay their way.

The Lewes to East Grinstead line was taken over by the London, Brighton and South Coast Railway before it was even completed, and they must have cursed their luck from the opening in 1882 until Grouping in 1923, when it became the responsibility of the newly formed Southern Railway. Lines like this did not need Dr Beeching to close them down; it survived until 1955, the time of the great Modernization plan. It didn't fit into British Railways' new scheme of things, and closure was inevitable. The last train ran on 28 May 1955.

But British Rail lawyers had not been doing their homework properly. And they had not been watching *The Titfield Thunderbolt*. These lines may not have been wildly successful, but they had entered the hearts of the local community. And the efforts of Rolt and Co. at the Tal-y-Llyn, and the publicity generated by the film meant that communities were not always willing to watch 'their' railway go to the wall. A local resident, a Miss Bessemer, whom I imagine as a little old lady much like the Vicar's housekeeper in *Titfield*, a bird-like figure with white hair and wire-framed spectacles, read the 1877 Act. And she pointed to the clause which said that the company had an obligation to run four trains a day over the line. The lawyers scratched their heads and admitted that she was right. They didn't have the legal right to close the line without an Act of Parliament, and in August 1956 the line re-opened. But British Railways had the political backing to obtain their Act; and the line was finally closed on 17 March 1958, which, not entirely by the by, was the day that Elvis joined the Army.

And at this point the preservationists stepped in; three students called a meeting to form a preservation society. How different were the students of the Fifties from those of the Sixties (drugs, free love, Maoism) or the Seventies (drugs, free love, Rock Against Racism), or today (drink, shopping, watching telly). The line was leased from BR, and the Bluebell became the second preservation society to re-open a standard-gauge line. (They were beaten by the Middleton in Leeds, by a few months.) Their first engine was an ex-London, Brighton and South Coast Railway *Stroudley Terrier*, the oldest steam engine at that time working for BR. It cost them 750 nicker, and was restored to the colour of the LBSCR locomotives, which is known as 'Improved Engine Green'.

This is my favourite colour. When I am famous, and do fatuous interviews for *Hello* and things, and people ask me what my favourite colour is, I will say 'Improved Engine Green'. All the LBSCR engines were painted this colour. What I like about it is that it is not, by any stretch of the imagination, even vaguely green. Not in the slightest. It is as green as red. Presumably, the man who came up with it was colour blind. It is a horrible diarrhoea-brown. If you have kids, and they have the Thomas the Tank Engine books, check out the story about this first engine, 'Stepney The Bluebell Engine', and you will see what I mean.

I left Minnie and Rebecca in the restaurant at Sheffield Park while I wandered through the loco shed. They now have a superb collection of engines and rolling stock, unrivalled anywhere except by the National Railway Museum in York. My favourite (and yes, I know, I'm talking about engines in a way I promised that I wouldn't but, as you've discovered, I'm a man who cheerfully lies to his own children, so what do you expect?) was 92240, a big black class-9F steam locomotive, built in the flush of the Modernization plan in 1954, and withdrawn from service in 1965. It seemed to symbolize perfectly the no-brain management style of the railways which has prevailed for the last sixty-odd years; obsolete as it came off the production line. The Bluebell does not own all of these engines; enthusiasts from all over the country buy up old engines and bring them down to Sheffield Park to work at restoration in their spare weekends. Then, while they are away doing this, their wives have affairs with the plumber. They get divorced, and have to take their children on access weekends. And so they visit preserved railways. It's a vicious circle.

The signal-box for this end of the line is on the platform at Sheffield Park station. There was a signalwoman in the box, pulling the great brass levers to signal the line clear. As on the Tal-y-Llyn, female volunteers are not entirely unknown. Our train pulled into the station; I pulled Rebecca and Minnie out of the restaurant and into the carriage. As we drew out of the station, Rebecca said, 'Did you know that people fall asleep on trains because the rhythm imitates your mother's heart-beat?' And Minnie said, 'People fall asleep on trains because they're so fecking boring.'

'You're going to be a comedian when you grow up, Min,' I said.

'I think so too,' said Rebecca.

I looked from the windows as we ambled through what I suppose is my native landscape. There were primroses all along the line, as there were when I was courting Minnie's mother, and I remembered all the times I travelled up from Brighton to visit her in Haywards Heath. Only today, there was the shadow of steam coming from the train, dimming the brightness of the flowers. It was this, and only this, which let us know that we were on a steam-hauled train. Minnie and Rebecca played Paper Scissors and Stones. The ticket collectors came round, two of them, genial old buffers, again with the sure badge of the preserved-railway volunteer, the fob-watch and chain. They clipped our tickets while I chatted to them about the Tal-y-Llyn.

'You're on the premier line now,' said the senior ticket collector. He told me that he had to buy his own ticket nipper; that there was still a place in Birmingham that made them, but that they were expensive. Even ticket nippers have a history, and people who collect tickets (as opposed to ticket collectors) can tell you a great deal about a ticket, and how it was used, from the way it has been nipped.

My mobile yabbered. It was my girlfriend.

'Hello?'

'Hello, darling. Where are you?'

'I'm on the train with Min.'

'Oh, let's have a word.'

I handed the phone to Minnie.

'Hi, Monique.'

(inaudible)

'Yeah.'

(inaudible)

'A bit.'

(inaudible)

'He said he wouldn't take us on another railway, but he has.'

(inaudible)

'Mon, will you take me to Alton Towers?'

(inaudible)

'OK. OK. Bye.'

Minnie handed me back my mobile. I held it to my ear; my girlfriend had gone.

'Oh, didn't she want to talk to me?'

'No.'

At Horsted Keynes, the *Golden Arrow* Pullman sat in the station, its restaurant car full of mid-Sussex Rotarians and their wives out for a stylish Sunday lunch. Once this train, these carriages, carried passengers for Paris and Berlin; now it chugged up and down this isolated piece of line. After Horsted Keynes, the line passed through the Kingscote Tunnel, an astounding piece of volunteer restoration. As is Kingscote station itself.

After the line closed, the station buildings were converted into a private house. The Bluebell ran on metals between Horsted Keynes and Sheffield Park only, but it has always been ambitious. The line now extends up to Kingscote; and over the next few years, it will reconnect with East Grinstead for the first time since Elvis joined the Army. The Society bought Kingscote station and converted it back into a station, the first time that the process has worked this way round. It is a fantastic piece of restoration; much less gimmicky than Sheffield Park or Horsted Keynes; much closer to the true atmosphere of the real country railway – except for the fact that it now handles hundreds of passengers a day.

So East Grinstead will be reconnected. Man, if anywhere was ever connected, it's East Grinstead. It has a bit of a funny name, doesn't it? It's in Surrey, or Sussex; somewhere like that? Other than that, people know very little of East Grinstead. But God knows it very well. As do Thetans, Mormon missionaries, Moonies, Members of the White Eagle Lodge, Anthroposophists, graduates of Steiner Schools, Rosicrucians, Ayurvedic medical practitioners, not to mention hordes of out-there Christian cultists. No one quite knows why, but this obscure corner of Sussex has all of these and more; it has the UK headquarters of the Scientologists, the Mormons and the Steinerites, plus all the other weird shit. Frankly, Glastonbury is nothing as a holy site next to East Grinstead.

In a few years' time, when the dedicated volunteers of the Bluebell Railway have completed their ambitious project and re-opened the whole of the northern part of their line, they will find some very odd cats standing on the platform at East Grinstead; some very odd cats indeed, waiting to go for lunch with the Rotarians on the *Golden Arrow*. There might well have to be macrobiotic sandwiches in the buffet.

We got back on the train for Sheffield Park. At the next table were a mother and father with two kids; to judge from the way conversation was spat from between clenched teeth, the parents were fairly close to the divorce courts themselves. Grown-ups are so stupid. Soon these two will stand at the ends of different platforms at opposite ends of the country, as my father stood waiting for me, and as I stand now at stations, watching anxiously for Minnie's pretty head to come bobbing through the crowd. She's allowed to travel alone now, and long journeys too; Lancaster to Brighton, Brighton to Exeter St David's. They are much more frightening for Lily and me than they are for Min. We phone each other in relief when we pick her up from the station.

The Railway Traveller's Handy Book says that we should place unaccompanied children in the company of family parties, and failing that, we should find a man travelling on his own and tell him that there is a lone child traveller, because

> *even the bare mention of such a fact to even the most inexorable of bachelors would prove a sufficient claim on his sympathies, and induce him to treat his little travelling companion with kindness and consideration.*

It is inexorable bachelors that we are most scared of letting near our children, 150 years later.

Yet another reason to be nostalgic about the Age of Steam.

Smug Oak

I'd been eyeing up the magazine for some time. There was something about the model on the cover that turned me on, turned me on big time. When I was sure no one was looking, I took it down from the shelf and turned the pages with a sense of rising excitement. I felt out of control. My palms were sweaty and my heart was racing. I knew I had to make the magazine mine. But I was embarrassed. I knew what the pretty girl on the till at Borders would think of me. She would think I was a stroker. So I hovered around, pretending to look at travel guides, until a till operated by a man became free. He would understand. We've all done it at one stage or another. I took the magazine to the counter, my hands shaking. He raised his eyebrows.

'Would you like a bag for that, sir?' he said, a superior smile playing over his lips.

'Yes. Yes, please,' I croaked, my mouth dry with anticipatory pleasure. He slipped the magazine into the bag, and I hid it under my coat and rushed out of the shop.

I had just bought my first copy of *Railway Modeller*.

I didn't have a train-set when I was a kid. Looking back, I am now convinced that I always wanted one. But I remember wanting Scalectrix for Christmas, and I got that, and I remember wanting a guitar, and I got that too. I can't really remember asking for anything for Christmas that I didn't get, so it seems odd that I now feel deprived because I didn't have a train-set. Perhaps I just didn't ask. I must have been bonkers. Both my daughters had train-sets, and I loved playing with those. My elder had a Lego set, and my younger had Tomy Train. I had hours of fun with them both. The kids were largely indifferent, obviously, but I loved them. I would sulk until they let me set them up, and then I would sit on the carpet and watch Thomas (inevitably) chug around on the plastic rails. But they never had a real set, a proper one, a Hornby one.

One of my pals from school, Mad Rikki, he had one. It was great. He didn't have a baseboard, so it wasn't a permanent setup. We'd sit on the floor of his room, setting up figure-of-eight tracks, and then we'd set the trains going so that they would smash into one another. Sometimes we'd put model soldiers on the trains, as part of a war game. Sometimes we'd set these model soldiers on fire, and watch them whizzing round the track, dripping plastic behind them. We were Subbuteo nuts, too. We'd set up the track around the outside of the pitch, and put our teams on the train, and pretend that the away team had to travel to the big game by train.

Another pal from school, Jack Easterby, used to live nearer Mad Rikki than me, and they played together a lot. Then, when we were about thirteen, there was a rapid cooling-off in their relationship. Boys, you may have noticed, are not like girls. Teenage girls talk about teenage friendship, and why Hayley is a bitch, and why Shelley is a slag, and so on. Boys are not like that. Boys talk about toys. Mad Rikki and Easterby had fallen out, and I never really wondered why. I certainly didn't ask.

But boys turn into men, kind of. And men often do feel able to express their teenage emotional angst. Adult women talk about adult friendship, but men are still struggling to sort out teenage stuff, especially since the advent of friendsreunited.co.uk. I'm lucky, in that I'm still friends with lots of the guys that I went to school with, even without the help of the website. I still see Mad Rikki. He's a durn fine guitarist, when you can persuade him to pick the thing up, and he currently plays with Arthur 'Fire! I'll teach you to burn!' Brown. I still see Easterby too. He's a durn fine bass player, and he plays in a left-field dance outfit called Blue Train. I once tried to get them both to be in a band with me. At first they seemed up for it, but ultimately they both refused, when they found out that the other was scheduled to be in the line-up. They never see one another to this day. They always ask after one another, though. Always. The last time I saw Mad Rikki, it was backstage at the Avalon Stage at Glastonbury, Rikki having just played a storming set with Arthur. We chatted and smoked a doobie. After a bit, Rikki said, 'Have you seen Easterby?'

'Yeah, a few weeks back.'

'How is he?'

'Fine.'

'That bastard ruined my train-set,' said Rikki. 'He knelt on my station when we were playing Subbuteo, and he never got me another one. It's just not the same when you haven't got a station. Where are the trains supposed to stop? Bastard.'

At last he was opening up to me. Thirty years too late, yes, but that was fine.

A few months later, I went out for dinner with Easterby. Inevitably, he asked me about Rikki.

'Seen Rikki?'

'Yeah, I saw him at Glastonbury, playing with Arthur Brown.'

'He's a fucking mentalist. Do you know, he nicked the floodlights for my Subbuteo pitch to use on the sidings for his train-set? When I went to get them back, he accused me of kneeling on his station! Can you believe it?'

Can you believe that two hip dudes in their forties are still bickering about train-sets and Subbuteo? I didn't know why they had fallen out at the time, but I sure as hell know now. These things run deep.

Boys grow up, as I say. Me and my friends grew into music; that was how we still stayed playing together. Other boys grow into railway enthusiasts, but they do *not* play together. What they do is *not* play. Model trains, I must tell you most emphatically, are not toy trains, no indeed. They are something much more than toys. They are an attempt to improve reality. Real train modellers would never try to make them crash. They would never set light to toy soldiers, and put them on top of carriages. They would never kneel on the carpet putting the tracks together. That is play; and model trains are a serious business.

But a love for model trains usually starts in childhood, and the first train a child receives is almost always a toy train (usually Thomas the Tank Engine now, of course). Modellers understand this in a child; they indulge it, even. As Gilbert Thomas says of toy trains in his railway memoir, *Double Headed* (written with his son, the railway publisher David St John Thomas), 'One had to be satisfied with toys . . . perhaps while one was very young, that was all to the good. Make-believe, not scientific realism, is the proper pabulum for young people . . .'

Who could argue with that? But Gilbert Thomas becomes sterner:

When, however, a boy reaches the age of eight or nine, it is natural and right that scientific interest should begin to come into play, and that toys should bear at least some likeness to the things they purport to represent.

Scientific realism is not necessary for girls of course. Get back in the kitchen, you pretty little scamps! Still, Thomas may have a point. Perhaps a disregard for 'scientific realism' explains why people are so confused these days. Those eight- and nine-year-old boys playing with Transformers and Tracey Island are in for a rude shock when they enter the real world and discover that there are no huge Japanese trucks that turn into robots, and that spaceships are not launched from beneath sliding swimming pools. Gilbert Thomas reflects an Edwardian world-view that play should be educative; but he also comes close to stating the modeller's unwritten law, that models should be better than the real thing, the so-called 'prototype'. They should be meta-real.

Toy trains are as old as the railways themselves. Made from wood, or more often tin-plate, they were supplied without track, and so had to be pulled along on string by the dear little Fauntleroys who were privileged enough to own such exotic fripperies. Hess, a Nürnberg firm, was advertising tin-plate trains as early as 1826, only a year after the opening of the Stockton and Darlington Railway. Nürnberg was a centre of German toymaking, and the earliest evidence of toy trains running on tracks is from advertisements by the firm of Issmayer, which was manufacturing clockwork trains which ran on rails by 1866. Toy steam locomotives were popular throughout the late Victorian period. They didn't look like real engines; they looked like those old Meccano stationary steam engines that boys still played with in my youth, except with wheels. You couldn't really control them; you just lit the methylated spirit-fired boiler, and set them running. Kids got burnt, but they were made of sterner stuff than us, those Victorian pioneers.

The first electric train-sets appeared in the 1880s. Since mains electricity did not exist, they were run off batteries. But all these early attempts to bring railways into the nursery were toys, rather than proper models. Although scale models had been being made for exhibition purposes since at least 1813, it wasn't until the early twentieth century that true model trains came on to the popular market.

Once again, like the toys, the first real models, roughly to scale, looking like real trains, were made in Germany. The first British models were built by Bassett-Lowke and designed by Henry Greenly, doyen of miniature railways, but also a hugely influential figure in the early days of hobby model-making. Greenly and Bassett-Lowke had visited the 1900 Paris Exhibition, and had been highly impressed by the German and French model railways on display. From 1903 onwards, Bassett-Lowke made Greenly-designed realistic models of British locomotives. We would regard them as whoppers. They were built to a much larger scale than today's generic Hornby-sized choo-choo, which appeared on the market from 1920 onwards.

Scale will drive you bonkers if you worry about it. But to get through this chapter, it will be a help to have a rudimentary outline of some of the issues. What I am going to tell you is that there are now three main scales of model train. The three most popular are 0, with engines about half the size of a cat (a smallish cat, about the size of my Aunty Pam's), OO, the one that ordinary train sets use (which is pronounced double oh, but really means half zero, i.e. 0, which is pronounced oh), and N, which is tiny enough to provide fascinating modelling opportunities in a small space (at a scale of 2.06 mm to the foot. Don't do the sums, or you'll go mad. Modellers call reality 'twelve inches to the foot', as well as 'the prototype').

And before people start writing in, just listen.

I was well aware, taking on a project of this nature, that I would get a lot of letters pointing out to me that, for example, there was no such train as the 16.27 Irish Mail running on Saturdays in the early 1960s, or that the sun really does shine through the Box Tunnel on Brunel's birthday, or that I have taken too lightly altogether the niceties of the rivet counter's art. That's fine; I shall be interested to hear where I have gone wrong. Hopefully, some readers, never previously interested in railways, will move on to find out more about them after reading this book, and one day they might find themselves standing in an Ian Allen bookshop holding a copy of *Branch Lines to East Grinstead*. In time, they may wish to return and check over a few facts. That's great.

BUT I'M NOT ANSWERING ANY RAILWAY MODELLERS WHO WRITE IN AND TELL ME THAT I HAVE MISREPRESENTED THE TRUTH ABOUT SCALE!

I know I have. Of course I have! This is for the general reader. Your general reader is not going to put up with hours of debate about scale, is he? Write about something else, and I'll gladly reply (ian@ ianmarchant.com, or care of the publishers). For the sake of argument, let's just hypothesize that there are three scales; big ones, (0), ordinary ones, (OO), little ones, (N). For me? OK?

Incidentally, I do know what a SPAD is. That was a joke. Don't write in about that, either.

The story of model trains is similar to that of most technologies in the twentieth century; they get smaller over time. The first models were built to run on 0 gauge tracks two inches apart, not very much smaller than some miniature railways which actually carry passengers. As electricity replaced steam and clockwork as the favoured method of propulsion, and as electric motors got smaller, so the trains shrank, over fifty years, down from 0 to Double-O and N.

And, yes, all right, there are other gauges. There are teeny-weeny trains, smaller even than N. They are Z-gauge trains, and they are as small and cute as a kitten's eyelid. Now cutting-edge model train engineers are pushing the envelope; sub-Z layouts are theoretically possible, but the theory has yet to be put into practical use. They will get there, those brave path-finders! One day there will be nano-trains, laid inside human blood vessels, carrying bored genetically modified anti-body commuters off for another shitty day attacking retro-viruses. But that lies sometime in the future. And I couldn't wait that long. I needed action, and I needed it now.

I searched through my by now sticky copy of *Railway Modeller*, and saw to my delight that there was to be a Model Railway Fair in St Albans. I had never been to St Albans. I could visit the famous old city, and see some model trains at the same time. St Albans is easy to get to if you live in North London. You just get down to King's Cross and get on the Thameslink train to St Albans. That's maybe a half-hour trip. I got on the Tube at Highbury and Islington, and travelled the one stop to King's Cross. It's quite a walk from the Victoria Line platform to the King's Cross Thameslink station. There are long tunnels and several steep staircases. There were a couple of old ladies on this trek, too; when we got to the bottom of the first staircase, I rather gallantly offered to carry their bags.

Why old ladies, given their relative infirmity, cannot travel light, I do not know. Readers who have got this far will know that my primary interest in life is smoking. Smoking and carrying two heavy suitcases up long flights of stairs are not compatible. I was gasping by the time we reached the level of the Thameslink platform. There was a grille across the entrance; it was closed. There was no sign to tell us why it was closed. The old ladies were upset. The ticket office was another steep staircase away. There seemed no option other than to start climbing again. By the time we got to the top, I felt like Brian Blessed after his attempt on Everest. The woman on the ticket barrier was almost helpful. She explained that the line from King's Cross to Kentish Town was closed for engineering works. There was no replacement bus service. We should go back down the two long staircases, back down the long, long tunnel, and down a further escalator, where we should take a Northern Line train for Kentish Town. Then we should haul our asses back up to the surface and schlep across to the overground station, where we would be able to pick up the Thameslink train.

'But why in the name of God weren't there any signs on the Underground telling us this, before we got up here?'

She shrugged. 'The Underground is nothing to do with Thameslink.'

And that's what Her Majesty's Government calls 'an integrated transport system'. Not so much as one lousy sign. Rise up, brothers and sisters! Smash the oppressors! Helping the old ladies back down the stairs with their bags full of breeze-blocks, I planned a revolutionary thrust against our political masters. I decided to keep on smoking blow and moaning about Blair to my girlfriend. That'll show them.

I managed to ditch the old ladies at the bottom of the steps, and I headed for the Northern Line, thinking about engineering works. They are fair enough. Britain's railway system was the first in the world. Our abundance of natural resources, our trading ships and the subsequent development of capitalist apparatus, our democratic system of government (which was the envy of free-thinking Europe), our leading part in the growth of scientific thought, our mild Protestant religion with its concomitant work ethic, our modern and efficient systems of agriculture, and the rapid growth of our canal system; all of this had kick-started the Industrial Revolution from the late seventeenth century onwards. Britain was the first industrialized nation. If anyone was going to be the first to develop new technologies it was going to be Britain. So we built the world's first integrated railway system. It was the steam-hauled train of the mid-nineteenth century which launched Britain into its era of greatest power and prosperity. The train gave us the key to the Workshop of the World. We all got rich on the back of the railway, and we still have cause to be thankful. But the fact that ours was the first railway system in the world also means that it is the oldest. And like the old ladies with the heavy bags, it is knackered. It can't go too far without stopping for a breather. It is tired, and needs replacing. That is why we have so many engineering works. It's not the engineering works I object to. It's the not explaining, the lack of information, the absence of helpful staff, the institutional indifference. That's what drives me mad.

When I got to the platform at Kentish Town, things were little better. There were no signs telling the hapless passenger which platform to use, no electronic departure boards. There was a member of staff trying to look inconspicuous, however.

'Excuse me,' I say, 'which platform for northbound trains?'

He sighed. 'Where are you going?' he asked suspiciously.

'St Albans.' He gestured with a nod of his head to the right platform. I really wanted to punch his sullen face. Look, I've had shit jobs. Anyone who has worked as a musician or a writer or an actor or any kind of 'artist' has had shit jobs. Anyone who comes from Newhaven has had shit jobs. Lots of people have shit jobs. It is not the customer's fault that you've got a shit job. Do something else if you hate it so much. There are friendly, helpful and enthusiastic people to be found working on the railway, and it's people like that schlong at Kentish Town who make their job harder. It's strange, how one irritating yet very minor incident can fill you with loathing and anger. But then, all the passengers that day had been pissed about beyond endurance. We needed a friendly face, and all we got was this miserable git. I hope you're out there, you . . .

Calm down. Deep breaths. Breathe in relaxation, breathe out tension. Go to St Albans and see lovely model railways. Lovely calm blue ones . . .

I must have dropped off; it really is a very short journey to St Albans. It had taken me much longer to get to Kentish Town than it did to get to St Albans. I was pleased to be there. Now all I had to do was to find the Alba Arena. I walked up from the station to the High Street. It was much like any other High Street in southern England, red brick, pantiled, Marks and Sparks, River Island, etc., except that hanging over the street was a banner advertising a forthcoming Gang Show. How utterly fantastic. I thought that Gang Shows had gone the way of music hall. Not in St Albans. In St Albans, Scouts and Guides still stand up on stage and do magic tricks, still perform comedy sketches, still play 'Oh Susanna' on the banjo; and at the end, they still all get up together and do 'Ging Gang Gooly'. Half an hour can take you a long way from London. Thirty-five years, in my case.

The Alba Arena seemed horribly familiar, resembling as it does every other civic centre opened since the 1950s. Forthcoming attractions included Sooty and Sweep (more intimations of my youth, like the Gang Show), the Paul Daniels Magic Show, and Rumours of Fleetwood Mac. There are similarities, it seemed to me, between the tribute-band movement of the last ten years and train modellers. Both wish to pay homage to illustrious antecedents, both take themselves rather seriously. The best model railways, like the best tribute bands, are those with high degrees of verisimilitude. Above all, both tribute bands and model railways seem cheesy, cheesy to an almost maggoty degree. Like bad cheese, yeah?

Well, tribute bands are bad cheese. Processed ersatz cheese. Cheese paste in a tube. There is only one good tribute band. Led by my pal Japanese John, they do Jeff Lynne songs translated into Arabic. They're called PLO. All the rest, you can forget. Model railways might seem just as cheesy, and they are, but they are a meaty Double Gloucester made with unpasteurized milk, an orchidaceous Stilton. All I know is, I'd much rather stare at model trains than sit though a Rumours of Fleetwood Mac gig. Or a Fleetwood Mac gig, for that matter.

The Arena was heaving with people, broadly divided into two camps, the committed fans and the merely curious. There were the devoted enthusiasts and modellers, 95 per cent of them men aged forty and above. These men had beards, and they wore sweatshirts saying things like Harpenden Model Railway Club. Some myths it would be good to debunk; but this one must move from the realm of myth into reality. These guys are not sharp dressers. One of the problems they have with being called anoraks is that they can't see what the problem with anoraks is. They all have anoraks, and jolly sensible coats they are too, especially if you're standing on Shap Fell in winter waiting to video the 11.57 Manchester Airport to Carlisle Sprinter come snorting up the incline like a throbbing, powerful beast.

It's odd. They could all wear Timberland boots, a pair of Gap jeans, a nice Next roll-neck sweater and a smart donkey jacket of some kind. They would still be perfectly respectable and conservative and comfortable and warm, but their wives wouldn't burst into tears every time the men-folk come home in their beards and anoraks and sweatshirts. If railway enthusiasts take anything away from this book, I hope that it is a somewhat heightened dress sense. Look at Michael Palin; your age, a trainspotter from his youth, and a nicely turned-out bloke. It's not hard, I promise.

Then I remembered the kinds of clothes that my mum used to buy me. Sensible, hard-wearing and warm, yes, but designed to awaken the interests of susceptible teenage girls, no. These guys look like they're wearing the sort of clothes that their mum would buy them. Perhaps their mums still buy their clothes? Or do they think, if it was good enough for my poor old mum, it's good enough for me? Again, I am led to suspect that many of these people come from stable, loving family backgrounds, which I find strange in this day and age.

As an example of what family life is like at the top end of modelling, we need look no further than W. A. D. 'Bill' Strickland's delightful volume, *Chronicles of a Garden Railway*, published in 1968. This neglected masterpiece is sadly now out of print. Masquerading as a 'How to' volume on the tricky subject of running an 00-scale layout through a suburban garden, *Chronicles* is, in actuality, a family saga played out between three generations of Stricklands – Bill, his mum and dad, and his son, 'Young Keith'. Bill's wife Sheila, whom he thanks for her support and tolerance, plays little part. The family, after some strife and upset, unite in their battle with the neighbour they call only 'The Enemy'. If you are lucky enough to come across this remarkable document, be prepared to search for the story amongst a great deal of sensible technical advice. For those of you who are unable to find a copy, here is the story in its essentials.

The year is 1951. Bill and his wife Sheila are living with Bill's mum and dad in what looks like a bungalow. No clues are offered as to location, but suburban London is a fair bet. Bill and Sheila have a son, Young Keith, a lively lad of seven or so. It is great for Bill and Sheila to be living with Mum and Dad, and Mum and Dad love Young Keith, but sometimes accidents can happen when there are small children in the house, and tempers can get frayed.

One day, Young Keith, meaning no harm, opened a long-closed cupboard, where, to his delight he found Dad's trains. Young Keith was as happy as Larry's mate, Barry, but Dad was upset and worried. Worried that his interesting and varied collection of model locomotives might have been damaged. Upset, because he knew what Mum would have to say. The layout had long been a bone of contention. Dad had many of the engines and much of the rolling stock when Bill was a boy, and they loved to set up the track together and get the trains running.

It drove Mum mad. She was always tripping over bits of track when she was trying to do. There had been hot words at one time. So most of the layout was disposed of, and for many years the trains had been lying dormant, waiting for a time when Bill and Dad might return to modelling and finally build the layout that the locos deserved. For Dad and Bill, the opening of the cupboard represented an opening-up of opportunity. Mum was having none of it. She ordered the trains to be put away. Mum never really liked them at all. But Young Keith was upset, and this upset Mum of course, so she said that they could set it up in the garden. Bill and Dad exchanged looks of triumph. At last, proper modelling could begin!

After the planning stage, when some of the problems of running 00-gauge outdoors were addressed, serious work started. Track was designed and eventually built; but within a few months, wind, rain and sun had warped the rails. As Strickland says, 'This was almost the end, but "no you can't bring that lot indoors" from the lady of the house was the deciding factor, we must not be licked.'

After more experiments with track, the railway slowly expanded into the garden. All seemed to be going well. Perhaps too well. In Strickland's words, 'Then catastrophe. Mum fell over one of the bridges in the dark; it should not have been left in place of course, but bruised shins are painful, Mum was insistent, the bridge must go.'

But Mum could see the pleasure that Young Keith took in the trains, and so when, 'diplomatic approaches were made concerning a right of way around Mum's flower garden', she was happy to help. Her bark was always much worse than her bite! And the garden railway was well established!

Years pass. Beatniks . . . Rock and Roll . . . The Notting Hill Riots . . . 'A wind of change is blowing!' . . . 'Blowing in the Wind' . . . etc.

Suddenly, we're in 1961. Bill and Young Keith have a garden shed each. Mum and Dad have disappeared. Have they died? Strickland doesn't tell us, but certainly he and Young Keith appear to have achieved suzerainty over the garden. Their railway dreams can at last come to full fruition.

At this point the nameless terror, 'The Enemy', enters the story.

'Have you ever had kids throw stones at your trains? I have,' says Strickland. Great troubles lay ahead.

New neighbours have moved in. It is the early Sixties. Standards are slipping. Bill and Young Keith are a last bastion of decency, yet forward-looking. They are Orpington Men. The Enemy, however, is a chill intimation of the changes in family life which would sweep through Britain over the next forty years. Bill paints a stark picture, which shows us what kind of people The Enemy were: 'Whilst we the model railway fraternity treat our hobby as it deserves, neighbours belong to that vast unenlightened group of people who look across the fence, shake their heads and give secretive smiles at one another as much as to say 'poor chap'. Others let their offspring express what they probably say indoors, by keeping out of the way when the kids and their pals feel like conducting 'bombing' raids on trains if they think you are looking the other way.'

Strickland increased his security: 'The exposed curve near the shed was roofed over, and the runner beans gave us reasonable privacy.'

But The Enemy had beans, too; remarkable electric beans. 'Some even blame your electrical gadgets for the 'blight' on their beans and of course you are fair game for every 'telly' addict who can't be bothered to erect a decent aerial and in consequence picks up every spark and click your gear makes.'

Bill was imbued with super-human powers: 'During "telly" hours we sensed the prying eyes and ears the other side of the fence.'

The end came in spectacular style, with The Enemy delivering the final denouement: 'Our old enemy showed his hand again, or rather his foot, because he put it through the trainshed roof.'

Years of interference during *Take Your Pick*, *Z-Cars* and *The Billy Cotton Band Show* had finally got to be too much to stand. The Enemy had had enough. And it was too much for Young Keith, too. 'Young Keith's exams and music and motorbike hobbies occupied all his spare time.'

Bill was left alone. A truce had been drawn up with The Enemy. Mum and Dad had disappeared, and now Young Keith was riding off into the sunset, his head full of O-level metalwork and boom-bang-bang music. At least Bill was now the master of his domain. 'I began to take an active interest in an allied subject that had always fascinated me – narrow-gauge railways.'

By the end of *Chronicles*, then, our hero has attained a quiet happiness. By 1967 Bill is less nimble than before. With Young

Keith off at the Ace Café feeding the jukebox, he has given up the hurly-burly of garden railwaying and has retired into his shed, to work, at last, alone and uninterrupted, on trains that don't take up much space. Mum, if she were still about, would be pleased. And in this process, wisdom comes. 'I can now appreciate the funny side of some of our most anxious periods.' We leave Bill in his train shed, pulling at his trusty old briar, smiling as he rewires his points.

Young Keith, if you're out there, get in touch. Come home. All is forgiven.

The other half of the audience, the merely curious, were mostly young families with small children. Mums predominated, of course, but there were a few dads, some grandparents and a fair smattering of couples. The kids ranged in age from eighteen months to maybe ten. After that, they are on the playstation, and you don't have to bribe them with visits to model-railway exhibitions in return for half an hour's shopping round the town. Model-train exhibitions must seem the ideal place to take the kids of a Saturday morning. There will be plenty to do, Mum thinks, and the children will probably get to see Thomas. With a bit of luck, everyone will be kept occupied until lunch. The kids were as happy as Larry and Barry's other mate, Gary, but I saw a lot of puzzled-looking mums by the end of the day, mums who did not know that there is a world of difference between models and toys.

There must have been fifty or more layouts. Some were vast club layouts carefully taken out for exhibitions year after year, with five or six club members standing at elaborate control panels and putting trains together in the fiddle yards. Others were operated by two or three operators; these, to my mind, were the best; models of country branch-line stations, or a fantastic steelworks with a narrow-gauge industrial railway serving the site. And finally, there were the one-man jobs; little slips of things in N-gauge, and, down in the basement, a layout in teeny-tiny Z-gauge; a railway running through an elaborate Alpine village and disappearing into tunnels through the mountains, the whole thing maybe three feet square. Fabergé's train-set, unbelievers.

This was the smallest-gauge railway that I'd seen; I thought of the broad-gauge trains that I'd seen in Didcot, the great Chinese train in the locomotive shed at the NRM; even of the wide gauge DART trains in Dublin. This was their tiniest brother. They all run on the same principles (flanged wheels, edged rails, metal wheels on metal track), but they are doing slightly different jobs. I like the little ones. If there is one thing I have learned from the writing of this book, it is that I would quite like a model train layout one day. In Z-gauge. When I'm old. It's a pleasure that I'm saving up, like bowls. No point in getting into it too soon, or you won't have anything to look forward to.

There were men crowded around each of the layouts, which made it difficult for the children to see what was happening. And on some of the bigger layouts, there was a great deal happening. Passenger expresses and stopping goods trains roared around the tracks. Little engines stood waiting for the connection, so that they could run up a branch line. The men at the fiddle yards were frantically busy, coupling and uncoupling the rolling stock from the engines, bringing new engines into use, making up new trains. I watched the trains go round, and then I watched the men who were watching the trains.

I haven't been to a strip show for a few years. It might have changed. In my day, if you went to a pub show, there would be a bit of talking and laughing going on, but if you went to a Soho joint, you'd find the thing was conducted in a church-like hush. The punters were concentrating very hard on the show, much too hard to talk, or smile. This is deathly serious. If anyone started to laugh, the whole thing would be blown. The men were staring hard, drinking in every detail. They are not nice places. Model-train exhibitions are much nicer, but the men have a seriousness of purpose, a reverent silence, an intensity of gaze, that I remember from my visits to the clubs in my youth. There is so much to take in, so much to think about. Like the sex industry, model railwaying is conducted with an air of slight embarrassment, which shades on occasion into straightforward shame. We've all been there.

I spoke to that rarest of beings, the psychotherapist with a lifelong interest in railways. He told me that he had been a trainspotter as a child, growing up as he did next to the Great Central Extension into London; that music and girls came along, and so he gave up on trains, until, in his fifties, his passion resurfaced, and he started to model. But as he says, 'There is always the shame. It's a big secret, not something I'd easily talk about.'

Many modellers, many rail enthusiasts in general for that matter, feel ashamed, and keep their peccadillo a secret. This is fascist, that people are driven to feel like this by the opprobrium of society. We are being nerdist. What these people do is not shameful. It is entirely harmless. They work at great length on artifacts of enormous intricacy. Sometimes beautiful artifacts. They are friendly and nice and highly skilled. But they are not cool. Their value system comes from another time. Cool is of no interest to them, that's all. For us, that's almost a crime. 'Moderns' share an ironic but largely classical worldview. Cool is a classical vice, and the modellers are romantics.

Classical restraint and ironic detachment were united in the modern ideal of 'cool' in the early 1950s. This particular, and now predominant, *Weltanschauung* takes its name from the 'cool jazz' emblemized by Miles Davis; restrained, laid back – chilled. 'Cool' came to represent to jazzers the attitude as much as the music. As 'teenage' took root in the 1950s, several musical cultures competed for dominance; rock and roll, jazz, and folk music. It was a close-run thing, up until the Beatles won it for rock and roll in the early Sixties. The three musical cultures informed one another; British Blues bands, such as the Rolling Stones and the Yardbirds, took cool with them from the jazz clubs to the pop charts. Sometime in the mid-1960s it became the dominant ideology for yoof. Before that date, a romantic worldview was dominant for the young and idealistic, and had been for some 150 years. The railways were built in the bright noontide of the romantic age, and trainspotting bloomed in its dimming twilight. People born much before 1945 belonged to a radically different age from those of us who were born afterwards; they are the last of the Middle Ages.

Daniel Defoe's view of nature, in his *Tour of the Whole Island*, was typical of eighteenth-century classical thinkers and writers. For Defoe, mountains and seas were 'awful' places, places of fear and loathing. Nature was best when it had been ordered by human agency. The greatest beauty that Nature had to offer was to be found in gardens. In Arcadia. By 1800, this way of thinking had become impossibly passé.

Mountains, natural untamed beauty, represented authenticity, which could be accessed by living closer to Nature. Nostalgic for the last romantic age, which was conceived as the High Middle Ages, the Romantics of the nineteenth century celebrated the Gothic, with crumbling ivy-clad towers standing above rocky chasms, incense burning on the dim holy altar. There were knights in armour slaying dragons and getting foxy hippy chicks out of trouble.

Commerce and its concomitant Industry, Science and its handmaiden, the milk-and-water Anglican Protestantism of the eighteenth century, were conceived of as the enemy. The railway could not be romantic, since it was spawned by industry, it might be argued. Wordsworth, self-crowned king of the English Romantics, disagreed, in his sonnet of 1833, 'Steamboats, Viaducts and Railways'.

> *Motions and Means, on land and sea at war*
> *With old poetic feeling, not for this,*
> *Shall ye, by poets even, be judged amiss!*
> *Nor shall your presence, howsoe'er it mar*
> *The loveliness of Nature, prove a bar*
> *To the Mind's gaining that prophetic sense*
> *Of future change, that point of vision, whence*
> *May be discovered in soul what you are.*
> *In spite of all that beauty may disown*
> *In your harsh feature, Nature doth embrace*
> *Her lawful offspring in Man's art: and Time,*
> *Pleased with your triumphs o'er his brother Space,*
> *Accepts from your bold hands the proffered crown*
> *Of hope, and smiles on you with cheer sublime.*

The railway was a 'lawful offspring' of Nature. Charles Vignoles, William James, the Stephensons, and above all Brunel were romantics, trying to get closer to the soul of the world. Wordsworth changed his mind, of course, as he did on everything else except the loveliness of trees, sky, daffodils, etc. By 1844, plans were afoot to build a railway into the Lake District. Wordsworth was aghast; he called upon 'thou beautiful romance of nature' to wash away the works. The other great sage of Lake District romanticism, John Ruskin, also disapproved of the railway, as we saw in Chapter 9.

As I have tried to argue, the railway could only have been built by romantics, a different generation of romantics. The engineers were . . . er . . . New Romantics, with Brunel as Spandau Ballet and the Stephensons as Duran Duran. These White Knights of Technology had tamed the dragon and harnessed it to pull their carriages. The knights bridged awful chasms, they tunnelled into the dark of the mountains, and did meet there much peril. They built fairytale castles like St Pancras, Hansel and Gretel gingerbread station houses steeped in Gothic idealism. Their vision was romantic to the point of madness, 'the Mind's gaining that prophetic sense of future change'. Robert Stephenson, we may recall, was rumoured to use laudanum.

Contemporary railway enthusiasm has as its key moment the availability of good model trains, from the 1920s onwards. Born in the Golden Age of Steam, modelling represents a romantic urge, first to freeze the past, and then to improve it, to make it better than it was, to bring it to life again. In most cases, modellers will tell you they like nostalgia and charm. Romantics have always liked charm. Charm does not just mean picture-postcard prettiness, but with its magical connotation also conveys a picturesque sense of loss, decay and abandonment, a nostalgia for a past which was more wondrous.

As popular consciousness has embraced cool, the idea of anyone finding almost anything remotely interesting has become ludicrous. Cool is a manifestation of the classical: cynical about nature, contemptuous of nostalgia (as opposed to retro). What could be more boring than charm? What is hollower than romance? Those who are interested in such things are anoraks. They have autism. They are wrong in the head. No wonder modellers feel as though they must go about their business in shame. They are out of time. They do not understand what they have done to upset everybody. As one of the exhibitors said to me, 'I don't like being categorized as an anorak. I don't see anything wrong in liking trains and buses, it is my hobby. I wouldn't want to sit on a riverbank trying to catch a fish, but I don't condemn people who go fishing. That is their hobby. I really don't see why people have to have a go at train enthusiasts.'

Why is it more boring to worry about the angle of repose of coal in your model coalyard than it is to be able to name all the B-sides of Elvis Costello's singles? Why is it bad to be uncool? Well, I'll make you cool, gluey-fingered ones! I'll prove that you are.

The Alba Arena was packed, and I was finding it hard to see all the layouts and talk at any length to the exhibitors. I left the show and went to find some lunch. In the Casa Bar, kewl boys and girls sat talking about clothes and makeup. They were sipping latte and eating biscotti. Music of some kind bleated on the verge of audibility. I can't say that I found the slack-jawed patrons of the Casa Bar the least bit cool either; less cool, since they were trying to be. So I finished my lunch and went back to the trains. A man in his sixties was hurrying through the exhibition hall, going choo choo choo. The woman on the ticket desk described the modellers as 'an odd bunch'. And so they are. That's all right, isn't it? I never met anyone who wasn't odd. Let he who is without oddness curl the first sneer.

My mobile tintinnabulated. It was my girlfriend.

'Hello?'

'Hello, darling. Where are you?'

'I'm in St Albans. I'm looking at model trains.'

'What are they doing?'

'Going round and round. Oh, hang on, I think this one's going into a tunnel . . . hello? Hello?' But she had gone.

There were fewer people around in the afternoon. The numbers of children had fallen. The afternoon children were a tatterdemalion crowd. Some were the children of parents who couldn't be arsed to bring them earlier, but fobbed them off with Thomas videos all morning while they read the papers in bed. Some enthusiastic children hung on from the morning, their flagging mothers bored to the point of utter despair. Fewer children gave me more chance to look around. Several of the exhibitors were running their railway to a timetable. I admire this.

Smug Oak was one such. Based on an imaginary suburban railway station a few miles outside Watford on the West Coast Line, the Smug

Oak team were running a busy weekday timetable, set sometime in the early 1960s, just before Beeching. This is a popular period to model. It gives opportunity for a pleasing mix of steam and diesel. Smug Oak formed the junction of a branch line with the West Coast main line. The afternoon children were able to watch mainline express trains, fast goods, suburban stopping and slow goods trains, all running to a timetable that the club members had devised for the show.

Operation is vital to the modeller. His model railway must do railway-like things, and this means being run like a real railway. Woe betide the model operator who, in the middle of a session controlling the down signal-box on the main line, loses his concentration for a moment and causes the 16.27 Irish Mail to be delayed for two minutes! The gentlemen who were running Smug Oak were kept busy to the point of frenzy as they attempted to show their exhibit at its best. Certainly, there were no cancellations or delays in the half-hour or so I stood watching the layout at work. The afternoon children hardly noticed the meticulous planning which went into the railways operation.

No less meticulously planned was the timetable being run by the proud members of the Biggleswade Model Railway Club. They hadn't made up a timetable for the show, like the Smug Oak boys. They were reproducing, exactly, a typical Saturday in 1955. Halwill Junction, the prototype of their station, was isolated at the junction of three almost forgotten lines, deep in the heart of Devon. Unlike Smug Oak, Halwill Junction is a real place. The timetable these guys were running was the real thing. There were, in total, five trains on a Saturday – four passenger trains and a slow freight. And so, at the St Albans Model Railway Exhibition, there would be five trains. No more, no less. Three inscrutable men in Biggleswade Model Railway Club sweatshirts sat with their arms folded behind the layout. A chalkboard gave notice of their timetable; the next train was in half an hour. I'd come back; I was not so sure of the afternoon kid standing next to me.

'Why isn't it working? Is it bust?'

'No, it's not bust. The next train's in . . .' One of the men looked at his fob-watch . . . 'twenty-seven minutes.'

'Why?'

'It's a West Country branch line, kid. There just aren't many trains, that's all. You'll have to wait.'

I wandered some more about the show, and came back to the Halwill Junction stand at the appointed time. The afternoon kid was there, as were a good crowd of visitors from the other clubs, come to pay homage to this exemplar of good model operation. The inscrutable men sprang into action, and a small locomotive pulling a rake of three carriages emerged from the fiddle yard behind the panorama card and came to a halt next to the platform. The enthusiasts murmured appreciatively and melted away. The men sat down again. Only me and the kid were left, staring at the newly arrived train.

'What happens next?' said the kid.

'Now she sits here for another . . .' the man looked again at his watch, '. . . hour and forty-three minutes.' He unwrapped some sandwiches from greaseproof paper and started to eat.

The modern cult of punctuality arose as a direct result of railway timetabling. Time all depends on where you are and how fast you're going. That's Einstein, baby. Most obviously, time changes as you travel from east to west, west to east. Australia is twelve hours ahead, New York five hours behind Greenwich. This time difference is dealt with by zoning, so that two places in the same zone share the same time. As the distance between two places becomes smaller, so does the difference in time between them. The UK is one such zone. But if rapid transport was not available, the zones would need to be much smaller. As the railways began to attain average speeds above 30 m.p.h., so time shrank in their smoke trail. Until the advent of the railway, different towns kept different times, local time. Liverpool was twelve minutes after London, Lowestoft half an hour before Land's End.

This was no use to the railways. As the network grew and enmeshed, the keeping of local time became potentially disastrous. If different companies kept to different times, it would not be possible to make connections or guarantee safety. And who would know what time to get down to the station to catch the train if every town on the line kept different time? The Great Western was one of the first companies to run London times throughout their network, which must have been confusing if you lived in Exeter, one of the last cities to use local time. Henry Booth, Secretary to the Liverpool and Manchester Railway, pleaded the case for a national standard of time: 'there is sublimity in the idea of a whole nation stirred by one impulse, in every arrangement one common signal regulating the movements of a mighty people!'

In the 1840s, the Railway Clearing House recommended that all its members adopt Greenwich time, so that the times of the companies would agree. At least one of them, the Chester and Holyhead, took no notice whatever. They continued to run their services by local time for some years. Unfortunate, since their trains were timed to meet the Irish Mail Packet, which ran on London time. Local time had in practice disappeared from the British Isles by 1852, with the advent of the Greenwich time signal, carried by the new-fangled telegraph to stations in all the major cities, but it did not end officially until the passing of the Definition of Time Act, in 1880. The railways had shrunk the island in space and time.

Clock towers in town centres started to make their appearance from the late 1840s onwards, as a result of the arrival of railway time and its increased importance in people's lives. The slow pace of medieval England was replaced by the regular time kept by beating pistons. This gave bosses a new tool – time management. Punctuality came to be seen as less of a virtue and more of a duty. The needs of good railway operation changed the way we live forever.

The first 'Time Table' was published by the London and Birmingham Railway in 1838. Timetable is a word invented by the railways; it was based on the idea of the Tide Tables that had been issued by ports since the fifteenth century. All the companies published their own timetables, but regular travellers changing between different lines came to rely on *Bradshaw's*. So did the companies. There was no national timetable other than *Bradshaw's* (the much more easily understood *ABC* gave times of trains only from London). For 120 years, travellers were driven to the brink of insanity by *Bradshaw's Guide*.

George Bradshaw was a Quaker printer, based in Manchester. Railway historians, with their slavish concern for fact, have bickered for almost a century about the date of publication of the first *Bradshaw's Guide*. Bradshaw's nephew recalled how, 'on a first day morning, whilst walking together from meeting, Mr Bradshaw remarked that he thought it would be a good thing to publish a table of times at which trains would run between Liverpool, Manchester, Bolton, and one or two other places connected by railways. The idea was voted a good one, and the first number of 'Bradshaw's Railway Time Tables' was given to the world during the year in which the conversation I have mentioned took place, namely in 1839.'

Herbert Spencer, in his autobiography, writes, '*Bradshaw's Guide* . . . did not commence till the autumn of 1838, when it made its appearance in the shape of some three or four leaves. There have been disputes as to the date of its origin, but I speak from definite remembrance.'

Both men were writing more than sixty years after the event; modern historians now agree with Spencer.

What is certain is that the fully realized *Guide* was first published in the form in which it was best known in January 1842, and continued to be published every month between 1842 and 1961. The months were listed in the Quaker style; 1st mo., 2nd mo., 3rd mo., etc., rather than the pagan January, February, March, just to add to the confusion. It was a beast. Dr Watson was always getting it off the shelf so that Holmes could find train times, but for anyone less gifted than Sherlock, the thing was a nightmare.

The print is tiny, and the narrow columns are packed with figures and dots and footnotes and ifs and buts and different kinds of squiggles, each of which means something; change here, don't change here, Saturdays only, never on a Saturday, no cats, cats must be carried, etc., etc. Just to make it harder, *Bradshaw's Guide* was packed with pages of advertising, which do not aid readability. Advertising banners run along the top of most of the pages, much like on a website today. I have a copy from July 1922, the moment just before the Grouping; my favourite banner advertisements are the ones for 'Bailey's Celebrated Trusses'.

I want to try an experiment. I want to try to work out some times. I've chosen two places, and I'm going to try to work out how to get from one to the other. I've chosen these places from my journeys, without sneaking a look at the actual timetables, to try to reproduce the difficulties the user must have faced. Maybe I've chosen two silly places – I don't know. It's 1.15 on Saturday afternoon. I'm going to time myself, to see how long it takes me to plan my route. I've decided I want to go from Abergynolwen, at the end of the Tal-y-Llyn, to Halwill Junction in Devon, the station so scrupulously modelled by the lads from Biggleswade. The year is 1922, but I'm really doing this, now. The clock is running . . .

I look up Abergynolwen in the index and turn to page 585. On a Monday only, there is a train for Towyn Pendre leaving at 6.50. The times are all listed by morning and afternoon; this was before the advent of the twenty-four-hour clock. Then, turning to page 583, I see I could get a train from Towyn Town station (*Bradshaw* tells me that there is a half-mile walk between Pendre and Town stations) for Aberystwyth, dep. 8.06, arr. 9.25. Hang on; there's a Z at the top of the column; what does that mean? Right – according to the notes, that means it only stops in Towyn on request. Fair enough. Must remember to raise my arm. Now then, Aberystwyth, page 578; oh no, that's not right; these are the down-train times, and I need the up line. (Down means coming away from London, up means heading towards it.) Hmmm hmmm hmmm, la la la, here we are, page 579, up trains, Aberystwyth to London Paddington . . . there's one leaving at 10.15, which gets me into Paddington on the dot of 5.00.

Bugger. I've missed the last train to Exeter. But if I pop out of the station and get a cab, I can whisk over to Waterloo, page 140, and make the 6.00 departure for Exeter Queen's Street, where I arrive at 10.07 at night. There are no trains to Halwill Junction, so I'd better put up in a hotel in Exeter. I turn to the advertisements at the back of the *Guide* . . . here we are. This one sounds dandy, The Rougemont, as 'Patronized by Royalty', 'near all stations' and with an 'omnibus that meets all trains'. That'll do. I spend the night there, and catch . . . let's see . . . page 143, the 8.31 train in the morning, which gets me into Halwill at 10.38.

Simple. Stop the watch. Ah. It is five to two. It took me forty minutes to pick out my route.

And I bet there's a better way. What if I went to Bristol from Aberystwyth instead of going via London? Hang on a mo, I'll just look it up . . .

After the last *Bradshaw's Guide* was published in 1961, rail travellers had to refer to six badly organized timetables issued by BR on a regional basis. BR was unable to offer its own national timetable until 1974.

These days of course, we have National Rail Enquiries, whose highly trained and enthusiastic staff carry in their heads an encyclopedic knowledge of the geography of the British Isles and its railway system. National Rail Enquiries are thinking of moving their call centres (currently in Cardiff and Newcastle) to India. If this happens, then 'highly trained', 'enthusiastic' and 'encyclopeadic knowledge' will be true, instead of ironic. Globalisation isn't all bad. You phone them up, they ask you what station you are travelling from, you say you don't know for sure, but you know which station you're travelling to, then they ask you what time you want to leave, and you say you don't know that either, because you don't know how long the journey takes, but you do know what time you want to arrive. Then they tell you a train time which will get you to your destination at that time, even though the route involves four changes and an hour's wait at Crewe; they do not tell you that if you were prepared to arrive, say, fifteen minutes earlier, there was a through train which would have whisked you there in a third of the time.

These public timetables were based on the careful calculations which the train schedulers had undertaken, and which were detailed in the 'working' or 'service' timetables. They included freight and special trains, and were printed only for the railway staff. If you thought *Bradshaw* was complicated, the working timetables leave it standing. All the detailed timings needed to run freight and passenger trains over the same line are included. All the movements of empty carriages or lone locomotives running to pick up a train are detailed. Special notices would be sent out to keep staff informed of any changes. Emergencies meant instant amendment, relayed by telegraph or telephone, and written into the working timetable by hand. Every working timetable had a set of instructions on how to cope with any situation which might arise to jeopardize the running of the trains to time. These rules became larger and more complicated over time, so they were published separately as the *General Appendix to the Working Timetable*. Staff were supposed to destroy their old copies, as new timetables and appendices appeared yearly, but luckily not everyone complied, and you can still pick up genuine *General Appendices* from the 1970s and 1980s for a song at enthusiast gatherings. Full of stickings-in and crossings-out, these unloved old documents give the best idea of the problems involved in running a railway.

Those guys running Halwill Junction had a copy of the working timetable for 1955, or else how would they have known what time to run their slow freight train? I looked again at their chalked-up timetable. The last train was scheduled to run at 8.33 p.m. But the exhibition closed at 6.30. I knew what those men were made of. They were going to sit there for two hours after the show closed, arms folded, watching the cleaners get ready for day two of the show. And, at 8.33 p.m. on the dot, the last train to Bideford would pull out of Halwill Junction. Then they could relax at last. They could turn everything off and go to the pub, looking forward to running a skeleton Sunday service on the morrow.

I was in the pub before them. I'd invited a few modellers to join me for a chat. As I've mentioned before, a successful model is one which mirrors the prototype as closely as possible, and a very successful model is one which improves on the prototype. In the greatest layouts, all the imperfections in the prototype are removed, and faultless running is within reach. The prototype railways are always in the news. There is horror, mismanagement, political upheaval, uproar, screeching brakes, cracked rails, calls for an inquiry . . . And yet here are a group of men who have been running railways perfectly for years. No under-investment, no crashes, no delays. Why has no one asked them what they think of the state of the railways? And what they would do to improve it?

Here then are the fruits of our conversation, my contribution to current political debate about the fate and state of the railway, the Modellers' Parliament.

MARCHANT: Are the railways any good now? Is it only nostalgia that makes us think they were better before?

BRIAN: Privatization has been a disaster for the railways. It could have been a good thing, but all the money has been put into the wrong places.

GEOFF: If BR had received the money that has gone into the railways since privatization, we would have the best railway in the world.

MALCOLM: A century and a half of operating experience was thrown away at privatization. Of course it's not nostalgia to think that things were better. They were better.

GEOFF: But there's some nice stock about. The new DMUs are comfortable.

BRIAN: Yes, but yesterday's passenger is today's customer. We're just packages to be whisked about.

MALCOLM: With steam, you knew you were on a train. The passenger was king.

DICK: I can't complain. Only once in two years travelling down from Sheffield to London has my train been delayed by more than two minutes.

GEOFF: GNER are good too. They recovered well after Hatfield.

BRIAN: I've seen some smart working with time lost being recovered. There are still good men on the railway.

MARCHANT: If you were running the railways, how would you go about it? You all run perfect railways. (Cries of 'We wish!)

DICK: You need to see railways as a long-term investment. The roads don't make money, why should the railway?

MALCOLM: When Railnet come in, they must be safety-led. There needs to be more people working on the railway again.

BRIAN: You say that we run perfect railways. But that's because we use the Big Hand of God if anything goes wrong. We can pick up wagons and Railtrack or whoever can't. There's no one to blame. Responsibility skitters away like water on a hot-plate. There needs to be a Fat Controller, someone who can be responsible. And the system needs to run by railwaymen and engineers and managers and passengers and accountants and politicians all working together. Simple.

We all laughed. It would work, though, wouldn't it, if good transport was the aim that all groups had in common? That would be something, wouldn't it? If transport became the primary aim of our transport system? It won't, of course.

My favourite contribution came from John Glasscock, who wrote to me after the show.

John worked as a volunteer on the Isle of Man Steam Railway in 1968. Sir Philip Wombwell had stimulated the railway into new life. He felt that railways should be carrying small amounts of freight over short distances. Where freight led, passengers would follow. The tourist trade on which the railway had previously depended would become the icing on the cake. The scheme worked brilliantly. Too brilliantly. The company carried fruit, vegetables, tins, Manx kippers, medical supplies, furniture, a Mini Cooper and a brown bear from the circus. Regular short freight runs brought goodwill. More and more Manx folk used the line. But thirty years of neglect meant that rails buckled under unaccustomed loads, and when the tourist season came, the company didn't have enough serviceable engines to keep the freight trains running. The railway went bankrupt.

The moral is, before you develop traffic, you have to have the infrastructure in place. The permanent way needs to be right. The engines and stock have to be in place, all before you start trying to increase your service. The new stock needs space for bikes and a luggage van, and should be wheelchair-friendly. Services would then be generated to meet local need, which will increase capacity over the system. Better local services mean more passengers feeding into the long-distance trains. People and goods would start to move efficiently. The people earn more, and so they pay more taxes, which support the infrastructure.

Mr Glasscock finished his letter with a proposal for an experiment.

I should like to see a relatively self-contained section of line of some useful length (Exeter to Salisbury springs to mind) handed over to the control of the county councils through which it runs. They would be given complete freedom to run it as they thought fit, provided they, a) levied a standard charge on the council tax for upkeep;

b) issued identity cards free for each member of each household affected.

c) charged only half the normal fare on production of such a card.

He concludes: 'We need schemes that give people a feeling of control over their local railway; without that feeling of control, I fear nothing will halt the process of decline.'

Oh, but then we'd have a democratically accountable transport system which took as its starting point the provision of local transport services. And that would never do.

I think Brian is right; there needs to be a Fat Controller. Transport should be the purpose of the railway, not profit. The passenger should be, if not king, then at least human. John Glasscock is a wise man. His ideas struck me as forward-looking and sustainable. If the railway is to be reorganized so that it becomes more accessible, accountable and responsible, I hope there are chairs at the table for these peaceable men who love trains. Love is still the main ingredient, kids.

I left the pub just as the Biggleswade posse emerged triumphant from the Alba Arena. The last train, a slow freight carrying local produce, had left Halwill for Bideford. They were smiling. They had done a beautiful thing.

On the train back to Kentish Town, I watched my reflection in the window. At night, there is nothing to see from the window but yourself. The reflection is reflected, much smaller, on to the window opposite; it is reflected back, smaller still. It is a series with no end, and there is a jewel at its heart.

All journeys are mythical journeys, journeys into ourselves. A model journey is the most inward journey of all, undertaken to find perfection. A great layout has been touched by the Philosopher's Stone, and turns to gold. It dissolves reality, which is distilled and remade in the crucible of the railway modeller's shed.

Which is cool.

All Change!

When I started writing this book, I lived in a large shared house next to the North London Line, which ran directly behind our garden. There were four lines at this point: a double set closest to our house, which were mostly used for freight traffic, and then the two platforms of Canonbury station on the North London Line proper. My bedroom was on the second floor. In winter, before leaves appeared on the trees which march along the trackside, I had an unmatched view of the lines, and of the station platforms.

From my bedroom I could hear the Tannoy from the station – the train is stuck at Hackney Wick, is thirteen minutes late leaving Camden Road. I would watch people waiting for trains; some of them, anxious like me, pacing around the platforms; others, more phlegmatic, sitting in the shelter or leaning against the upright of the station sign. In the early evening, dozens of passengers would spill from the train on to the platform nearest our house, hurrying up the steps, carrying briefcases and bags and bikes. By day, women with pushchairs would bump their children down the steps, rushing to catch the train as it pulled in from Dalston. I liked to watch the runners, sprinting through the entrance and leaping down the steps. Sometimes they made it to the train, sometimes they would have to wait on the platform for another twenty minutes, and sometimes, on very cold mornings, they fell over.

In the late evening, and on weekend afternoons, kids took over the station. I could watch them jumping up and down on the roof of the shelter and running across the line. Their favourite game was to touch the live line with their feet as they jumped over it. I used to think of the Darwin Awards, the annual prize given to those who die in the most stupid way. The award is given by a grateful world to a total dunce, who has done the decent thing and removed himself from the gene pool. Who was I to buck evolution? I never shouted at them to stop, but I watched from my window, waiting for the day when they would kill themselves. I always thought that since I was probably the person who spent most time looking at the station, I would be the one to phone the Emergency Services.

Trains rolled by my window. From six in the morning till gone twelve at night, the passenger trains on the North London Line came and went, came and went, one every twenty minutes in either direction. On the two lines nearest the house, goods trains ran all night. I watched them pass; long trains of containers from China, Africa, South America, crossing London from Harwich and Felixstowe, bound for the great trans-shipment yard at Willesden.

All night long, I could feel the rumble of the trains through my bedroom floor. This is when they move the flasks containing low-level nuclear waste; sometimes, I sat up to watch them pass on their long trip to Sellafield. They were the trains that made me the angriest, but it was the car transporters, wagon after wagon of new cars, hundreds of cars pulled behind a solitary diesel engine, that made me the saddest. You could see, right in front of your eyes, the exact numbers of cars that one train could keep off the road. Hundreds and hundreds of them.

Often there were lone engines, moving from one part of the network to another, or hurrying to pick up a train at Stratford. Once, just once, like something leaked from another world, there was a steam loco-motive, running without a train. I heard it coming while I was sitting at my desk, and hurried to the window just in time to see it pass, a small loco in the colours of the Midland, its smoke filling our garden.

For those who regularly use the North London Line, it is a little bit of hell on earth. It creeps around some of the least attractive parts of the north of the city like a nun on downers. The trains are always filthy, and usually late. In the mornings and evenings, they are packed full of workers, crushed against the doors, filling the corridors. The passengers always looked poor to me, much less prosperous, somehow, than on the Underground. You never see City types on the North London Line. The stations are badly lit, and they feel dangerous; it is difficult, travelling at night, to read the signs on the platforms through the grubby windows. Regular passengers navigate by counting stops.

It has its moments, though. Once, when I was travelling from Canning Town back to Canonbury, a couple of teenage black guys got on and started a rapping contest. One was fat and oily, and the other had specs and a face covered in bumfluff, but they were so cool that I wanted to weep. I'd never heard better street rapping; the fat guy was fast, rhythmical and funny, but the speccy guy blew me away with a virtuoso display of crackneck mouth music. When he finished, the five or so people in the carriage applauded, and the speccy guy grinned and took a bow.

And once, when my girlfriend and I were going home on the last train, happily pissed and stoned after watching Panorama, the steelband contest that takes place on Kensal Road the night before the Notting Hill Carnival really gets going, one of those Peruvian bands in ponchos who play dead armadillos and pan pipes got on with us, and started to jam, really for their own amusement, in a corner of the carriage. They were so good that they were the first pan-pipe players I'd ever heard that I didn't want to throttle; the first pan pipers I'd ever heard who didn't play Mull of Kintyre.

The best thing about the North London Line, though, is that it is free to use. No one ever comes round asking to see your ticket, and for much of the day most of the stations are unattended. Even when they *are* attended, the ticket-office workers never look up from their papers as you stroll past their window. This is because Silverlink are subsidised by the state to run the line; ticket money is the icing on the cake. If you turned the subsidy into investment, you could upgrade the track, run more frequent, more punctual services, put in new rolling stock, humanize the stations, build in proper ticket controls, and then, Bob's your mum's live-in lover, you'd have a functioning railway that served its community. And one train, I never forgot, can pull hundreds of cars.

It's all a matter of how you do the sums.

The North London Line isn't romantic, but then it doesn't need to be. It needs to do the job it was built to do much better.

Soon, the Tube, the East London Line, the orange one, will snake north from Shoreditch to meet the North London Line at Dalston, and when it gets there, the North London Line will need to get real. It could be an Outer Circle if it was run right, but at the moment, it isn't.

In May 2002 I moved with my girlfriend to North Devon. If you drew a line south from Bideford, and a line east from Bude, the place where they crossed would be the village where we live. If you look at this area on a map, you'll see that there is nothing here. It is empty. This is not the cream-tea Devon, where the tourists come, but a place of peace and beauty, where agriculture is virtually the only employer. From my office window, I look out on to a cobbled courtyard, where roses grow and birds come to feed. There is a gate that opens on to a well-ordered garden. Behind the garden are fields and woods rising to the top of low green hills.

God, I miss the trains.

The nearest thing North Devon has to the North London Line is the Tarka Line from Exeter to Barnstaple, but it's miles from here. It is named after the book by Henry Williamson, *Tarka the Otter*, which was set in North Devon. Williamson was a fascist; the only English fascist, so far as I'm aware, to have a major tourist attraction named after his work. Exeter St David's is a fine station, but that's an hour's drive away. It's unsurprising that there are no railways through here; there are, as I say, very few people, and no industry, save for a small china-clay pit a few miles to the north.

But there used to be railways here, until quite recently. After admiring the smart operation of the Halwill Junction layout at the St Albans Model Railway Exhibition, I was pleased to find myself living just five miles up the road from the prototype. Looking at the local Ordnance Survey map, I noticed that it was cross-hatched by abandoned lines. There may not have been any real reason for building these lines in the first place, but everywhere had to have a railway, whether there was any traffic to carry or not, so the 'no-man's land of the North Devon plateau', as David St John Thomas calls the area, had to have its railways too.

There was a line from Exeter that used to run up to Okehampton, down through Tavistock, and on to Plymouth. This was once the London and South Western's main line from Waterloo. It's closed now; the only line from Exeter to Plymouth is the old Great Western Line, along the South Devon coast. In places, this remaining line goes along the sea wall. Waves break over the line. Virgin have just invested a vast amount of money in new trains to run their cross-country services from Penzance and Plymouth to Bristol and beyond. These trains keep breaking down every time they go along the sea wall. Salt gets into their delicate parts, far more delicate than on any of the steam engines which used to navigate the line. Richard Branson, for one, must wish that the other mainline route to the South-West was still open, rather than truncated at both ends. It was closed under the Beeching cuts of the 1960s, though Beeching himself had not recommended it as one of the lines to be axed in his original report.

Halwill wasn't on this main line. It wasn't important enough for that. Halwill stood on a branch line that left this old Plymouth route near Okehampton and ran for thirty miles across the peninsula to Bude. Nobody used the line much. The main traffic was in manure. Then Halwill was chosen as the start of another line, running fifty miles through the deserted North Cornwall countryside to Padstow. They expected a tourist trade, but it never really materialized. Nobody used this line a lot either, certainly not outside the tourist season. Now Halwill had two lines that nobody used very much. Clearly, what it needed was a third.

Railway construction was even more developed in the far north of Devon, especially around Barnstaple. Five lines converged here, one of which ran on to Bideford and up the Torridge Valley to Great Torrington, where it stopped. Mostly, this last part of the line from Bideford to Torrington carried china clay. Somebody must have looked at the map and thought, 'Ooh, look. If you ran a line from Great Torrington to Halwill, then you'd have that essential third traffic-free line.'

So they built it. It was called the North Devon and Cornwall Junction Light Railway. Incredibly, it was built in 1925, by when, surely to God, people should have known that branchline railways through empty countryside could never be much use. But no.

The only town that the railway even came near to serving was Hatherleigh. Hatherleigh is the nearest town to where we live. When we first moved down here, I took my girlfriend to Hatherleigh and told her, 'Honey, this is our nearest town.'

She looked up the High Street, with its handful of shops, and said, '*This* is a *town?*'

The population of Hatherleigh is maybe 1,500, just. It is seven miles by road from Okehampton, the nearest town of any size. From Hatherleigh to Okehampton by rail, changing at Halwill Junction, was twenty-two miles. Hatherleigh's railway station, when it opened, was two miles outside the town down a single-track road. No one used this line at all. Hatherleigh only really remembers its railway because of the night in 1925 when the hundreds of navvies, constructing what must have been almost the last railway in Britain, rioted and attacked the police in what would be the final hurrah in a spree of terrorizing country folk that had lasted for nearly 200 years.

In *Double Headed* David St John Thomas wrote about the line in the 1950s, '*a single empty coach (empty apart from a few pieces of luggage and at busy times rabbit boxes piled in the first compartment as well as the guard's van) passed through Hatherleigh each way twice daily, the driver, fireman, guard and signalman being amazed if a passenger was seen*'.

From Great Torrington down to Petrockstowe, there were occasional passengers. But from Petrockstowe to Halwill via Hatherleigh, there was nothing. Nobody. Not a soul. This surely, was a job for Dr Richard Beeching.

As mentioned earlier, Beeching was appointed chairman of British Rail by the pro-road Transport Minister Ernest Marples in 1962. Beeching was not a railway man. Previously, he had been technical director of ICI. Marples had been looking at the books. British Rail had lost £87 million in 1961, the equivalent of about £1.2 billion today. Marples didn't believe in railways, so he gave Beeching a brutally simple task. No matter what it cost in social terms, the railway must be made to pay. Dr Richard went away and did his sums. In 1963 he published his report, which highlighted the gross inefficiency of British Rail. As an example of that inefficiency, twice a day, in both directions, the empty trains ran between Great Torrington and Halwill, via Hatherleigh. Such traffic as there was in the area was carried in buses; the most serious accident on the line was when an empty train ran into a full bus at an unmanned level crossing.

In his report, Beeching recommended that 10,000 of Britain's 17,830 miles of railway be closed. Over 2,000 stations would close. In 1965 Beeching presented another report, which called for the closure of all but 3,000 miles of line; essentially, just the InterCity network would remain. It was Harold Wilson's government which implemented Beeching, and luckily, like all Labour governments, they went about things in a half-assed way. They dithered and compromised for so long that they accidentally saved much of the railway. In 2002, about 10,500 miles of line survive, and I still haven't coloured in more than about half. Among the 7,000-odd miles of line that were closed, inevitably, was the North Devon and Cornwall Junction Light Railway. The last train passed through Hatherleigh in 1965, full of railway enthusiasts out to say goodbye to this least used of lines. It was only the second time the carriages were full; the first was on the opening day, only forty years previously.

That's now my local line, and I went out in search of what is left. Perry Venus came out with me. We drove in his car to Meeth, the stop north of Hatherleigh. The old station is still there, Meeth Halt. A road cuts the railway in half; once there was a level crossing. The line on the Meeth Halt side of the line is now part of the Tarka Trail, the only major long-distance bicycle path named after a work by a leading English fascist. On the other side of the road, the old track is unconverted. Where the rails were, now there are ruts. It looks like a typical sunken Devon lane. The ruts are muddy and full of water. It would not be surprising to see a horse pulling a farm wagon with wheels four feet, eight and a half inches apart, so that it fitted into the ruts. The line is barred by a gate which has a notice on it asking people not to climb over it owing to foot and mouth. Hatherleigh was at the centre of the epidemic, and the farmers do not like walkers.

Hatherleigh station can still be traced, too. North of the town there is a tiny lane to the left, signposted Totleigh. If you follow this lane for two miles, you will cross the line as the little road is carried on a railway bridge over a deep cutting. Perry and I got out of the car to look. The cutting was like a mini Rhine gorge, carved through rock. This was a Gothic railway, decaying in romantic and almost decadent luxuriance. Trees were growing in the trackbed, British racing-green ferns were growing up the damp rock. Water lay stagnant on the trackbed. Hard by this bridge is the track that led to Hatherleigh station; it is a private house now.

Back towards Hatherleigh, and then out on the road towards Holsworthy. A double line of trees swings in from the right; this was the railway. It once crossed the road by a level crossing; again, where the line crossed, it has turned into an unused country lane, its eloquent ruts almost hidden underneath the overgrown hedges, the encroaching bracken. It runs parallel to the road before heading away towards Halwill. We found it hard to trace the line across country. It doesn't come anywhere near a road for the run into Halwill Junction, but we could just make out the line of trees as we drove into the village. There was not much evidence of the railway left in Halwill Junction. A small housing estate has been built over the old station yard. North of Halwill, though, there is a forest walk, part of which uses the old line.

Perry and I parked, and followed the waymarked path through the forest. For much of its course it uses the forest roads, laid to hard-core and well drained. But as the forest road crosses the old railway line, the waymarked path leaves the road and continues along the abandoned trackbed. The hedges close in; the way is no longer well drained, and the ruts where the track once lay are full of mud. The sun struggled through to the trackbed between the overhanging trees.

Perry touched my arm. 'Jesus! What is that?' he said.

Fifty metres in front of us, a large creature had come through the hedge and was standing on the line of abandoned railway. It was looking at us. We stood and looked back at it.

'Oh my God, it's the biggest dog I've ever seen,' I said. 'Get ready to run.'

'It can't be,' Perry whispered. 'No dog is that big.'

'It's one of those beasts of Bodmin, then, or something. It's going to have us,' I whimpered.

'Shut up, speccy,' said Perry. 'It's a deer.'

Perry was right. It was a red deer, a hind. The deer kept looking at us, and we kept looking at the deer. Perry moved slowly for his camera, and the deer walked through the hedge and away into the forest. When we got to where it had been standing, we could see no sign of it. The deer have reclaimed the line. So this was the perfect romantic railway; although no one ever used it, it offered unlimited opportunities for nostalgia, and was in a state of decay so advanced that it had almost returned to the state of nature.

Yes, very romantic, but the lines, the parallel lines, have gone.

It's not real any longer.

Perry and I walked on down the old line and back to his car. Then we drove into Halwill Junction again, this railway village that owed its existence to a series of railways that probably shouldn't have existed, and went for a drink in the Junction Inn.

Railways are leys; lines of connection. They connect places, and they connect us with time, and the ghosts of time. The railway is a road of memory. When you go from London to Birmingham, you are following in the path of millions of other passengers who have used the line. Robert Stephenson, prematurely aged from the strain of building this colossal enterprise, stands at the head of a ghostly procession; behind him are countless stout Birmingham businessmen, London money changers, excited holiday-makers, doomed lovers, overloaded shoppers, trippers, spotters, bashers, spies, *femmes fatales*, all pulled along in his train.

The railways are the arteries of England's potentially terminal desire for nostalgia, a conduit for sentiment.

Nostalgia isn't what it used to be, runs the old joke. When the railways first came into early maturity, in the 1830s, Britain was close to revolution. When Wellington went to Manchester for the opening of the Liverpool and Manchester, the town greeted him with bricks. A riot ensued. Catholic emancipation had recently been granted, albeit reluctantly. The Church of England was going through its period of greatest upheaval since the end of the Civil War, almost 200 years before.

Based in Oxford, the Tractarians were calling on the Church to renew its spiritual life. One of their leading lights was Richard Hurrell Froude. His younger brother William was shortly to become an assistant to Isambard Kingdom Brunel, working on the Great Western Railway. After his early death, his friends published Richard's auto-biographical writings under the title *Remains*. It is almost certain that if he had lived, Froude would not have wanted them published. The *Remains* reveal Froude's disgust for the Reformation, and a sentimental nostalgia for Charles I, neither of which was a popular position in the 1830s.

Charles I had looked back with disgust at the Reformation, too. He had a sentimental regard for the great old days of the Renaissance princes, when nobody argued with the idea of the Divine Right of Kings. The Renaissance princes were sponsoring the greatest revival in learning since the collapse of the Roman Empire. Plato had just been rediscovered in the West, and scholars looked back on Greek Civiliza-tion as a Golden Age. Plato, meanwhile, claimed that the charts were rubbish now, and just full of manufactured boy bands, but in his day, they'd been fantastic, because you'd had Bowie and T-Rex and The Clash.

Oh no, hang on. That's me.

It's got to stop somewhere, this nostalgia.

This book arose, at least in part, from the events of the morning of 11 September 2001.

I was working in a second-hand bookshop on London's Charing Cross Road. A man brought in some books, which I bought for a tenner. Among these books was one I'd never seen before; the *abc Guide to Miniature Railways*, published by Ian Allen. This fantastic book lists all the details (including all the engine numbers) of all 160 of Britain's Miniature Railways.

Miniature railways include things like the La'l Ratty and the Romney, Hythe and Dymchurch, as well as the little ones you sit on while an old boy drives a tiny engine round an 800-yard track through landscaped garden areas past plastic models of small animals. It occurred to me, looking at the *abc Guide of Miniature Railways*, that I could perhaps go on all of them in the course of a year. What a trip. I would call the project *Great Miniature Train Journeys of the World*. Of course. I'd sell the idea to the telly. Michael Palin could do episode one, 'Ruislip Lido'. Marvelling at my own creative flair, I set out for lunch. It was a beautiful late-summer day in London. I was in a very good mood.

When I got back from lunch, my colleagues told me that there probably wasn't going to be much call for a book about miniature trains; not for a while, at least.

I'm still holding out for the TV rights, though.

The world didn't change that day, but it did push Britain's railway to second place in the news. If I'd tried to keep up with political developments on the railway during the writing of this book, I would now be in a home.

There were reports and inquiries by the dozen. There was at least one major accident (Potters Bar) which seemed to have its causes in the botched privatization of the railways. Liartrack was finally done away with, and Network Rail ushered in. The Strategic Rail Authority was set up to be, if not a Fat Controller, then at least Fat Controllerish. The unfortunate Stephen Byers lost his battle to try to cling to power at all costs. There was a man who never took responsibility for his own skidmarks: 'It's a shame my Y-fronts are stained, but you must understand that I'm not responsible. It was the civil servants who briefed me.'

The politicians are re-drawing, in one of their favourite phrases, the map of the railways. Watch them as closely as they will allow you, and see where they are drawing their lines. If you look at a map of European railways in 1945, you will see that all the lines met at Auschwitz.

One railway, the railway that you sit on every morning on your way to another shitty fucking pointless day in a drab office in the company of drab work-related acquaintances, is the fruit of political corruption, institutional indifference and short-term profiteering. No one loves it, because it is unlovable.

The other railway, the romantic railway, the railway of memory and dreams, the one that fills the St Albans Arena with starry-eyed dreamers with sticky fingers, the railway that thousands of volunteers give up all their spare hours to running and maintaining, this railway is deeply lovable because it isn't entirely real.

In Euclidian mathematics, the ordinary everyday mathematics of a three-dimensional world, it is axiomatic that parallel lines can never meet. In the 1820s and 1830s, about the time the first real railways were being laid, mathematicians got bored with Euclid and started imagining a world where his Elements didn't hold. Then weird stuff could happen. I suppose the best-known consequence of this is the Mandelbrot Set, the infinite fractal ammonite, posters of which hang on student bedroom walls.

In a non-Euclidian universe, parallel lines could meet quite happily, enjoy latte and a biscotti together, and then drift apart again. What we need is a non-Euclidian railway. We need to mix reality with a dash of romance. Instead of harping on about the Good Old Days, we need to imagine a better way to allow people freedom of movement, a better railway, a railway that answers local transport needs, is democratically controlled and is altogether more pretty, charming and downright good old-fashioned nice.

It's worth doing, because the railways are worth fighting for. More people die on Britain's roads in a year than died in the World Trade Center. In 1998, the last year for which comprehensive figures are available, 1.2 million people were killed on the world's roads.

We need a War on Speed.

In the Junction Inn with Perry, my mobile giggled. It was my girlfriend.

'Hello?'

'Hello, darling. Where are you?'

'I'm in the pub with Perry.'

'You lying bastard. You're on a bloody train somewhere, aren't you?'

Me and Perry left the pub and got into his car, and we drove home so that she could smell our beery breath, and set her mind at rest. There isn't really any other way to get around in North Devon. If the slow empty train from Halwill had still been running, then we'd have caught it, and walked the five miles from Hatherleigh station back to our house.

The Railway Traveller's Handy Book recommends it:

To the jaded and toilworn we would say, close your books, leave the desk, fly the study, hasten to the nearest railway station, and take a return ticket for some twelve or fifteen miles. On arriving at your destination, scud down the green lanes and across the fields, setting out at a brisk pace and maintaining it until your return to the departure station in a couple of hours' time. The journey homeward will appropriately cap the achievement; which, although we do not vaunt as a panacea for all the ills of life, we nevertheless declare, from experience, to be one of the very best repairers of health and restorers of spirits.

LIST OF ILLUSTRATIONS

1. Cambrian Coast Line, Towyn
2. Midland Grand Hotel, St Pancras
3. Wagon wheels, Tal-y-Llyn Railway
4. Diorama, Narrow Gauge Railway Museum
5. Underpass, Stratford station
6. Photographs in carriage window, Henllan
7. Crossing sign, Tal-y-Llyn Railway
8. North Devon and Cornwall Junction Light Railway, Meeth

All photographs are by Paul Williams.

ACKNOWLEDGEMENTS

Many thanks to everyone I met and corresponded with in the course of writing this book, and in particular, John Glasscock, Chris Drake, Richard Salmon, Joe Macnally, Gilly Johnston, Tracey Mansell at Atticus Books, Chris Howard at the Hay Cinema Bookshop, Dave at Motor Books, and the Cambridgeshire Society of Imaginary Psychology. Thanks too to Deirdre Rusling, Ian Willson, Johnny Dodd, Dr 'Big' Dave Littlewood, Jillian Stuteley, Saleel Nurbhai, Madeleine Weymouth, Shevaughn Williams, Alan Cox, Stephen O'Laughlin, David Brown, Jane Brocket, Sorcha O'Brien, Peter Young and Esme and Eleanor, always. Thanks to The Arvon Foundation, in particular Julia Wheadon, for their support. And to Monique Roffey, whose patience kept her from killing me while I explained the difference between gauge and scale at some length, over several months, and whose love, phone calls and packed lunches sustained me on many a chilly platform . . . poop poop!

The author and publishers gratefully acknowledge permission to quote from the following works: (page 69) *The Book of Railways* by Arthur Groom, published by Birn Brothers Ltd; (page 86) *Notes on the Underground* by Rosalind Williams, published by The MIT Press; (pages 89–90) The Metropolitan Railway' by John Betjeman from *Collected Poems* by John Betjeman, courtesy of John Murray (Publishers) Ltd; (page 160) *Broken Rails: How Privatisation Wrecked Britain's Railways* by Christian Wolmar, published by Aurum Press Ltd; (pages 161–2) 'A Slice of Wedding Cake' by Robert Graves from *The Oxford Book of Twentieth Century English Verse* published by Oxford University Press and Carcanet Press Limited; (page 279) *Chronicles of a Garden Railway* by W. A. D. Strickland, published by Model & Allied Publications; (page 301) *Double Headed: Two Generations of Railway Enthusiasm* by David St John Thomas and Gilbert Thomas, published by David & Charles Publishers.

A NOTE ON THE AUTHOR

Ian Marchant is the author of two novels, *In Southern Waters* and *The Battle for Dole Acre*. He has run a second-hand bookshop, and is a comedian, singer, songwriter and cabaret performer. *Parallel Lines* is his first work of non-fiction. Visit Ian's website at www.ianmarchant.com.

A NOTE ON THE TYPE

Linotype Garamond Three – based on seventeenth-century copies of Claude Garamond's types, cut by Jean Jannon. This version was designed for American Type Founders in 1917, by Morris Fuller Benton and Thomas Maitland Cleland and adapted for mechanical composition by Linotype in 1936.